Career Theory, Development, and Appraisal

A GUIDE FOR HUMAN SERVICES

Louis A. Busacca
Mark C. Rehfuss
Old Dominion University

Lomar Academic Books, LLC

Cleveland, OH

Lomar Academic Books, LLC
P.O. Box 24193
Cleveland, OH 44124
https://lbusacca.wixsite.com/lomar

Library of Congress Cataloging-in-Publication Data
Names: Busacca, Louis A., author. | Rehfuss, Mark C., author.
Title: Career theory, development, and appraisal: A guide for human services / by Louis A. Busacca and Mark C. Rehfuss.
Description: Cleveland, OH: Lomar Academic Books, LLC, 2019. | Includes bibliographical references and index.
Identifiers:
LCCN 2019902249
ISBN 978-0-578-44075-0 (pbk.: alk. paper)
ISBN 978-0-578-47386-4 (ebk.)
Subjects: LCSH: Vocational guidance. | Career counseling. | Career development. | Human services. | Career assessment.

Dedication

To my late loving father, grandmother Sarah and family.
—*Louis A. Busacca*

To Tracie, Adelyn, Taylor, and Claire, the most incredible women I have ever known, and loves of my life.
—*Mark C. Rehfuss*

Table of Contents

Forward

Ed Neukrug, Ph.D.[1]

One of the most important areas for all helpers to embrace is career counseling. Unfortunately, this critical area is often not taught, taught ineffectively, and even maligned as a specialty area. Since all individuals face a myriad of career transitions throughout their lifetime, often with a fair amount of stress and despair, this is indeed regrettable. It is with this in mind, that I am excited to see the publishing of *Career Theory, Development, and Appraisal: A Guide for Human Services.*

A critical aspect of what all helpers do, this book is a thorough overview of the theory and skills needed to assist individuals with a wide range of career needs. One of the first books that focuses solely on the work of the human service professional, the book is comprehensive, yet down to earth. The book begins with the essentials—the importance of a solid helping relationship when conducting career guidance, a history of vocational guidance in America, and an overview of career services needed by clients. It then offers the basics on career theory, assessment, and occupational and career information. Importantly, it covers how to assist a wide variety of special populations when conducting career guidance, including diverse individuals, dislocated workers, offenders/ex-offer enders, veterans, individuals with substance abuse, individuals with disabilities, the chronically ill, individuals with disabilities, and others. It also zeros in on the role of the school counselor in career guidance. Importantly, it focuses on ethical issues for human service professionals when conducting career guidance. The final chapter examines how meaning-making is critical when clients are facing transitions related to the world of work.

An important and well-need addition to the human service field, I highly recommend this book for those becoming human service practitioners and those already working as human service practitioners.

---

[1]Dr. Ed Neukrug is an American Counseling Association Fellow & recipient of the President's Award from the National Organization of Human Services. He is Professor of Counseling and Human Services for the Department of Counseling and Human Services, Old Dominion University.

Preface

From an early age, Ashish Alfred struggled with addiction while tenaciously pursuing his passion for cooking. But one day, his mother intervened, and everything changed. Ashish's parents were immigrants from India and had adopted three children with disabilities. He was the youngest, and was born in Maryland. His mother, a Seventh-Day Adventist, had been a professor in Pune, India. From an early age, however, Ashish and his mother both experienced abuse by his alcoholic father. Ashish turned to drugs to cope with his personal insecurities. He stated that his family were the only Indian people he knew. In fourth grade, Ashish felt that he didn't fit in because he was smaller than most of the students in his class and was often bullied by his peers. By eighth grade, Ashish stopped doing homework, got suspended, and was buying marijuana, stealing liquor, and drinking all day. In ninth grade, he failed the grade and was required to repeat his freshman year. Along with abusing drugs, Ashish engaged in fighting and theft. He felt this fueled his own popularity among his group of at-risk teenaged peers. By age 17, Ashish was addicted to cocaine and on a path toward abusing heroin and other opioids.

When Ashish was about to graduate from high school, he realized that he had a passion for cooking which had been quietly developing over the previous years. He convinced his mother to let him attend the International Culinary Center (ICC) in New York City. However, the potential that Ashish showed as a chef throughout his training wasn't enough to help him conquer his addictions. Shortly after moving to New York, he sold a precious crucifix necklace that his mother had given to him in order to buy cocaine. Despite his gifts and accomplishments, he remained addicted to drugs. Two years after graduating from ICC, 25-year-old Ashish opened his first restaurant—an endeavor he now feels was irresponsible given the poor decisions he made while struggling with chemical dependency.

One night, Ashish found himself breaking into his own restaurant and stealing $4,000 from the company safe to buy more heroin. During these dark times, he even contemplated suicide. Ashish said, "Why stick around? I was failing everyone around me. I had lost the respect of anybody close to me. The one person I really did care about, my mother, at one point, she couldn't stand the sight of me." That was the day his mother told Ashish that he had to go to rehab or she would never speak to him again. After 28 days of detoxing in a rehabilitation center in Pennsylvania, Ashish was sober for the first time in a decade. He returned to his restaurant, determined to stay sober and truly experience the sense of meaning and purpose in life that cooking gave him.

Ashish is now 33 years old and five years sober. He lives in Baltimore Maryland, and opened three restaurants there in just three years. He has appeared on hit Food Network TV shows such as *Cutthroat Kitchen* and *Chopped*, and was even invited to cook at the prestigious James Beard House in December 2018. Ashish Alfred appeared on *The Today Show* on March 19, 2019 (Wida, 2019) to tell his story and impress upon others that his passion for cooking and love for his mother saved his life. Speaking of his mother's view of his work, Ashish stated, "It really took a long time for her to understand and respect what it is that I actually do. But I know she's happy, and she's happy with me and how far I've come. I mean, five years ago I was almost dead, and now I'm cooking at the Beard House. That's a big deal." For Ashish, cooking helped him escape a life of addiction and start fresh. Today, he is known by his customers as Chef Al.

Work and Career Issues are Personal

As a current or future human services practitioner, you probably feel moved by Ashish's journey from a rough start as a teenager and young adult engaged in dangerous behavior and battling substance addiction to becoming a rising culinary star and successful business owner. We could formulate a variety of hypotheses and consult theories and models to gain insight into why and how Ashish was able to overcome his addiction, and perhaps focus on the effects of childhood abuse, family dynamics, or methods of relapse prevention. Learning how to assess and conceptualize client problems is necessary for one to learn how to select appropriate interventions to help clients solve their problems and achieve their goals (Busacca, 2002). An important aspect of doing so is taking into account the complex mix of factors underlying those problems. Progress for clients with both career and personal needs may be limited unless practitioners address the interrelationship of concerns (Zunker, 2008). We recognize that Ashish's struggles with addiction intersected with his career issues. When discussing his sobriety and work Ashish stated, "It keeps me sane, the business of it keeps me going." Ashish's story illustrates that his passion and motivation for becoming a chef likely influenced his eventual recovery, which underscores that personal and career concerns are inextricably intertwined.

From the 1950s through the 1980s, career counseling and personal counseling were viewed as separate disciplines in both training and practice. This false separation appears to have been generated by scholars and practitioners who took a compartmentalized view of career issues, which historically had focused on helping clients only through developmental or preventative approaches (Hackett, 1993). Career theories primarily addressed helping students and clients make an optimal career choice. Viewing a career concern as exclusively developmental in nature can lead to a passive view of people that assumes that some unfolding developmental process underlies change or lack of change. This narrow view conceptualized individuals' issues and concerns as things that would resolve with time or do not involve maladaptive emotions, cognitions, and behaviors, and thus would not benefit from personal interventions. Over time, however, this view has changed. Krumboltz (1993) clarified that "When we discover the complex circumstances that are interwoven into our clients' problems, it becomes almost impossible to categorize any given problem as either 'career' or 'personal'" (p. 143). Since the 1980s, our thinking about the relationship between career and personal issues has changed significantly (e.g., Niles & Harris-Bowlsbey, 2017; Zunker, 2008). By its very nature, career issues involve grappling with a range of emotions and thoughts, which ventures into a subjective experience for an individual.

The subjective nature of work is what makes an individual's career concerns personal. People are strongly motivated to find meaning in life, which can arise through various life roles. Frankl (1984) voiced that striving to find a meaning in life or *will to meaning* is the primary motivational source in people. Meaning-making provides an individual with a sense of value and self-worth, a basic need necessity for life to have sufficient meaning (Baumeister, 1991). People are particularly vulnerable to meaning making when they are faced with urgent experiences or significant life-changing events (Cohen, 2003). Work can be perceived as generally meaningful when individuals' needs for self-worth and value are both met (Hall, Feldman, & Kim, 2013). Yet, in the 2012 Kelly Global Workforce Index survey of 168,000 Generation Y, X, and baby boomer workers in 30 countries, slightly fewer than 50% said that their current employment provided them with a sense of meaning (Kelly Services, 2012). This study illuminates the notion that we have both an objective and a subjective career. According to Savickas (2019), an individual's objective career refers to what is publicly observable over time, such as their success or failure; conversely, their subjective career symbolizes the story or meaning they construct about their working life and their evaluation of their own career, and may include outcomes relating to purposiveness, satisfaction, fulfillment, self-worth or even frustration, anxiety, and depression. Individuals' subjective career is also related to their self-image and personal engagement in the work role.

Work and Identity

Work as personal identity can be an expression of self-image. It is through work that we exercise our talents and build an identity. "Using work to become the sort of person one imagines can be a potent source of motivation in any form of work" (Lent & Brown, 2013, p. 3). We see this when an individual considers work as a calling (i.e., a transcendent summons to purposeful work that serves the greater good) or when their personal story captures the sense that work can play a valuable, self-defining role in their life. When an individual invests self in a social role such as work, it forms an identity, provides meaning, and creates a story of who the individual is, in relation to work (Savickas, 2012). Baumeister (1999) suggested that an identity comprises three essential elements in the form of self-questions: "Who am I in this role?" "Who am I becoming in this role?" and "What is important to me in this role?" Some individuals, however, overemphasize the work role, which can lead to workaholism because it provides a feeling of self-worth that they cannot find anywhere else (Robinson, 1996). For traditional men, gender-role expectations are central to their personal identity and self-esteem. As a result, a conventionally gendered man often has trouble with transitions and needs special assistance navigating life's unpredictable events (Kilmartin, 2009). For a traditional man who has been socialized to think of himself as synonymous with his work, layoffs, downsizing, and retirement often result in feelings of emasculation or in depression (Hollis, 2005). Such a substantial crisis of identity occurs when individual experience loss and discontinuity.

In the book titled *Counseling Adults in Transition* (Anderson, Goodman, & Schlossberg, 2012), I [Louis] came across a profound sentence that resonated with me, "Today, continuity is the exception, and adjusting to discontinuity has become the norm of our era" (p. 3). This statement reflects the fact that because the nature of work and the meaning of career have been restructured over the last three decades, adults increasingly find themselves confronted by frequent transitions. In the work role, transitions include developmental career tasks (e.g., occupational choice), occupational transition (e.g., new work arrangements), or a work trauma (e.g., reduced hours, layoff, termination, and illness) (see Busacca & Rehfuss, 2017). Identity, in an age of uncertainty, brings challenges when people experience unwanted transitions and unwanted traumas.

The nature of personal identity is becoming more fluid. Social philosopher Anthony Giddens (1991) stressed that the demand on the individual to define her- or himself has become a major social fact and a characteristic of our societies. That is, when confronted by transition, individuals may find that their sense of who they are and where they fit in, in relation to occupation and work, loses continuity. Nevertheless, as Savickas (2019) noted, "identity is seldom an individual project" (p. 19), especially in collectivist cultures. Identity emerges and exists because of interaction with others, and is embedded in culture and context (LaPointe, 2010). Individuals, therefore, must adapt by repeatedly revising their identity to integrate new experiences into their ongoing sense of self (Savickas, 2012). Unfortunately, this is often accompanied by discouragement, anxiety, and frustration. We now recognize that identity development is a lifelong process and people often seek career services when the content of their identity is insufficient or unable to support them when confronting the demands imposed by society's new economy. As career trajectories become marked by unpredictability and frequent transition, individuals may experience threats to their sense of purpose, self-worth, and personal identity related to the work role.

Precarious Work

The 21st century world of work has been restructured. Major shifts are occurring in the demographics of the workforce, and career trajectories are now marked by nonlinear, unpredictable, and constant transition. The new economy has changed jobs in profound ways. In general, there are new technologies, organizational designs, industries, and markets. In particular, Sweet and Meiksins (2017) identified major changes that characterize work in the new economy which include "decline of mass production and manufacturing work, new skill requirements, the emergence of new cultures of control, the gradual decline of organized labor, the rise of flexible work arrangements, and globalization" (p. 28). From the point of view of the worker, work is now characterized by uncertain, insecure, and risky employment opportunities. Kalleberg (2009) has labeled this *precarious work*. Precarious work undermines workers' control and their capacity to engage in planful action. In reality, the loss of a job or fear of losing a job, lack of alternative livable employment opportunities, diminished freedom to obtain and maintain skills, and the nonexistence of advancement options in a position impact people in profound ways.

The possible effects of insecurity are strikingly harsh and have a broad impact on individuals. They include a sense of oppression and exploitation, demoralization, loss of motivation, and ill health (Standing, 1999). Precarious work and the results of its stress will be seen by human service professionals working with almost any client. Given this situation, it is often only those individuals in advantaged positions or those who can adapt quickly and decisively that are put in the best position to survive and thrive. For others, making a commitment to an occupational choice has become increasingly difficult as more people face uncertainty about what type of work will be available and others have trouble coping with career tasks, occupational transition, or work trauma (Busacca & Rehfuss, 2017). Thus, human service professionals need to be equipped to meet the complex needs of individuals preparing for and participating in the new world of work. Whether we consider it a calling or a curse, work plays a central role in the lives of most people.

Centrality of Work

To a considerable extent, Western culture defines people by what they do occupationally. Everyone works—including those engaged in unpaid activities—and everyone is connected to people who work. As Alfred Adler (1927/1954) noted years ago, the human community sets three fundamental life tasks for every individual: work, friendship (i.e., social relationships), and love. These tasks are central to healthy human functioning, which embraces the whole of human life with all its desires and activities (Dreikurs, 1989). They are critical in that each must be addressed and integrated to achieve optimal well-being. Every human services professional will encounter individuals with career- and work-related concerns, whether they confront normal career development tasks, crisis situations such as job displacement and dislocation, coping with a disability, the transition from military to civilian life, offender/ex-offender adjustment, or individuals struggling with chemical dependency. Therefore, having a basic awareness of and competency in providing career services is essential, regardless of the setting in which you will be working.

Most people experience work as central to their lives. Work centrality can be defined as "individual beliefs regarding the degree of importance that work plays in their lives" (Walsh & Gordon, 2008, p. 46). Although other roles in life such as play, family, relationships, and spirituality may be complementary and convergent for some cultures (Hartung, 2002), most adults spend more time engaged in work (including non-paid activities) than in any other waking activity—roughly six times the amount we spend with our families. We can observe and study the importance of work in people's lives through its representation in media including narratives, memoirs, art, literature, and music

(Budd, 2011). Thomas Jefferson wrote, "It is neither wealth nor splendor, but tranquility and occupation, which give happiness" (qtd. In Rather, 2001, p. 71) (Jefferson, 1788). In addition, work has been viewed as essential for psychological health and to the welfare of communities. Blustein (2008) stated that "working is a central ingredient in the development and sustenance of psychological health" (p. 230). We know from research and practice that when career and work situations go off-center, mental health issues increase. Work plays a role in serving our needs, promoting or inhibiting well-being, and establishing the basis for healthy, safe, and nurturing communities (Blustein, 2013; Fouad, 2007; Juntunen, 2006).

Work Fulfills Needs, Purpose, and Belonginess

When we define work, it conjures up different things for different people. Work is often judged by its most measurable component: income. Yet, the work we choose serves interpersonal needs, psychological needs, family needs, and social needs (Herr, Cramer, & Niles, 2004). Work means different things to different people. For some, a job is a necessary evil, a requirement for paying the bills. For others, work is a gauge for testing their self-worth. For some, work provides a ladder to advance in one's career and value-driven rewards for evaluating professional progress. For others, work enables their personal growth, helps them optimize their inner potential, helps them make sense of life, and gives them a path to pursue their purpose (Dik, Byrne, & Steger, 2013).

Adler (1927/1954) stated that human behavior can be understood based on what the individual perceives as being meaningful and goal-achieving. That is, people strive to fulfill their purpose. Purpose refers to "people's identification of, and intention to pursue, particular highly valued, overarching life goals" (Steger & Dik, 2010, p. 133). The motivating factors that underlie striving for purpose include our needs and values. Work can meet someone's needs, but values refer to *how* someone fulfills their needs. Values foster motivation and allow individuals to contribute to the welfare of their social and cultural groups (Neff, 1985). In brief, needs and values strongly influence career choices, satisfaction from work, and adjustment to work. Rosso et al. (2010) asserted that belongingness is a mechanism through which meaningfulness is created.

Work is a significant channel for a sense of belonging. Because many of us strive to find our place in the social world, Adler (1927/1954) believed that the goal of all people is to strive for a feeling of belongingness. Adler also believed that work is socially embedded, and that people have a need for social connection. In trying to fit in, we ask questions such as, "Where can I make my place?" and "How can I contribute?" Recognizing the human need for striving for relatedness, career theorists emphasize that relationships in work provide a means of understanding how we matter to others (e.g., Blustein, 2011; Schultheiss, 2003). On an episode of *The Andy Griffith Show*, the English butler Malcolm Merriweather, a character played by Bernard Fox, responds to the question of young Opie Taylor (played by Ron Howard). Opie says, "Mr. Malcolm, do you always sing when you do the dishes?" Malcolm replies, "Well, you'll understand this better when you're older, but you see, you're happiest when you're working, because it makes you feel useful." Feeling useful—feeling that you matter—provides individuals with a sense of social meaning and relatedness and contributes to their sense of belonging. Some individuals, however, struggle with the absence of connectedness and meaningful relationships in the workplace, and this can result in a sense of isolation and alienation (Schultheiss, 2003; 2006). Therefore, because individuals may identify the work role as a source of meaning in their lives (Baum & Stewart, 1990), an understanding of the role of relationships in clients' lives is essential as we help people with their career and work issues.

In Ashish's story, we see a young man who strives for purpose through gaining status and popularity among his peers, and then through his motivation in becoming a chef, and ultimately in his career success. Recognition from significant others heightens one's sense of belonging (Savickas, 2004). But, during this process, they may engage in behavior that appears to be helpful to self, but often disruptive to others (Carlson & Englar-Carlson, 2017). It appears that the value that Ashish placed on achievement, financial prosperity, and belonging was a factor in motivating him to become a chef ever since his teenage years. Unfortunately, these needs were instead fulfilled for many years through at-risk behavior and substance abuse. For Ashish, the pursuit of his dream job was thwarted by faulty goals met through his addiction. Working is related to psychological health, and this has been shown by the positive, stabilizing effect that Ashish's career has had on his life since he achieved sobriety.

Work and Mental Health

Work can contribute to mental health issues. Various symptoms of poor mental health have been associated with problems in the work role. Involuntary unemployment, among both youths and adults, is associated with numerous negative health outcomes including increased depression and anxiety (Paul & Moser, 2009). Perhaps the most obvious indication of how important work is to mental health is shown by the frequency with which individuals who lose their jobs struggle with depression, anxiety, substance abuse, and alcoholism (e.g., Lucas, Clark, Georgellis, & Diener, 2004; Vinokur, Schul, Vuori, & Price, 2000). In addition, work stress and subsequent problems in relationships at work can spill over into conflicts in the home and other relationships (Zedeck, 1992). This underscores the interrelatedness of personal and career/work issues. In addition to influencing problematic symptoms and outcomes, work has the potential to foster and sustain positive mental health.

Work promotes well-being by serving a protective function in the face of aversive life events and experiences. That is, work can ameliorate or even prevent mental health issues. Occupational health psychology (e.g., Quick & Tetrick, 2002) has generated keen interest in the way in which work functions in the context of health and wellness, such that changes in the work environment can lead to improvements in worker well-being. For example, being employed has been shown to correlate negatively with criminal activity (e.g., Sampson & Laub, 1993), substance abuse (Bellair & Roscigno, 2000), and other mental health concerns (Keyes & Waterman, 2003). In addition, multiple studies conducted over the last 50 years have found consistent correlations between job satisfaction and life satisfaction (Moser & Schuler, 2004), and work satisfaction is positively related to satisfaction in other life roles such as that of student, leisure-seeker, spouse, homemaker, and parent (Swanson, 2012). Furthermore, individuals who report a satisfying work life also report greater happiness and fewer psychological problems (Fritzsche & Parish, 2005). In our vignette, Ashish's passion for becoming a chef, although complicated for a time by his addiction, may have served a protective function in his recovery. Given the interacting influences of work and mental health, the separation of work from personal issues seems counterintuitive from a holistic perspective.

Holism of Work and Life

Ashish's story can be viewed from a holistic perspective. Holism refers to the concept that individual humans should be viewed as unified wholes that are more than the sum of their respective constituent elements (Sweeney & Witmer, 1991). This view has its roots in the work of Adler (1927/1954), who was emphatic in his belief in the unity and indivisibility of the self. We can gather from the aforementioned literature that work often intersects with other life roles, cultural variables, and psychological health. For Ashish, it appears that his enduring passion to be a chef and entrepreneur and his desire to maintain his relationship with his mother helped him in his recovery.

Adler also viewed clients as whole individuals embedded within dynamic social contexts (e.g., family, society) that require a sense of purpose or movement toward achieving desired goals (Ansbacher & Ansbacher, 1956). As such, work is a social phenomenon that must be understood in the context of social institutions and structures. For Ashish, we can see various facets of culture and context embedded in his story. These include his ethnicity, youngest child status, childhood abuse, victimization by bullying, peer relationships, school environment, and his relationship with his parents. Any combination of these factors may have influenced the trajectory of Ashish's life journey. In light of the aforementioned literature, we believe that it is important for human services students to recognize the potential intersection of work with the behavioral, emotional, and physical aspects of health and wellness, and recognize that embedded in career and work concerns are the cultural and social context of the client.

Purpose of the Book

In writing the first edition of this book, our primary goal was to offer students and human services educators a textbook choice devoted to the typical career and work concerns entry-level practitioners will encounter in various roles and settings. Additionally, this book can serve as a useful resource for students in counseling, rehabilitation, and social work programs. We hope to covey to our readers the respect we have for career theory and practice. We emphasize this in the preface, as there are few things more personal than career and work, and remained aware of this as we prepared each chapter.

Given the centrality of work in the lives of individuals, we suggest that entry-level human services students be trained in providing basic career services to clients and students from diverse backgrounds, and that they consider holism and inclusiveness as an integral concept in the ecological sphere of the client and in human service delivery. As a current or future human services practitioner, you may work in different settings with diverse client populations, and as generalists, you may also work in a variety of roles, including as crisis intervention specialists, substance abuse counselors, social service workers, case managers, probation officers, or mental health aides (Neukrug, 2017). But intertwined within these roles, and others, is exposure to various work and career-related concerns that clients will bring with them. We emphasize, therefore, that career theory and practice need to be culturally inclusive; thus, we provide a chapter on culturally competent career services and a primer on the postmodern perspective on working with culturally diverse clients. Because a lack of awareness of the various career paths in the human services may limit students' options, we believe that it is important to inform students about the role of the career services provider, promote interest, and ensure that qualified individuals pursue the necessary degrees and training in this area if they so desire (Dice & Rehfuss, 2017).

We avoid viewing people's career and work issues as isolated events. It is important to recognize that the intersection of work with other aspects of life makes it likely that work-related concerns can emerge in multiple settings, and competency in this area is not limited to specific career services such as helping an adolescent or young adult choose an occupation. To gain familiarity with clients who are recipients of services requires the integration of knowledge from a wide variety of academic disciplines (Johnson, Sparkman-Key, & Kalkbrenner, 2017). Thus, human services students are trained to meet the needs of diverse clients through an interdisciplinary knowledge base that focuses on prevention and remediation of issues (Council for Standards of Human Service Education, 2015). Given the rich support for the efficacy of career interventions (Whiston & Rahardja, 2008), and the evidence that vocational well-being influences emotional well-being, career and work must be considered vital to the welfare of all clients.

Overview of the Book

The chapters in this book discuss career counseling theory, development and appraisal as ways to augment and enrich the human service professional's work with diverse clients. This guide provides an overview of career services. Chapter 1 sets the scene for the material you will encounter in the book. It discusses the role of the human services professional in the provision of career services, and core ingredients for establishing an effective helping relationship. In Chapter 2, we provide an overview of how vocational guidance served a need in evolving American society. We also take a brief look at several early pioneers of the vocational guidance movement, followed by notable landmarks in early legislation. Chapter 3 presents an overview of the various career service areas, and discusses the typical career problems clients present with, the implicit question that clients want resolved, and the helper's objective in providing career interventions and typical assessment tools used for each service area.

Chapters 4 through 7 provide an overview of career theory, assessment, and occupational and career information. Learning about career theory and assessment provides the foundation for competent career interventions, and familiarity with career information and resources represent important aspects of the career development process. Chapter 4 discusses several guidelines to consider when learning about career theory, and presents a primer on several career theories that are popular and applicable today. In Chapter 5, we provide an overview of several career-related inventories and assessments that can be administered by entry-level human service professionals. Quantitative and qualitative instruments are contrasted, and multicultural considerations in the selection and use of assessment tools are discussed. We focus on some of the most popular sources of career information in Chapter 6, and cover tips and guidelines for evaluating the quality of web-sourced occupational information. Chapter 7 covers the career resources available for identifying competencies, and guidelines for helping clients and students in their job-search process.

The next four chapters emphasize culturally inclusive career development interventions as a standard of practice in career services. In Chapter 8, we discuss the basics of multicultural career services, and examine the multicultural movement and the need for culturally competent services. We also look at the cultural limitations of traditional career theories, and the postmodern view of career and culture. Chapter 9 introduces adult career transitions and looks at several special populations that human service professionals will typically serve in any setting. The populations covered in this chapter will be displaced or dislocated workers, offenders/ex-offenders, veterans, and people with chemical dependencies. In Chapter 10, we present an introduction to providing human services to people who have disabilities. We discuss typical phases in the vocational rehabilitation process when assisting chronically ill and disabled people with employment issues. Chapter 11 begins with the role of the school counselor in providing career guidance and education to high school students, followed by a brief overview of the history of career and college readiness in schools. Some developmental issues are examined, along with approaches for helping adolescents become college and career ready.

The last two chapters present the role of ethics in providing career services and a primer on the new landscape of working in the 21st century. The desire to engage in ethical practice is a standard in the field, and the changing nature of work has resulted in an emphasis on postmodern models and methods in career assessment and counseling. Chapter 12 provides working definitions of some typical terms encountered when discussing the topic of ethics, the need for ethical codes, and some typical ethical conflicts that human service professionals may face when delivering career interventions. An ethical decision-making process is described. This book concludes with Chapter 13, which introduces you to why we need more professionals trained in career counseling, especially postmodern approaches, and how career assessment and intervention is adapting to the changing nature of work. We discuss the new social arrangements in work and career, and then introduce the concept of precarious work along with its features. We then introduce you to the importance of constructing meaning making in helping clients with their career issues, and conclude with four features of culture and context in postmodern thought which has shaped career counseling in the 21st century.

Conclusion

In a world in which career planning has become precarious and work more contingent, human service professionals and career practitioners must now help clients to achieve self-definition, create meaning, and live within their sociocultural context. In a new social organization of work, employees feel more anxious, discouraged, and frustrated because of perceived job insecurity, coping with multiple transitions, and multicultural imperatives (Savickas, 2012). As we have emphasized in this preface, working can be a curse for some or a blessing for others. Yet, it plays a central role in our lives. The provision of career services requires more professionals trained in models and methods to help clients shape their lives to successfully cope with career tasks, occupational transitions, and work trauma in the 21st century.

Acknowledgements

We thank the Department of Counseling and Human Services at Old Dominion University for making this book a reality. Thank you for the fine work of our editorial assistants Nicola Meade and Charlie Loudin.

About the Authors

 **Louis A. Busacca, PhD,** received his doctorate in counseling and human development from Kent State University and holds licensure as a professional counselor in Ohio and as a national certified counselor. He received special recognition as a master career counselor from the National Career Development Association (NCDA), is certified in clinical rational hypnotherapy from the National Association of Cognitive-Behavioral Therapists, and as a Certified Clinical Trauma Professional from the International Trauma Training Institute.

He is currently an adjunct assistant professor of counseling and human services at Old Dominion University and adjunct professor of behavioral sciences at Lakeland Community College. Prior to this, he was adjunct professor of counseling for Youngstown State University and an instructor at Northeast Ohio Medical University. Dr. Busacca has 7 years' experience as an administrator in higher education as director for the U.S. Department of Education's TRiO Veterans Upward Bound in Cleveland, Ohio.

Dr. Busacca was a member of the board of directors for the Council for Accreditation of Counseling and Related Educational Programs (CACREP). He served as president of the Ohio Career Development Association and on several committees for CACREP and American Counseling Association. He was on the editorial board of *Counselor Education and Supervision,* the *Journal of Humanistic Counseling, Education and Development,* and currently serves on the editorial board for the *Journal of Employment Counseling* and *Journal of Counselor Practice.*

Dr. Busacca's interests include postmodern paradigms in career counseling, counselor trainee development, and stress and trauma. He has peer-reviewed publications in the areas of constructivist career counseling, career assessment and counseling, counselor trainee career development, and neurobiology in counselor preparation. He is a member of the American Counseling Association, American Psychological Association, National Career Development Association, and Ohio Counseling Association.

 **Mark C. Rehfuss, PhD,** received his doctorate in counseling and human development from Kent State University and holds licensure as a professional clinical counselor in Ohio and as a professional counselor in Virginia. He is currently an associate professor and director of the human services distance program in the Department of Counseling and Human Services at Old Dominion University, Norfolk, Virginia.

Dr. Rehfuss is Editor in Chief of the *Journal of Employment Counseling* and sits on the national executive board of the National Employment Counseling Association. He has served as National Treasurer for NOHS, chair of the NCDA Research Committee and as president of the Virginia Association for Counselor Education and Supervision. He has 24 years of experience in higher education administration, curriculum development, counselor and human services education. He has over 45 peer-reviewed publications and has delivered numerous professional presentations at international and national conferences.

Dr. Rehfuss' research interests include career counseling and guidance, narrative career interventions, counselor education and supervision, online learning, human service education and the integration of behavioral and mental health professions into integrated medical practice settings.

Dr. Rehfuss is an active member of the National Organization for Human Services, the American Counseling Association, and the National Employment Counseling Association

Chapter 1

THE CAREER-SERVICE PROFESSIONAL AND THE HELPING RELATIONSHIP

"Agreement on means and end, along with a warm bond developed in elaborating the problem, establishes a working alliance to undertake the next episode."

~Larry Cochran, 1997, p. 51

CHAPTER HIGHLIGHTS
The Career Services Professional in Human Services
Competencies of the Human Service Professional in Career Services
Preparation and Education for the Career Service Professional
Core Ingredients for Developing a Helping Relationship
Who Needs Help with Work and Career?

Everyone knows work, and everyone is connected to people who know work. As Freud (1930) noted, "Love and work are the cornerstones of our humanness," while Alfred Adler believed that everyone confronted three tasks in life: work, friendship, and love (Ansbacher & Ansbacher, 1964). Working is a fundamental aspect of life, providing a source of structure, a means of survival, connection to others, a sense of purpose, and a means of self-determination (Blustein, 2006). Because there are few things more personal than work and career, every human service professional will encounter clients with career challenges such as difficulty coping with career transitions, making high-stakes occupational choices, and addressing significant work challenges involving layoffs, illnesses, and terminations. We know that when people experience such problems in their professional lives, they often get discouraged and feel stuck. Thus, having a basic knowledge of career issues, processes, assessments, and

1

interventions is essential regardless of the human service setting in'which one works.

This chapter discusses the role of the human service professional in the provision of career services. It includes definitions of some common career terms, explanations of career service competencies relevant to human service professionals, and a discussion of preparation and education for the career service professional. Core ingredients for establishing an effective helping relationship as it relates to providing career services are also presented, including during the career-intake process. Next, the National Survey of Working America is examined. This provides the reader with an opportunity to see what Americans currently think, feel, and believe about the state of the workforce and career development, and to determine how those attitudes and beliefs may affect future career development actions. This chapter concludes with a look at common career myths held by the public and even some mental-health professionals.

The Career Services Professional in Human Services

Whether you have entered or are thinking about entering the human services profession and providing career services, you probably have some intuition that this field fits your sense of who you are. You may even have an image of what personal characteristics professionals who enter the field possess. Perhaps you think a human service professional is an altruistic person—a person who want to help others; a person who is introspective, intuitive, and social. This relates to a person's values, which are a source of motivation for individual action or objectives that one seeks to attain to satisfy a need and are central to an individual's self-definition and decision-making process (Rounds & Jin, 2013). Values are not only a relevant aspect to consider with a client when providing career services, but awareness of one's value orientations becomes more salient when a student, for instance questioning self-concepts and the personal characteristics needed for the field being studied (Ronnestad & Skovholt, 2003). As you become socialized into the human service profession, whatever path you may take, you will develop a sense of identity. This sense of identity relates to the conception of self-perceived attributes, such as values, interests, and abilities that individuals consider relevant to the profession (Skovholt, 2001).

Some of the personal motivations for pursuing training in the various human services fields have been explored empirically. The purpose of some of these studies were to investigate variables related to student's career development. For example, in a national study by Busacca, Beebe, and Toman (2010) of master's-level students in community counseling; mental health counseling; school counseling; and marital, couple, and family therapy programs, the general life values that students brought to their respective training programs were benevolence, self-direction, and achievement along with work values such as lifestyle, supervision, and achievement. Lower emphasis was placed on the life values stimulation, tradition, and power and the work values creativity, prestige, and income. Hazler and Kottler (2005) noted that it is important for students to evaluate their personal motives and professional aspirations early in their training. Self-reflection and awareness of one's value orientations early in training may diminish issues of role conflict, incongruence, and ambiguity. Thus, we encourage students to reflect on their work values and how those values are congruent with the profession of helping others.

Role of Career Professional in the Human Services

The role of the career services professional for human service professionals can be regarded as a generalist position that involves a variety of opportunities to help people with career and work-related issues. Although the undergraduate human services professional is not equipped to provide in-depth career counseling or psychotherapy, he or she may be well-equipped to facilitate client change and growth. Recently, competencies and skills that are necessary for human service work have been identified (Diambra, 2001). These are known as the **Skill Standards**, and they encompass 12 competencies that have been formally defined by the National Alliance of Direct Support Professionals (2011). These competencies delineate the roles and functions of the human services professional. They include competencies 3 [assessment] and 9 [vocational, educational, and career support parameters] in which the human service professional can perform his or her services.

Terminology

It is important to define some common career terms used in career services today. These terms are valuable for the human service professionals to know. The following definitions, synthesized from some prominent authors, are terms related to the career development process (Brown, 2016; Dik & Duffy, 2009; Herr, Cramer, & Niles, 2004; Savickas, 2019; Sharf, 2013). Some of these definitions may not be the same as our common, lay definitions. The following terms will be elaborated upon throughout this text:

Avocation. A chosen activity that is pursued by an individual because it gives satisfaction and fulfills an important aspect of the person's life. It may or may not be income generating.

Calling. "A transcendent summons, experienced as originating beyond the self, to approach a particular life role in a manner oriented toward demonstrating or deriving a sense of purpose or meaningfulness and that hold other-oriented values and goals as primary sources of motivation" (Dik & Duffy, 2009, p. 427).

Career. The combination of activities performed at any given life stage in all roles of life, including the role of worker.

Career Advising. A process that "helps students understand how their personal interests, abilities, and values might predict success in the academic and career fields they are considering and how to form their academic and career goals accordingly" (Gordon, 2006, p. 12).

Career Assessment. A process of using an instrument with clients to gather information about their self and occupations with the goal of helping them understand their career needs and possibilities so that they can make well-informed decisions about their future.

Career Counseling. "Career intervention that uses psychological methods to foster self-exploration as a prelude to choosing and adjusting to an occupation" (Savickas, 2011, p. 151).

Career Counselor. A licensed professional whom provides career interventions by use of psychotherapeutic methods to foster self-exploration and help clients choose and adjust to occupations.

Career Development. The sequence of career-related choices and transitions made over the life span.

Career Education. The systematic attempt to influence the career development of students and adults through various types of educational strategies such as infusing career-related concepts into the academic curriculum.

Career Guidance. A planned, sequential program of services provided by a professional to individuals or groups to assist them in increasing self-knowledge, finding career information, making decisions about a career, and/or conducting a job search.

4

Career Intervention. A deliberate act aimed at enhancing some aspect of a person's career development, including influencing the career decision-making process (Spokane, 1991).

Career Placement. The process of organizing and placing individuals in job positions; this includes writing a resume, practicing interview techniques, and going out on job leads, and may also involve helping students and graduates secure internships, work-study opportunities, and part-time employment.

Career Planning. The steps an individual takes to plan a career.

Career Services Provider. A person who has completed the Facilitating Career Development Training Program (National Career Development Association) and works in any career development setting or who incorporates career development information or skills in their work with students, adults, clients, employees, or the public.

Job. A group of similar positions in a single business or organization.

Leisure. Time taken from required effort (e.g., job or occupation) to pursue self-chosen activities that express one's values, abilities and/or interests.

Occupation. A defined set of work tasks commonly performed to make a particular product or perform a specific service.

Position. A group of tasks performed by one individual. As many positions exists as the number of individuals working.

Work. Effort expended at a job, occupation, or avocation to produce or accomplish something.

Competencies in Career Services

Human service professionals may work in a variety of career development settings. The work of a human service professional may include serving as a career group facilitator, job search trainer, career resource center coordinator, career coach, career development case manager, intake interviewer, academic or career advisor in higher education, occupational and labor market information resource person, human resource career coordinator, employment/placement specialist, or workforce development staff person. They may also work in rehabilitation counseling. We believe that the 12 core competencies addressed in the National Career Development Association's *Facilitating Career Development* curriculum (NCDA, 2018a) are relevant for human service professionals. Most of the chapters of this text are organized around seven of these competencies:

- *Helping Skills.* Be proficient in the basic career-facilitating process while also fostering productive interpersonal relationships.
- *Career Development Models.* Understand career development theories, models, and techniques as they apply to lifelong development, gender, age, and ethnic background.
- *Assessment.* Comprehend and use *(under supervision)* both formal and informal career development assessments with an emphasis on selecting appropriate ones for the population being served.
- *Labor Market Information and Resources.* Understand the labor market and occupational information and trends and be able to use current resources.
- *Employability Skills.* Know job search strategies and placement techniques.
- *Diverse Populations.* Recognize special needs of populations being served and adapt services to meet those needs.
- *Ethical and Legal Issues.* Follow the Code of Ethics of the human service professionals' parent organization and know current legislative regulations.

Preparation and Education

Most professional jobs providing career services start with bachelor's degrees in areas such as human services or psychology. Those with a desire to focus on career services often continue their education with additional certificates. If a person wishes to focus even more on providing career services, attending graduate school would be the path to become licensed as a counselor or other human services provider.

Generally, career service providers should be licensed. This is especially important if they are providing services under the title counselor, school counselor, rehabilitation counselor, social worker, or psychologist, choose to open a private practice, or if the human service organization or practice in which they are employed requires licensure. Along with meeting several strict education requirements, the student will also usually need to complete about 3,000 hours of supervised fieldwork (The exact number will depend on the specific guidelines of the state in which they will be practicing). Students should be sure to check with their state's licensing board to ensure that they are aware of current licensure requirements.

The counseling profession has made great progress in defining and creating a formal distinction between professional counseling and career counseling. However, several professional groups have recognized that many individuals who are currently providing career assistance are not professional counselors. In order to further clarify and differentiate these two levels of career practice, the Facilitating Career Development training program was developed by the NCDA (2018b). This program provides standards, training specifications, along with Certified Career Services Provider (CCSP) and Global Career Development Facilitator (GCDF) credentialing opportunities for these career providers.

Human service professionals without a license can undergo training as a Career Services Provider (CSP). The CSP is a person who has completed the *Facilitating Career Development Training Program* (formerly called the Career Development Facilitator Training Program) and can work in a variety of career development settings or who may incorporate career development information or skills in their work with students, adults, clients, employees, or the public. A CSP has received in-depth training in the field of career development through 120+ class/instructional hours provided by a nationally trained and qualified instructor.

Core Ingredients for Developing a Helping Relationship

Before a human service professional can assist a client in undertaking steps to address their career issues, it is essential to establish an appropriate helping relationship and a working alliance. The working alliance refers to the strength of the bond developed through the helping relationship. It is closely related to the ability of the client and helper to set and work on attainable goals (Gelso, 2009). The six core ingredients of the helping relationship are **acceptance, respect, empathy, understanding, trust,** and **genuineness** (Egan, 2013). C. H. Patterson has clarified that these attributes are essential to any good relationship, whether it exists in the context of vocational guidance, counseling, or psychotherapy (Freeman, 1990). Many scholars have agreed that these qualities are a vital component in enabling clients to engage in the self-exploration that leads to increased self-understanding and improved decision-making. Because these ingredients are discussed more thoroughly elsewhere, they will only be briefly defined here:

- *Acceptance.* Refers to the act of relating to another person without judgment. This is also referred to as "unconditional positive regard" (Rogers, 1957). This means acceptance of a person as worthwhile and valuable, regardless of age, sex, race, ethnicity, religion/spirituality, disability, sexual orientation, or other cultural attributes, and regardless of choices they have made in the past.

- *Respect.* Refers to the attitude of treating people with dignity. We convey respect when we show interest and concern for the client as a unique individual rather than because of their social status, education, or accomplishments.

- *Empathy.* Considered a critical factor in the helping relationship, empathy allows us to put ourselves in the other person's place to gain a deeper understanding of their issue. Hoffman (2000) defined empathy as "the cognitive awareness of another person's internal states, that is, his thoughts, feelings, perceptions, and intentions" (p. 29). When we work to understand and convey empathy, the client will feel heard and validated.

- *Understanding.* Use of empathy to gain a deep understanding of another person's point of view. When we communicate that we have heard what they have told us and provide them with the space to clarify or expand on anything that remains unclear and conveys understanding.

- *Trust.* Considered the most essential ingredient to develop in the helping relationship, trust is a feeling that the client experiences when we are consistent, reliable, and responsible. Thus, it creates a sense of security and safety for the client. When trust has been established, clients are more likely to be open and honest in sharing their experiences, thoughts and feelings, enabling us to connect with them on a deeper level.

- *Genuineness.* The alignment between our emotional response and behavior. Warmth and genuineness are conveyed though our tone of voice, eye contact, facial expressions, attentiveness, and body language. Rogers (1980) felt that genuineness—or sometimes called congruence—meant being in sync with one's own feelings and behaviors.

Using Helping Skills in the Career-Intake Process

The **career-intake interview** allows a professional to use helping skills to learn about the client, their needs, and how the available services can be used to address their situation. During the intake interview, the career services professional gathers work and career-related information from clients in a private and confidential setting. This first visit typically provides an in-depth look at the client's employment history, training, education, and current needs. The intake interview is an important opportunity to establish a working relationship with the client. By integrating basic interviewing skills with the core ingredients of a helping relationship, you will be able to convey genuine interest and concern while gathering the information you need to offer relevant career services. There are four basic purposes of the career intake interview:

1. to develop an understanding of the client's history and current situation or problem;
2. to identify and define a client's career goals;
3. to recognize barriers to and resources for goal attainment;
4. and to match the client's needs with appropriate services offered by your employer and assess whether any referral to other agencies or organizations are necessary.

Who Needs Help with Work and Career?

In the *National Survey of Working America,* Harris Interactive was commissioned in early 2011 by the NCDA (2011) to conduct a survey of U.S. adults with the following objectives: 1) to better understand how adult attitudes about work and career development have changed since 1999; 2) to see what Americans currently think, feel and believe about the state of the workforce and career development, and 3) to determine how those attitudes and beliefs affect the career development actions they may take. Some of the survey results are presented and discussed below:

- 21% of respondents in the labor force reported needing help in making career plans, selecting, changing, or getting a job (7% increase since 1999 in adults needing help in the past year).
- 24% say they have visited with a career practitioner about possible career choices.

The data suggested that individuals have a need for greater career assistance, and many have sought career help:

- Respondents reported seeking help to select, change, or get a job from, friends, relatives, and associates (70%); online career sites (57%); newspapers (46%), and co-workers (46%).

- 61% would seek help from a counselor, at their place of employment (37%), a counselor in an education-based setting (30%), a career specialist in private practice (28%), and in a public employment or welfare agency (27%).
- 57% now cite the internet as a source of information for selecting, changing or getting a job (up from 13% in 1999).

Adults value the importance of quality career information in making career decisions. However, it is possible they are not accessing the best or most useful resources. Many believe they need more training or education in the future and feel it would be difficult for them to find jobs similar in compensation and skill to what they have now:

- 59% of adults in the workforce would try to get more or different information about their options if they could start their work life over again.

Fewer employees who left their previous job did so because they wanted to (46% in 2011 vs. 60% in 1999) rather than because they had to or for some other reason. A large majority of respondents report various impacts of increased global competition:

- About three in four respondents who said that the US economy had been affected by globalization believe that millions of jobs have been outsourced (79%); that it has forced people to learn new skills (77%); that it has forced people to be retrained (76%), and that many middle-class Americans are forced to accept lower paying jobs (74%).
- In terms of individuals' personal situations, adults personally affected by globalization most commonly cite the following kinds of impacts: significant changes in how they work (36%); having to learn new skills (36%); and globalization having a significant impact on job or career prospects (35%).

The workplace and workforce environment remain less positive and more challenging for younger adults, minority adults, and those with lower levels of education:

- Blacks and Hispanics are more likely than Whites (32% and 31% vs. 10%) to report needing help in the past year.
- Blacks (15%) are more likely than Whites (6%) or Hispanics (4%) to expect that they will be forced to change jobs because of downsizing or the company going out of business.

These results reinforce the federal agenda related to developing career readiness, which includes learning how to make career decisions effectively, being aware of occupational and educational opportunities, and knowing how to gain access to such opportunities. Despite a decade which had the highest unemployment rates seen in many years, career specialists are underutilized relative to the present need and potential value. Significant numbers of employees are less than fully satisfied with their current jobs; employment that provides a livable wage is harder to find, and a majority of workers continue to report that they wish they had known more when they started their careers. Certain segments of the population who have historically faced greater challenges in gaining full employment—members of minority groups, younger adults, and unemployed adults—continue to face obstacles and are more likely to report needing help and more training.

The NCDA has provided the following recommendations in response to the findings of the study. Employers can make career development more of a priority by adding a focus and emphasis on those employees who are not fully satisfied in their current jobs. This could lead to not just greater satisfaction but greater productivity, commitment, and loyalty from employees. Regardless of one's education, every individual should have access to quality career planning and information. Human services practitioners are a vital resource for the livelihood of our nation's workforce and they are underutilized in terms of the need for and value of their services.

Common Career Counseling Myths

There are some myths about the scope of practice and process of what career counselors and practitioners really do. Amundson, Harris-Bowlsbey, and Niles (2014) have identified **common career myths** held by the public and even some licensed professionals. These misconceptions have been adapted here for human service professionals:

1. career service professionals use standardized assessments to tell people which occupation they should choose
2. work-role decisions can be made without consideration of other life roles
3. career services do not address personal issues
4. career service professionals do not need extensive training to do their work competently
5. career services do not address the client's culture and context
6. career services are required only when a choice must be made (p. 5)

These myths play themselves out in various ways. First, *many clients seek career services expecting to take a "test" that will "tell" them what occupation they should be in.* This is the old **test-and-tell** notion or client expectancy toward career counseling. Accordingly, it is important to provide appropriate structure and address client expectations. When practitioners use inventories or assessment instruments, they are primarily using them with the client to explore client concerns and problems and to help teach them about how the model or theory behind the assessment tool works.

Second, *life roles interact, and clients may expect that the only issue they talk about with a career practitioner is the work role.* Work-related decisions affect other roles in life, including one's place in family relationships and friendships, or status as a student or member of a community group. The life roles we play throughout our day are not isolated and separate. Career counseling is a highly personal matter that concerns the whole self and its relationship to life and work.

Third, *a client's personal concerns can significantly affect work roles and career development over the life span.* Today, many career and vocational scholars agree that work-related issues can often be intertwined with psychosocial and interpersonal problems in complex ways (Betz & Corning, 1993; Blustein, 2001; Krumboltz, 1993). Unfortunately, personal and career counseling have generally been viewed as separate entities in both training and practice.

Until recently, many mental health practitioners and educators viewed the career field as devoid of psychological processes and focused instead on outcomes and methods. Some scholars have even viewed career and personal counseling as a dichotomy that should be dealt with separately. Yet, more sophisticated career development approaches and counseling interventions have developed since the latter part of the 20th century and have dramatically expanded the role and scope of career counseling. With the call for the counseling profession to integrate career and personal counseling, which notably heightened in the 1990s, career theories now address a wide range of client concerns, including multiple life roles, learning deficiencies, cognitive difficulties, emotional problems, multicultural issues, and social barriers (Zunker, 2016). We, along with other scholars, believe that personal concerns should not be ignored in career-related programs and that human service professionals should take a holistic approach when working with a client's career concerns—including referring the client to a licensed career counselor or mental-health professional for further assessment when necessary.

The role of work in a person's life can vary in relation to their culture, race, sex, or social class, ranging from promoting health to distress and strain (Quick & Tetrick, 2010). In light of this variability, career intervention may directly benefit well-being by providing a helping relationship and emotional support, building confidence or competence beliefs, promoting optimism by identifying future goals, and clarifying one's identity. Indirect benefits of career interventions may arise through promoting participation in employment or alternative activities that provide access to meaningful work. The client may then have the opportunity to use skills and develop a sense of control, gain social-group membership, and earn income to address financial anxiety (Robertson, 2013).

On the other hand, career concerns can be strongly affected by a variety of interpersonal stressors and intrapersonal concerns. Sources of stress may include workload, number of hours, shiftwork, travel, and physical risk, along with psycho-social risks like bullying, sexual harassment, discrimination, and isolation. Work tasks such as repetition, control, burnout, and precariousness due to the threat of restructuring, downsizing, outsourcing, and other types of job insecurity can affect an individual's emotional and mental health. Further, mental-health disorders such as depression, anxiety, alcohol/drug addiction, and personality disorders can all serve as underlying sources of problems in the work role. Although more research is warranted, the available research does imply that it is reasonable to expect that when work situations are positive, the likelihood of experiencing positive mental and physical health increase (Zunker, 2008).

Fourth, *given the interrelationship between career and personal concerns, mental health clients with career-related issues require an advanced level of training, competence, and experience.* As covered in the "Preparation and Educational Requirements to Provide Career Services" section that appears earlier in this chapter, human service professionals, career practitioners, licensed counselors and others must possess a substantial combination of training, knowledge, and skills, as well as the licenses or other credentials required in their state to help clients from diverse backgrounds with career-related concerns.

Fifth, *the human services and career counseling profession embraces all expressions of diversity.* Unfortunately, the history of career counseling and intervention does not reflect a strong commitment to being sensitive to diversity in clients. Many of the standardized assessments used in career guidance for example lack cultural equivalence or appropriate norm groups. Additionally, some of the traditional theories and model of career development, although appropriate for their time, are now considered culturally biased. Blustein (2006) postulated that many traditional career theories and models appear irrelevant to some groups because they remain based on cultural assumptions that emphasize freedom of choice, affluence, the centrality of the work role, and notions of career success. Thus, the dialogue in multicultural career counseling has slowly evolved from a monocultural to a pluralistic perspective of culture which includes not only race and ethnicity but also gender, sexual orientation, disability, age, religion, and spirituality—along with intersectional identities (Busacca & Rehfuss, 2017).

The contextualist worldview considers knowledge about ourselves that is derived from social interaction and the active nature of individuals. Contextual variables that can have an influence on a client's experience of a career problem include socioeconomic status, workplace, employment market, educational institutions, geographical location, peers, political decisions, family, historical trends, media, globalization, and community groups. These types of context are highly individual: two clients may grow up in the same city and culture but have vastly different contextual exposures, expectations, and perspectives. Cultural context becomes increasingly essential as the labor force becomes more diverse, with marked increases in the number of women, non-White and immigrant workers, and older workers (Arabandi, 2015). It is important that human services practitioners take a universalistic stance, which assumes that every client has a unique cultural background embedded in and influenced by context.

Finally, *career services are not designed and used only to help a client make a career decision involving occupational choice.* Career concerns span the life course and continue beyond the point at which a choice has been made. The word career denotes course or passage, having evolved from the medieval Latin word *carraria*, meaning road for vehicles, and the middle French word *carrier*, meaning streets. Helping professional, therefore, can view a student or client's career task as choosing a direction at a crossroads or turning point. Savickas (1998) suggested that career practitioners may relate this metaphor to client's career experiences by "describing the career paths that they have already traveled and project the paths over the horizon" (p. 351). Career choice and adjustments are continual, ongoing processes because our self-concept, or the individual's view of the situation in which she or he exists, changes with time and experience (Super, 1990).

A wide range of career concerns may emerge for people especially when engaging in their work role. These concerns often manifest as decreased job productivity, low work satisfaction, and the struggle for meaningful work. Some triggers may involve navigating relationships with coworkers and supervisors, coping with job demands, burnout, layoffs, career transitions, discrimination in the workplace, and searching for one's sense of meaning, purpose, or calling in work. All can affect how present we are in our work. In the Gallup (2017) study *State of the American Workplace,* of 195,600 U.S. employees and 31 million respondents, the aggregate data collected in 2015 and 2016 indicated that just 33% of employees are engaged in their job. Work engagement denotes that an employee is psychologically present in a particular organization role (Saks, 2006). It is often defined as "...a positive, fulfilling, work-related state of mind that is characterized by vigor, dedication, and absorption (Schaufeli et al., 2002, p. 74). Actively disengaged employees are almost twice as likely as engaged employees to seek new jobs. These individuals often have difficulty coping and lack personal resources such as hope and optimism.

Career professionals should foster a sense of hopefulness when working with clients. Hope and optimism provide the foundation for career success and job satisfaction. Hope allows a person to consider pathways to desired goals and drives the individual to take action (Niles, 2011). As Neault (2011) stated "Without hope, clients are unlikely to be motivated to engage in career planning activities or ongoing career management." Proverbs 13:12 declares, "Hope deferred makes the heart sick, but a longing fulfilled is a tree of life." In today's uncertain and unpredictable work economy, career services will increasingly focus on work adjustment, meaning-making, and transition. Thus, strengthening hope in clients and having a basic knowledge of career issues, theories, and assessments constitute the basic essentials for human service professionals.

Conclusion

This chapter discussed the basic landscape of career issues, processes, assessments, and interventions that are essential to human service professionals. The role of the career services professional for human services as a generalist position was addressed. Definitions of key career terms and explanations of career service competencies relevant to human service professionals were provided. An overview of the preparation and education required for the career service professional was covered. Core ingredients for establishing an effective helping relationship and working alliance with a client were listed and explained. The National Survey of Working America was examined to show its impact on current career counseling theory in general and this text in particular. The chapter concluded with a look at several common career counseling myths and provided arguments that debunk those misconceptions. The topics covered in this introductory chapter will be explored in greater detail in the remaining chapters.

Key Chapter Terms

Skill Standards	Job
Avocation	Occupation
Calling	Leisure
Career	Position
Career Advising	Work
Career Assessment	Acceptance
Career Development	Respect
Career Guidance	Understanding
Career Counseling	Empathy
Career Counselor	Trust
Career Education	Genuineness
Career Intervention	Career-Intake Interview
Career Placement	National Survey of Working America
Career Planning	Common Career Myths
Career Service Provider	Test-and-Tell

Web Resources

Note that website URLs may change over time.

2011 Harris Interactive Survey on Working America
https://ncda.org/aws/NCDA/pt/sd/news_article/48270/_PARENT/layout_details/false

Career Theory, Development, and Appraisal

2017 Gallup Report-State of the American Workplace
https://www.gallup.com/workplace/238085/state-american-workplace-report-2017.aspx

Career Providers Comparison Chart
https://www.ncda.org/aws/NCDA/pt/sd/news_article/15416/_blank/layout_details/false

History of Career Services Provider Credentialing in the USA
https://associationdatabase.com/aws/NCDA/asset_manager/get_file/156400?ver=438

Certified Career Services Provider
https://ncda.org/aws/NCDA/pt/sp/credentials_ccsp

National Career Development Association
https://ncda.org/aws/NCDA/pt/sp/home_page

National Employment Counseling Association
http://www.employmentcounseling.org/

Occupational Outlook Handbook-Community & Social Service Occupations
https://www.bls.gov/ooh/community-and-social-service/home.htm

Human Services Career Network
http://www.hscareers.com/

Chapter 2

FROM VOCATIONAL GUIDANCE TO CAREER COUNSELING

"...cultural transitions prompt vocational guidance experts to reflect on where they have been in order to consider where they will take their profession."
~Mark L. Savickas, 2008, p. 97

CHAPTER HIGHLIGHTS
The Need for Career Helpers Through the Eras
Forerunners of the Vocational Guidance Movement
Early Legislation, Professional Organizations, and Journals

We will start our look at history by journeying into the distant past and exploring some of the precursors to the career counseling field. Some students of human services may wonder, "Why learn this information?" One concept can shed light on why historical events are important in the helping professions. In 1962, a provocative book by Thomas Kuhn called *The Structure of Scientific Revolutions* stirred debates within the social sciences *and* had a profound impact on the way we view scientific progress. In particular, his concept of **paradigm shift** proposed that knowledge builds upon itself and new discoveries are based on the evolution of past knowledge. For instance, for many years psychoanalysis was the treatment of choice for most mental illness. However, research on the effectiveness of other forms of treatment and the advent of new theories and methods revealed that other treatment methods should be considered the treatment of choice. Kuhn stated that when a paradigm shift occurs, our conceptual schemas or perspectives change. Consequently, we begin to view the world and those in it differently. The paradigm shifts we are going to discuss during these periods of recent U. S. history were also successful solutions to the pressing social problems of each period. This chapter does not go into detail about the challenges faced by society, its workers, women and minorities, but paradigm shifts were often driven by societal unrest and groups of individuals acting to create a better life for themselves and those around them. A detailed description of such events can be found in Howard Zinn's (2003), *A People's History of the United States*. Guichard (2015) emphasized that career theories and interventions met a societal need in the early to mid-20th century because of the changes in work organization and in the scientific models within which research questions were formulated at the time. With knowledge of the historical process involved in shaping the profession, human service professionals can be ready to provide the leadership required in times of societal transition and crisis (Pope, 2000).

This chapter provides an overview of how vocational guidance served a need in evolving American society. Five economic eras guided adaptation to the changing conditions of work along with the methods helpers used to assist and support people experiencing work issues. Next, we look at the changing narratives in society as prompted by the eras and ensuing impact on career counseling. We will also take a brief look at several early pioneers of the vocational guidance movement, followed by notable landmarks in early legislation. This chapter will conclude with a discussion of the evolution of vocational professional organizations and journals related to the career profession.

The Need for Career Helpers Through the Eras

Based in sociological theory, we will briefly describe in the following section ways in which working lives were shaped by agrarian, artisan, industrial, modern, and postmodern economies. The dominant shared assumptions, implicit values, and ideals inherent to life during these five eras guided adaptation to the changing conditions of work during each time-period (see Figure 2.1). In response to the migration of people from rural areas to the city, an increase in occupational alternatives, social reform, and the needs of a country at war, helpers adapted to the transitions by creating methods to assist people in making occupational choices.

Agrarian Society

During the colonial period, which began with the arrival of the first English settlers in North America and lasted into the 18th century, country life and the Puritan ethic largely shaped American values. In the **agrarian society**, the Puritan ethic emphasized hard work, frugality, and diligence as constant displays of moral character for a person seeking salvation in the Christian faith. People progressed in work through self-motivation and individual efforts that led to success and personal fulfillment. Work was shaped into chores, and men predominantly held occupations that commonly continued through successive generations within families, such as being a farmer or a craftsperson.

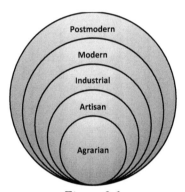

Figure 2.1
Five Eras of The Working Economy

For many people during this period, family, religion, and the Puritan ethic provided structure and predictability. Personal relationships and collectivist values unified agricultural communities. The community expected everyone to be of good character: honest, moral, and hardworking. This was consistent with Calvinistic teachings. Because most people were simply assigned a work role that they inherited from their parents, society offered few occupational choices. Thus, to choose a life's work did not pose a problem for many people. This began to change with the advent of the artisan era.

Artisan Society

During the late 18th and early 19th centuries, artisans or craftsmen worked independently. In the **artisan society**, people refined their skills, owned their own tools, and served an apprenticeship to learn their trade (Applebaum, 1998). More than 80% of workers were farmers, craftspeople, and small business owners (Maccoby, 1983). As a secular version of the Puritan ethic, the value of work began to be based on pride in workmanship and the maintenance of self-reliance in one's own work, along with the provision of economic independence for the family, rather than being rooted in religion. Although workers felt a responsibility to serve their communities, they "performed work for its own sake, beyond the ulterior motivation as a means to livelihood" (Applebaum, 1998, p.

21). A sense of purpose through tradition and social responsibility provided a great deal of structure and predictability for artisan workers during this time. Most people still did not worry about choosing an occupation. With the arrival of the industrial revolution, however, an enormous change in social organization took place.

Industrial Society

With the advent of the first phase of the American industrial revolution during 1790 to 1850, significant cultural changes occurred in the institutions of work. During the **industrial society**, the war of 1812 especially made it apparent that America needed greater economic independence. In the past, agricultural society offered freedom of activity and the joys of craftsmanship. During the industrial period, there was conflict between the traditional values associated with holding a craft and the new model of industrial factory work (Applebaum, 1998).

From approximately 1850 to 1914, the time-period regarded as the second phase of the Industrial Revolution, people moved from the farm or village to the city. They had to choose one major job or focus on a single task in a manufacturing industry rather than do the variety of chores they had done at home. For many workers, the assembly line in machine-aided production factories provided a career. Working life went from the leisurely style of the colonial period to a standardized one with clearly delineated rules, procedures, boundaries, and requirements. As Applebaum (1998) noted, workers no longer found themselves as self-employed producers providing a service to customers, but as wageworkers dealing with owners of capital.

Considering this new form of social organization, society devised **mentoring** as a mechanism to help youth choose occupations from an increased range of options. Mentoring became systematized in informal guidance programs such as C. C. Robinson's (1922) *Find Yourself* program. Robinson called his approach to vocational mentoring a friendly method because advice was provided as a friend, not as an expert (Savickas, 2008). **Friendly visitors,** who were volunteers, helped youth choose among alternatives and were eventually offered to every boy who entered a Young Men's Christian Association (YMCA) program.

To improve the spiritual condition and mental culture of young men engaged in drapery-making and other trades, the YMCA was founded in 1844. As part of the relief efforts in the USA, the organization opened employment bureaus to address the employment needs of Civil War veterans. By the 1870's, the individuals who staffed the YMCA employment bureaus engaged in mentoring as part of their employment programs. The bulk of the mentoring provided by the YMCA consisted of placement services along with character education (i.e., building self-discipline and habits of responsibility and morality). These mentoring programs reached their peak in the 1920s and 1930s. The YMCA's friendly visitors eventually became organized within the community as the profession of social work emerged to address the ills of society. With the arrival of the second phase of the industrial revolution, however, helping new workers through the assistance of friendly volunteers and mentors became ineffective in meeting the needs of city youth (Savickas, 2008).

From 1900 to 1949, views of success espoused by corporations, educational institutions, and the family served as socializing agents in preparing youth for lifelong jobs. Jobs became standardized for efficiency and uniformity, making advancement in a career possible. Although this brought people and groups closer together, sociopolitical limitations and resistances in the form of stratification, inequality, and differentiation by gender, ethnicity, race, and social class remained (Savickas, 2009). The change in population distribution caused by the movement to commercial cities led to problems such as unemployment, immorality, alcoholism, delinquency, and crime.

By 1910, 50% of the population of the USA lived in cities. Terrible working conditions and low wages led to the growth of labor unions. Organized labor came about because workers, many of whom were immigrants and women who were not allowed to vote, had little political support. The problems of the city, including the ability of people to choose and find jobs, overwhelmed the volunteers and required the attention of experts.

The experts viewed science as the panacea for society's ills. The science of helping soon came to embrace the idea of individual differences in abilities and personalities, rather than the assumed uniformity of character espoused by the Agrarian and Artisan societies. School personnel and social workers in many countries needed to design an innovative model for helping adolescents make vocational choices. In the United States, vocational guidance was quickly integrated into the schools. Science was used to devise vocational guidance as a new mechanism for assisting youth to choose among their occupational options (Savickas, 2008).

In early 20th century American society, the focus on psychological testing and assessment was referred to as the measurement movement. Psychological testing became an important part of vocational guidance and eventually gave career counseling respectability. A key type of test that sustained early vocational guidance as a science was measures of ability, devised by the psychologist **Alfred Binet**, who studied the differences that separated the normal child from the abnormal child. In 1916, Binet constructed the intelligence test for French school children. Testing also received a huge push at the beginning of World War I, as it became necessary to classify almost 1.5 million soldiers into appropriate positions. Due to this need, Robert M. Yerkes chaired the committee that created the first group-administered intelligence tests. These tests became known as the Army Alpha and Beta Tests and were made available to counselors of the public following the war.

During the next two decades, special aptitude tests, interest inventories, and achievement tests were developed. These assessments were instrumental in linking the measurement movement to the guidance movement and provided standardized support materials for the vocational guidance field. In addition, these early tests were influential in the development of the trait-and-factor career theory discussed further in Chapter 4 of this text. Today, vocational guidance remains closely associated with tests and test interpretation.

In general, social reform was linked to vocational guidance advocacy efforts by the growing exploitation of people (Aubrey, 1977). The need for vocational guidance has been described by historians as a "progressive social reform movement aimed at eradicating poverty and substandard living conditions spawned by the rapid industrialization and subsequent migration of people to major urban centers of the 20th century" (Whiteley, 1984, p. 2). Vocational guidance, as a function of social reform, rested on the promise of social efficiency in matching workers to work and of fostering the personal development of workers (Savickas, 2008).

Modern Society

The period from 1950 to 1999 is referred to as **modern society** or high modernity. While modern industries and their employees remained in the city, large numbers of workers moved to the suburbs and commuted to work. In addition, high modernity was characterized by growth of national and multinational corporations. With the hierarchical structure in corporate society came the image of the corporate ladder. Rather than having one job for life, the possibility of advancement and improvement along an established path emerged (Savickas, 2008). Because of this paradigm shift in the nature of work, career experts now needed to assist people in coping with, preparing for, and managing a series of stages and tasks along with concerns related to their life-long career, and in balancing work with other life role activities (career stages and tasks are discussed in Chapter 4). As Savickas (2008) noted, "each time the social organization of work changes, so does society's methods for helping individuals make vocational choices" (p. 97).

The shift from company to corporation foreshadowed the change in vocational intervention models. Theories started to focus on the person rather than the occupation and helping individuals with career issues changed from providing guidance to providing counseling. To begin to address these changes, a major theory was proposed by **Donald Super,** who in 1953 published his theory of vocational development and career patterns. Super continued the development of his theory with the publication of the instrumental book *The Psychology of Careers* (Super, 1957). He concentrated on the process of developing a career rather than on the content involved in matching oneself to a fitting occupation, as would occur in vocational guidance.

The transformation that occurred during the end of the corporate era made career choices for many people more difficult. Because developmental career theory, such as Super's theory, is rooted in assumptions of stability of personal characteristics and secure jobs in hierarchical organizations, one's career was conceptualized as a progressive sequence of stages. Concepts such as career planning, career development, and career tasks were each used to help people advance in work environments with relatively high stability and clear career paths. Although valuable and effective for their intended purpose, these theories do not adequately account for the uncertain and rapidly-changing occupational structure of the present day—nor do they address the needs of peripheral workers (Savickas, 2019). Career paths are not as clear as they once were. By the end of the corporate era, commitment to an occupational choice was difficult for some people due to lack of stability in social structures. With the lack of a stable framework to guide one's career, professionals and counselors trained to understand the occupational landscape of the 21st century was needed.

Postmodern Society

A focus on career counseling rather than on vocational guidance and career development has become the distinguishing feature in career theory and intervention since 2000. The nature of work and the meaning of career have been restructured and reinvented. Because **postmodern society** is characterized in part by a global economy and information technology, work is increasingly more uncertain, unpredictable, and risky from the point of view of the worker (Kalleberg, 2009). Consequently, commitment to an occupational choice, career progression, and coping with unanticipated transitions have become more difficult for many people. This section presents a condensed version of postmodern career counseling, a topic discussed in greater detail in Chapter 13.

Organizational restructuring for lower costs and greater efficiency has resulted in a transformation of working lives. Layoffs, unanticipated transfers, offshoring (i.e., contracting out the performance of service sector activities to businesses located beyond U. S. borders), career destabilization, and non-standardized work contracts (Inkson & Elkin, 2008) are characteristic of work in a postmodern society. Standing (1999) cited sources of work insecurity including loss of a job or fear of losing a job, lack of alternative employment opportunities, and diminished freedom to obtain and maintain skills in order to advance in a position. According to Standing, possible effects of insecurity include a sense of oppression and exploitation, demoralization, demotivation, and ill-health. As established career paths disappear, many companies today expect their employees to take responsibility for the direction and evolution of their own career pathways (Arthur & Rousseau, 1996), which leaves many people feeling anxious, depressed, and frustrated.

In response to the massive changes taking place in the world of work at the end of the 20th century, many of the core concepts in vocational psychology were reexamined and broadened, and new theories were proposed to help clients affected by these changes. In fact, career and vocational scholars proposed a redefinition of the term *career* to fit the postmodern economy. **Postmodernism** is an intellectual movement that rejects the fundamental assumptions of modernism regarding objective truths, and in general asserts that individuals construct meaning or perceive their own reality or truth (Busacca & Rehfuss, 2017). So, career scholars believe that identities, anchored in family and community, no longer provide the meaning they once did (Richardson, 2015). People not only construct their own meaning, but they also revise it across time and life span. As sociologist Anthony Giddens (1991) stressed, the demand on the individual to construct him- or herself has become a major social reality and a defining characteristic of our societies. Because of the increased importance placed on individuals becoming more self-directed in making meaning of the role of work in their lives and managing their careers (Richardson, 1996), people required help with a new form of career problem.

Career counseling in a postmodern society began to distinguish itself from vocational guidance and career education by focusing on the integration of a process-oriented, subjective, and emotional domain. In the traditional view of career guidance, there is minimal emphasis on the subjective nature of career problems such as meaning, how individuals cope with the career process, their emotions, and the counseling relationship. Postmodern career counseling models and methods therefore take a more facilitative, more collaborative, and less directive focus when helping clients.

Forerunners of the Vocational Guidance Movement

The forerunners of social reform included social workers, lawyers, economists, psychologists, and teachers. These pioneers propelled the movement and established the profession of vocational guidance, which later evolved into the field of career counseling. Reformers hoped that teachers and social workers would use scientific methods of guidance to replace 19-century charity work with 20th century professional service (Savickas, 2009). The following introduces several notable people who were instrumental in the early vocational guidance movement in America.

Lysander S. Richards

Two early pioneers influential to the eventual formation of vocational guidance for youth in America were Lysander Richards and George Merrill. **Lysander Richards** was a school science teacher, horticulturist, and leader in reformatory and progressive movements. He served as a Massachusetts state senator and was author of several literary and philosophical works. Richards (1881) book *Vocophy: The New Profession. A System Enabling A Person to Name the Calling or Vocation One is Best Suited to Follow* envisioned the role of career counselor and advocated for the need for a new profession to provide vocational assistance to youth. Richards believed that a fitting occupation was paramount, and the lack thereof was the source of poverty. In his book, he states that a "fit" was synonymous with a calling, subsequently the conversation of calling shifted from glorifying God through work, to a more secular view of working.

George Merrill

Vocational guidance began in Cogswell High School in San Francisco in 1888 lead by **George A. Merrill**. In 1894, he was hired as the Director of the California School of Mechanical Arts, which offered free education to boys and girls. The curriculum combined a general academic preparation with technical and vocational instruction. Merrill's goal was to create the "educated craftsman." In 1900 Merrill became the head of Wilmerding School of Industrial Arts, and in 1912, as a nationally recognized pioneer in vocational education, he founded and became the head of The Lux School for Industrial Training for Girls. George Merrill implemented a unique plan wherein the teachers observed and counseled students about appropriate occupational choices and trade preparation (Savickas, 2008).

Frank Parsons

One of the best-documented stories of the origins of modern vocational guidance began in 1908 in Boston. **Frank Parsons** started his career as a social worker influenced by the work of Jane Addams in Chicago and was later trained as a civil engineer. He settled in Boston in 1885 after returning from a hiatus in the southwest. Parsons ran for mayor of Boston in 1895 and taught political economy at Kansas State University until his resignation in 1899. During this time, there was increasing disparity between the status of the rich and the poor. He was a prominent early leader in the struggle to eliminate child labor exploitation which culminated in the passage of the 1938 Fair Labor Standards Act.

In 1906 Parsons gave a lecture to the Economic Club of Boston entitled "The Ideal City." He stressed the need to assist youth in their vocational decision-making (Savickas, 2008). Because of his lecture, he was asked to present a similar lecture to a graduating class at a local night school. From this beginning, Parsons was asked to formulate a plan for systematic vocational guidance. This request led to the creation of the first institutionalization of vocational guidance in the U.S. In 1908, The Vocation Bureau at Civic Service House opened in Boston and Parsons served as director and vocational counselor. It was at this time that Parsons coined the term "vocational guidance." In a relatively brief period, his vision was implemented—most schools had some form of vocational guidance program by 1920.

At the same time as the inception of the Bureau, Parsons was developing a training program for educational and vocational guidance experts. He was scheduled to be Dean of the new training program but died prior to its implementation. One of the most important contributions Parsons made was his conceptual framework for helping individuals choose careers (Parsons, 1909). He consulted with leading psychologists about using tests and rating scales to study self and occupations. **Parson's three-step model** for vocational guidance is outlined as follows:

1. *Self-Assessment.* A clear understanding of yourself and your aptitudes, abilities, interests, resources, limitations, and other qualities;
2. *Information Gathering.* Knowledge of the requirements and conditions of success, advantages and disadvantages, compensations, opportunities, and prospects in different occupations;
3. *Decision-Making.* True reasoning in comparing self and occupational information to make a realistic vocational choice.

In the United States, Parsons's seminal book ignited the vocational guidance movement. For the first fifty years of the 20th century, Parsons's three-step process served as the theoretical framework used by vocational counselors to provide vocational guidance and formed the basis for the trait-and factor model. Parsons's work "continues to be a remarkable milestone in the evolution of career development practices" (Herr, 2001).

Jesse B. Davis

Considered to be the first school guidance counselor, **Jesse B. Davis** is credited for helping achieve the goal of Frank Parsons. From 1898-1907, he was the first person to implement an 11th-grade systematic guidance program at Central High School in Detroit, Michigan. In 1907, he became principle of a high school in Grand Rapids, Michigan, where he required English teachers to have students in the seventh grade write weekly compositions on their occupational interests. Davis's (1956) influential book, *Vocational and Moral Guidance,* was published in 1914 and became the model used for implementing vocational guidance in public schools in the U.S. from 1914 to 1916.

Edmund G. Williamson

At the University of Minnesota in 1931 **Edmund G. Williamson** joined the faculty as assistant professor of psychology and was named director of the University of Minnesota Testing Bureau (now the University of Minnesota Counseling and Consulting Center). He became the Dean of Students between 1941 and 1969. Much of the research on psychological assessment took place at the Minnesota Employment Stabilization Research Institute (MESRI). The Minnesota group, led by Williamson, developed psychometric instrumentation and occupational classification systems to assist with the placement of workers who had been displaced during the Great Depression. As the country moved into World War II, the contributions of the Minnesota researchers were widely applied in classifying and assigning military personnel. This effort operationalized Frank Parsons's concepts of matching the characteristics of workers with jobs and came to be labeled trait-and-factor counseling (Savickas, 2009). The term **Minnesota point-of-view** was also sometimes used because of Williamson's prolific and influential writings on trait-and-factor counseling.

Williamson successfully adapted the methods developed by the MESRI to address the career development concerns of college students. He emphasized the importance of reliably and accurately assessing career problems and individual characteristics, and viewed counseling as facilitating self-understanding, realistic planning, and decision-making skills (Williamson, 1965). Under Williamson's leadership, the University of Minnesota Testing Bureau became the prototype for all future college counseling centers. For several decades, the trait-and-factor approach enjoyed considerable success and up until the 1950s was the essential career counseling approach. The prominence of this approach started to lessen, however, as Rogerian psychotherapy permeated the counseling field and developmental and social learning approaches to career counseling matured.

Early Legislation, Professional Organizations, and Journal

Laws supportive of vocational guidance began to receive considerable social support in the early 1900's. The landmark Smith-Hughes Act of 1917 established secondary school vocational education training. This legislation was strengthened in succeeding years by the George-Reed Act of 1929, the George-Ellzey Act of 1934, and the George-Deen Act of 1939. The passage of these federal laws supported vocational education as an important part of the public-school system. Also, in 1913, the U.S. Department of Labor (DOL) was founded, and the Bureau of Labor Statistics was moved under the auspices of the DOL.

Out of this transition came the founding of the National Vocational Guidance Association (NVGA) in 1913 in Grand Rapids, Michigan. NVGA was founded five years after the death of Parsons. In brief, the first journal of NVGA was the *Vocational Guidance Bulletin* in 1915. In 1952, the name changed to the *Personnel and Guidance Journal* (PGJ, now the *Journal of Counseling & Development*) and became the journal of the new American Counseling

29

Association. The National Vocational Guidance Association (NVGA, now National Career Development Association in 1984) was one of its four founding divisions. NCDA, wanting to maintain a journal of its own, began publishing the *Vocational Guidance Quarterly* in 1952 now *The Career Development Quarterly.*

Conclusion

This chapter began by describing how working lives have been shaped through history by agrarian, artisan, industrial, modern, and postmodern economies. Career counseling today requires human service professionals to consider the impact of dominant narratives, and how individuals construct their own ideas about their world and try to make meaning out of the career transitions confronting them. We then took a brief look at several early pioneers of the vocational guidance movement, followed by notable landmarks in early legislation. These pioneers propelled the movement and established the profession of vocational guidance, which later evolved into the field of counseling. Career counseling today is a product of all these changes and the work of key thinkers over the years. We also briefly discussed the evolution of vocational professional organizations related to the career profession, and birth of the premier journal of the National Career Development Association. The human service field has undergone, and will continue to undergo, paradigm shifts. By studying the history of the field and gaining knowledge about its roots, human service professionals are in a better position to help clients adapt to the challenges inherent in the new organization of work that is evolving in a global and information-age society (Savickas, 2008).

Key Chapter Terms

Paradigm Shift	Postmodern Society
Artisan Society	Postmodernism
Agrarian Society	Lysander Richards
Industrial Society	George Merrill
Friendly Visitors	Frank Parsons
Mentoring	Parson's Three-Step Model
Alfred Binet	Jesse B. Davis
Modern Society	Edmund G. Williamson
Donald Super	Minnesota Point of View

Web Resources

Note that website URLs may change over time.

Pope, M. (1997). *History and Development of Career Counseling in the USA.* https://eric.ed.gov/?id=ED439332

National Employment Counseling Association
http://www.employmentcounseling.org/about-neca.html

NCDA (2013). National Career Development Association's Annual Conference, Mark Savickas Keynote speaker [Video File]. Retrieved from https://www.youtube.com/watch?v=rJC6e2caZ6E

Revise Sociology (2016). From modernity to postmodernity. Retrieved from https://revisesociology.com/2016/04/09/from-modernity-to-post-modernity/

Chapter 3

CAREER SERVICE AREAS: A FRAMEWORK AND OVERVIEW

"Helping to develop schemata that students can use to conceptualize clients and their concerns is a much more complex process than skill development."
~Ann L. Cummings et al., 1990, p. 120

CHAPTER HIGHLIGHTS
Five Career Service Areas
Career Guidance
Career Placement
Career Development
Career Education
Career Counseling

Many human-services and related programs teach students about various theories, models, and career assessment measures during their training. However, the transition to practicum and internship often challenges students with regards to when to apply career theories and measures to specific client problems (Busacca, 2002). Determining the best way to begin work with clients who present career issues can be confusing because career theories can be abstract, while client problems are more concrete. Herr (1996) stated that the abstract language and definitional distinctions used in career services, such as vocational guidance and career counseling, raise the issue of semantics. Over the years, vocational scholars have proposed diagnostic classifications to help them understand a client's career problem and where to begin the helping process (e.g., Savickas, 1996). The present chapter presents an overview of the major career service areas. We discuss the typical career problem clients present, the implicit question that the client wants resolved, the helper objective in providing career interventions, and typical assessment tools used for each service.

Five Major Career Service Areas

Out of vocational guidance, distinct models and methods for helping people with career issues have emerged. To place vocational guidance into perspective, we will look briefly at the purpose of **five career service areas** adapted from Busacca (2002): career guidance, career placement, career development, career education, and career counseling (see Table 3.1). The discussion includes a brief mention of select career inventories and scales which are discussed further in Chapter 5 of this text. It is important to note that the terms career guidance (e.g., vocational guidance), career development, and career education have distinct meanings with origins in the historical perspectives of society during specific periods that reflect the societal, political, and economic conditions of those times. Thus, one can see a natural progression toward career services that require fewer objective tests and more subjective approaches to helping people cope with work and career. The five career service areas are discussed as follows.

Table 3.1			
Five Career Service Areas and Problem, Question, Objective			
Career Service	*Career Problem*	*Implicit Client Question*	*Helper Objective*
Career Guidance	Making a career choice	What shall I choose?	Explore match between self-concept and jobs.
Career Placement	Starting a job	How do I get a position?	Prepare, refine, and help secure a position.
Career Development	Managing & coping with career	What should I expect?	Enhance awareness and develop skills to negotiate career tasks, and balance life roles.
Career Education	Developing a career	Why Career/work?	Foster autonomy, foresight and self-management attitudes.
Career Counseling	Self-concept & identity	Who am I within my career?	Develop insight, self-reflection, and meaning-making.

Career Guidance

The first career service area concerns matching people to jobs. Clients present the problem of making a career choice with implicit question, "What shall I choose?" Also called the 'matching model,' the goal of **career guidance** is to match people to occupations or positions based on individual differences. Career guidance (or vocational guidance) is often provided by human-service professionals, professional counselors, career counselors, school counselors, vocational rehabilitation counselors, social workers, and psychologists.

Career guidance shows clients how to gather information about themselves and the world-of-work. Thus, career guidance is considered a **content model** which focuses on *what* occupation to choose, rather than *how* one makes decisions. The idea was, and continues to be, that a "fitting match of individual ability to job requirements leads to occupational success; while a fitting match of interests to job rewards leads to work satisfactions; and finally, that success and satisfaction combine to promote stability or tenure" (Savickas, 2008, p. 104).

Interests, abilities, values, and personality traits can be measured separately or in combination. Services may be delivered to individuals or groups or may even be self-directed. Although there are many tools used in career guidance, the most widely used interest inventories are based on the popular Holland (1997) theory of career choice. These include the *Self-Directed Search* (SDS; Holland, Powell, & Fritzsche, 1994), and computer-scored inventories such as the *Strong Interest Inventory* (SII; Harmon, Hansen, Borgen, & Campbell, 1994).

Career Placement

Career placement was embedded within vocational guidance during the late 19th and early 20th centuries. Career placement, formally referred to as mentoring, helped clients develop and plan ways to attain jobs. In its modern form, this service begins with the client's implicit question, "How do I get a position?" The primary goal of **career placement** today is to help people overcome the challenges and difficulty involved in obtaining a position. Career placement is often provided by human-service professionals, professional and career counselors, vocational rehabilitation counselors, social workers, and psychologists.

Placement activities relate minimally to theory. Instead, they involve practical interventions such as skill training, gathering information, writing resumes, networking, searching for opportunities, preparing for interviews, and refining self-presentation behavior. In helping clients develop new skills, human-service professionals can apply specific interventions to aid transition into a job. These interventions include increasing a client's self-efficacy and job search activity, assertion-training for job interviews, developing social supports, and connecting clients with job clubs, organizations, and people in their community.

Career Development

Beginning in the mid-20th century, helpers focused on managing worker and other life roles over the life span. **Career development** involves addressing the problem of managing and coping with career and life roles. The client's implicit question is, "What shall I expect?" The term career development came into more common usage in the 1950's through the work of Donald Super. Super (1957;1980) shifted attention away from occupations and which people *fit* them (e.g., guidance) to a focus on careers and how people *develop* them (Savickas, 2008). Thus, the goal of career development is to enhance awareness and develop skills to negotiate career tasks, and balance life roles. Career development is considered a **process model** which concentrates on *how* to make decisions, rather than on *what* occupations to choose. Career development services require more expertise and are often provided by professional counselors, school counselors, social workers, and psychologists.

Increasingly, adults struggle with issues relating to how to best prepare for career developmental tasks and the intertwining of life roles. Super identified **career stages** throughout the life span: growth, exploration, establishment, maintenance, and disengagement--each with its own set of tasks (Super, Savickas, & Super, 1996). Special career development inventories can be used with clients to indicate what stages and tasks of career development they are currently engaged in (Super, Thompson, & Lindeman, 1988). These measures also identify the degree of concern expressed by clients for the major developmental tasks associated with each stage of an adult occupational career, and help clients develop the skills needed to cope with specific stage tasks.

As work becomes more contextualized, individuals may not be able to balance the life roles in their life space. Super proposed nine major **life roles** that people take on at various ages: Child, Student, Leisurite, Citizen, Worker, Spouse, Homemaker, Parent, and Pensioner. Super (1980) stated that the importance of life roles and the nature of involvement at any stage of a person's life span can change. This involvement can be measured in terms of participation, commitment, knowledge, and value expectations. Special career development inventories can focus on the client's life structure, the importance placed on the work role, and how various roles meet a variety of work values (Nevill & Super, 1986). For example, if the work role appears relevant, then further career development and career guidance will be more meaningful for the client. Career development may also explore the role of leisure as a primary means for attaining life satisfaction outside of the work role (Liptak, 1991).

Career Education

Career education prepares youth for career tasks such as choosing an occupation or college major. Typically, a student may present with indifference with the implicit question, "Why career/work?" The primary goal of **career education** is to orient individuals and groups to pending tasks of career development and provide strategies to cope with them. The term *career readiness* is commonly being used today to refer to career education and is discussed in Chapter 11 of this text. Career education imparts a set of general employability, adaptability, and promotability skills to K-12 students, primarily through being infused into regular classes. In the view of career educators, these skills include academic skills, good work habits, personally meaningful work values, and career decision-making skills (Hoyt, 2005). Career education services are often provided by professional and school counselors, teachers, and career educators.

In the early 1970s, the career education concept became part of education reform. **James Allen** (1970), U.S. Commissioner of Education, initially used the term career education when he addressed the National Association of Secondary Principals Convention in 1970. Among those who were central to the subsequent career education movement was **Kenneth Hoyt**, who was instrumental in improving connections between education and work. He served as the Director of the U. S. Department of Education's Office of Career Education. In a seminal book by Hoyt (1972) entitled *Career Education: What It Is and How to Do It*, the assumption of career education was that work is an example of the human need to do, to achieve, and to know that someone needs them for something. An important part of its focus was the integration of work values into one's personal value system. By 1975, numerous definitions of career education had been formulated and promulgated. But it was the definition by Evans, Hoyt, Mackin, & Mangum (1972) that became the standard in the career education movement:

> Career education is the total effort of public education and the broader community to help all individuals become familiar with the values of a work-oriented society, to integrate these values into their personal value

system, and to implement them into their lives in such a way that work becomes possible, meaningful, and satisfying to each individual (p. 1).

As you may notice, career education is related to the career development service area. Career education interventions center on Super's exploration stage where the tasks of crystallization (i.e., making a tentative career choice) is expected for many 9-12 grade students. Students during this period should have a general understanding of the world of work, as well as of their interest and abilities and begin to engage in activities to acquire more specific information about occupations to narrow down their choices. Because the goal is to prepare youth for such career tasks, career education fosters **career maturity** or self-management attitudes such as future orientation and autonomy. Fostering career maturity engages students and clients in discussion about their competencies to help them cope with tasks like planning and decision-making. As such, career education requires a more process-oriented approach. Teaching and fostering mature attitudes and competencies help develop career readiness and prepare students to transition from high school to college, employment, or the military.

The *Career Maturity Inventory-Form C* was designed to measure career attitudes and competencies (CMI; Busacca & Taber, 2002; Crites & Savickas, 1996, 2011), or one's *readiness* to engage in and cope with imminent career tasks. Busacca and Taber suggested that the CMI-R be used by counselors, teachers, and career educators as a process-oriented supplement to career guidance and counseling. In addition, time-perspective interventions (Savickas, 1991) designed to increase future orientation and planfulness, especially for at-risk students, can provide good experiential activities for educators.

Career Counseling

The most recently-developed career service area, introduced toward the end of the first decade of the 21st century, includes the term *counseling*. **Career counseling** uses models focused on meaning-making and the process of *how* individuals make vocational choices. The client presents a problem with self-concept and identity through the implicit question, "Who am I within my career?" The goal of career counseling is to develop insight, self-reflection, and meaning-making. Career counseling services are often provided by professional counselors, career counselors, and psychologists.

The **subjective process** of career counseling focuses more on the characteristics of a quality counseling relationship, such as the core conditions proposed by Carl Rogers (Bedi, 2004; Granvold, 1996). Also, because emotions are embedded in all aspects of the client's experiences, consideration of this subjective component is particularly suited to the models and methods of career counseling (Hartung, 2011). The role of emotion factors prominently into career counseling methods such as narrative career counseling and career construction counseling (discussed in Chapter 4 of this text). This increased emphasis on the personal experience aspects of career choice and development became known as *career counseling* (also referred to as postmodern career counseling) and generated a paradigm shift in vocational guidance (see Busacca & Rehfuss, 2017 for a review).

Conclusion

As the 5C's framework aids in the understanding of the distinct career service areas, it also serves to guide career intervention planning. Differentiating between career service areas, helps one to organize data into meaningful categories, reduce conceptual confusion, and ease the transition from theory to practice. It can provide human service professionals with a conceptual tool that will help guide the use of career theories and measures with the complex problems presented by clients.

Key Chapter Terms

Five Career Service Areas	Life Roles
Career Guidance	Career Education
Content Model	James Allen
Career Placement	Kenneth Hoyt
Career Development	Career Maturity
Process Model	Career Counseling
Career Stages	Subjective Process

Web Resources

Note that website URLs may change over time.

Career Guidance

MBTI Career Report sample
https://www.cpp.com/en-US/Products-and-Services/-
/media/cpp/files/sample-reports/smp262153.pdf

Career Theory, Development, and Appraisal

STRONG Interest Inventory profile sample
https://www.cpp.com/en-US/Products-and-Services/-
/media/cpp/files/sample-reports/smp284108.pdf

Self-Directed Search sample
http://www.self-directed-search.com/Sample%20Reports/SDS-Standard-
Report%20RIE.pdf

Work Values Inventory
https://humwork.uchri.org/wp-
content/uploads/2015/01/Workvaluesinventory-3.pdf

Career Placement
Resume Writing and Interviewing Skills
http://www.hcpss.org/f/newlanguages/docs/eng_resumewriting.pdf

Resume and Interview Guide
https://www.k-state.edu/careercenter/documents/resumeinterviewguide.pdf

Career Development
The Salience Inventory
http://www.vocopher.com/SII/Salience%20Inventory.pdf

Career Development Inventory
www.vocopher.com/2005_ACA/ACA3.ppt

Career Education
Career Maturity Inventory-Form C
http://www.vocopher.com/ms/cmic/CMI_C_Master.pdf

Virginia Department of Education Career Connections
http://www.doe.virginia.gov/instruction/career_technical/career_connections/
index.shtml

Virginia's Workplace Readiness Skills
http://www.doe.virginia.gov/instruction/career_technical/workplace_readines
s/wrs-research-report.pdf

Virginia Administration Code-College and Career Readiness; (Middle and High School)
http://lis.virginia.gov/cgi-bin/legp604.exe?000+reg+8VAC20-131-140

Career Counseling
Career Construction Interview
http://vocopher.com/CSI/CCI.pdf

Life-Design Counseling Manual
http://www.vocopher.com/LifeDesign/LifeDesign.pdf

My Career Story Workbook
http://www.vocopher.com/CSI/CCI_workbook.pdf

Chapter 4

CAREER THEORIES AND MODELS

"A theory is just one way of oversimplifying a complex situation so that it is easier for you to see the big picture."

~John D. Krumboltz, 2005, p. 34

CHAPTER HIGHLIGHTS
Nature of Career Problems
Trait and Factor Theory
Developmental Theories
Career-Decision Making Theories
Social Learning Theories
Postmodern Theories

What does theory have to do with practice? Why is it important to include theory in a book on career issues and interventions? To begin with, **theory** provides us with a way to see and understand human behavior. Anderson, Goodman, and Scholssberg (2012) stated that "a theory is a set of abstract principles that can be used to predict facts and to organize them within a particular body of knowledge" (p. 4). Thus, theories provide basic knowledge from which you may draw useful concepts and language to explain client behavior.

Nature of Career Problems

How do the helping process and theory interact? Clients often seek career services when they are in a transition. Whether a transition is due to an anticipated or unanticipated event, individuals often feel as though their life is going off-course. This experience can be characterized by a lack of control, an urgent but vague sense of uncertainty about the future, and general confusion that permeates their attitudes and behaviors. Cochran (1997) noted that a problem "is a gap between what is and what ought to be" (p. 36). Clients seeking career counseling are often uncertain how to bridge this gap. Their means might not be clear, barriers may seem overwhelming, and resources may seem inadequate. The way they think about their problems and the questions they have about how they can resolve them often come across at first as jumbled and not clearly formed. Thus, we need a map to identify and interpret clients' presenting problems. Theory provides us with a way to conceptualize and give meaning to the thoughts and feelings of clients (Gysbers, Heppner, & Johnston, 2014). This meaning, once it has been made clear, can then be connected to practical strategies and interventions for assisting our client in pursuing their identified career goals.

There are many different types of career theories. It is important to remember that theories have strengths, but also limitations. Nevertheless, they are the best way we have to guide both our knowledge and our practice. The following are some guidelines to consider when learning about career theory, including both advantages and inherent limitations in several prominent theories:

- Each theory views career choice and development from a different perspective or **epistemology**. Theories originate from a point of view that encompasses shared assumptions, common understandings, and collective values (Savickas, 2015). As such, epistemology validates the source of knowledge or what we know about career issues, counseling orientations, and interventions. Because each theory focuses on a specific aspect of the career process, no one theory is able to provide a complete picture that can be applied to every client's situation. Rather, different theories leave it to the practitioner to use their professional training, experience, and judgment in choosing the best way in which to help the client. As discussed in Chapter 3 of this text, when selecting a theory, human service professionals must first identify the relevant career service area based on the needs of the client. Then helpers can be flexible or eclectic by using various theories and models that have been developed for the problem area.

- Career theories stimulate research to help clarify career choice, development, and behavior. Although many theories are supported by considerable research, minority groups and people with ethnic differences have historically been underrepresented in sample populations. That is, much of the research in the past has been conducted with white middle-class men, though women have been much better represented in studies from the last

15 years or so. Despite the recent shift toward more inclusive research, students should keep in mind that some theories may still not apply as well to minority groups as they do to dominant groups.

• The theories reviewed in this text were developed in the United States and were historically situated in the social, economic, and cultural values and norms of their times. Therefore, you should be aware of and remember their limitations, and how well they can be applied to individuals from other countries and cultures. Multicultural strategies for career services are discussed in Chapter 8 of this text.

A Review of Major Career Theories

The remainder of this chapter is dedicated to introducing several career development theories. Like human development theories, career theories consider the process and influences in the step's individuals take throughout his/her lifetime as related to career and work. The five major categories of career theories are trait-and-factor, developmental, career decision-making, social learning, and postmodern. Human service professionals should be familiar with these theories and their associated models. This section presents a primer on several career theories that are popular and applicable today; the reader is referred to the resources and references at the end of the chapter for more information.

Trait-and-Factor Theory

Frank Parsons developed a three-step conceptual framework for helping individuals choose careers. This framework required a clear understanding of self, knowledge of different lines of work, and an understanding of the relationship between these two things. Parsons' view became the foundation for what later evolved into **trait and factor theory** (Hartung & Blustein, 2002). Trait and factor theories incorporate these assumptions.

The first term, **trait**, refers to individual characteristics that can be measured through testing and assessment. The second term, **factor**, refers to work or environmental characteristics required for successful performance in a job. When these two vital components are combined, the result is a theory that assesses and matches the characteristics of a person with the characteristics of a job.

Assumptions of Trait and Factor Theory

Trait and factor theory embody a broad category that overlays several career theories. The theory makes the following assumptions:

- Individuals have unique characteristics related to interests, abilities, needs, values, and personality traits.
- Occupations and jobs have unique characteristics related to work tasks, skills, demands, and rewards.
- The characteristics of both individuals and occupations can be measured.
- Workers and employers are most satisfied when there is a good match or 'fit' between the characteristics of the worker and the occupation/job.

Terminology

It is important to revisit and define several terms in trait and factor theory that are common throughout most career theories. Assessment tools related to each of the following traits are listed in Chapter 5 of this text. The following defines the traits in trait and factory theory:

- *Interests.* At a fundamental level, interest are activities for which we have a liking or disliking and which we move toward or away from. They may or may not be preferred to other interests. Interests are viewed as dynamic, rather than stable traits (Strong, 1955).
- *Abilities/Aptitudes.* Ability refers to a person's maximum performance and reveals the level of a person's present ability to perform a task. An aptitude test reveals a person's probable future level of ability to perform a task in their educational endeavors or occupational training (Sharf, 2013).
- *Values.* Values are a source of motivation for individual action or objectives that one seeks to attain in order to satisfy a need. Values are central to an individual's self-definition and decision-making. Work values are what one seeks to express in the work environment in pursuit of job success and satisfaction (Rounds & Jin, 2013).
- *Personality.* A personality trait refers to the unique and relatively enduring internal and external aspects of a person's character. Personality traits are ways or styles of acting to meet a need in a given situation. Vocational personality is defined as an individual's career-related abilities, needs, values, and interests (Savickas, 2005).

Several popular career theories based in the trait-factor approach are used in career guidance today. One popular theory has been classified as a typological theory and was developed by John Holland.

Holland's Theory

No theory of career development has had a greater influence on the practice of career counseling and education than **John Holland's** theory of vocational personalities and work environments. Holland believed that vocational interests are an expression of an individual's personality. According to Holland, personality describes a pattern of values, attitudes, and behaviors that represent distinctive ways people think and act (Holland, 1959). Personality develops because of the interaction of innate characteristics, activities to which the person is exposed, and competencies and interests that develop from these activities (Holland, 1997). Holland's theory suggests that people try to find work in occupations that have environments compatible with their personalities.

Holland (1997) maintains that by late adolescence most people come to resemble a combination of six vocational personality/interest types. **Personality types** are groups of traits that describe the similar characteristics of groups of people and are used to help describe a person. He labeled the six personality types as Realistic, Investigative, Artistic, Social, Enterprising, and Conventional. These types are graphically depicted on a **hexagonal model** and referred to as **RIASEC** (see Figure 4.1 and website resources for a diagram). On the hexagon, letter R (Realistic) is placed on the top left point and the remaining letters follow clockwise in order.

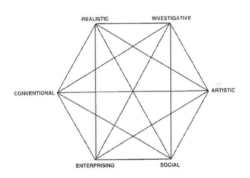

Figure 4.1

Holland's Hexagonal Model

Holland also assigned the same labels to work environments that he did to personality types. Just as individuals have codes, so do occupations, majors, and leisure activities. A **model environment** is an interpersonal atmosphere created by the people who dominate a given setting (such as work) and can be viewed as having a distinctive pattern of values, attitudes, and behaviors. Occupational environments are assigned a Holland code and are found in the *Dictionary of Holland Occupational Codes* (DHOC; Gottfredson & Holland, 1996). The DHOC enables users to link their personal characteristics to the major educational and occupational classifications in use today. O*NET online which is supported by the US Dept of Labor/Employment and Training Administration has integrated this tool with other tools such as the O*NET interest profiler and is free to use. The six personality types with corresponding environments are briefly defined below.

Personality & Environmental Types

Realistic Personality Type (R). People with realistic personalities prefer working with their hands and using tools to build and repair things. They prefer to work outside or with a machine. Construction workers, mechanics, farmers, paramedics, foresters, and fish and wildlife managers can all be said to have Realistic occupations.

Realistic Environment (R). Realistic work environments call for the manipulation of tools, objects, machines, and animals. These settings include machine shops, farms, service stations, military settings, and construction sites.

Investigative Personality Type (I). People with investigative personalities like research activities that involve ideas in mathematics and the physical, biological, and social sciences. Research laboratory workers, biologists, pharmacists, chemists, physicists, veterinarians, surgeons, programmers, and design engineers can all be said to have Investigative occupations.

Investigative Environment (I). Investigative work environments call for research and exploration of biological, cultural, or physical knowledge. These settings include research laboratories, hospitals, universities, and libraries.

Artistic Personality Type (A). People with artistic personalities like opportunities for self-expression and artistic creation in writing, music, art, and theatre. Authors, artists, musicians, poets, actors, composers, photographers, and interior designers can all be said to have Artistic occupations.

Artistic Environment (A). Artistic work environments are creative, artistic, and interpretive and usually require intense involvement for prolonged periods of time. These settings include concert halls, dance studios, libraries, art studios, theatres, museums, and galleries.

Social Personality Type (S). People with social personalities like to work cooperatively with other people. They have a strong concern for the welfare of others, like to train or inform others, and want to help others solve their personal problems. Teachers, social workers, police officers, occupational therapists, nurses, political scientists, personnel managers, and counselors can all be said to have Social occupations.

Social Environment (S). Social work environments interpret and transform human behavior through frequent and extended personal relationships. These settings include counseling offices, schools and colleges, health-care agencies, churches, recreational centers, and nonprofit agencies.

Enterprising Personality Type (E). People with enterprising personalities like activities where they can lead, control, or persuade other people, in order to attain a personal or organizational goal. Lawyers, business executives, realtors, salespersons, project directors, marketing managers, and insurance agents can all be said to have Enterprising occupations.

Enterprising Environment (E). Enterprising work environments use verbal skills to manage and persuade other people to reach organizational or personal goals. These settings include various businesses, restaurants, insurance agencies, real estate offices, advertising agencies, stock brokerage firms, and car lots.

Conventional Personality Type (C). People with conventional personalities prefer structured jobs and activities. They like everything neatly in place. Accountants, bank tellers, editorial assistants, website editors, bookkeepers, secretaries, file clerks, and computer operators can all be said to have Conventional occupations.

Conventional Environment (C). Conventional work environments perform systematic, detailed, routine, and repetitive processing of verbal and mathematical information. These settings include business offices, banks, accounting firms, post offices, and file rooms.

Diagnostic Indicators for Holland's Model

In helping to better understand the relationship between the various personality types and work environments, Holland proposed three important constructs to help make predictions about people's career choices, satisfaction, and performance: congruency, consistency, and differentiation (see Reardon and Lenz, 1998 for a discussion). The three constructs serve as diagnostic indicators in application of the model and are described as follows:

Congruency. The term **congruency** refers to the relationship between the personality type and the work environment. It assesses the degree of agreement or fit between a person and a work environment with the Self-Directed Search. Another tool that uses this same theoretical framework is the O*NET Interest Profiler. In assessment and intervention, the career professional uses the individual's highest three letters from the Self-Directed Search, which is referred to as the **summary code**. The summary code is also referred to as a **subtype** and can be a two- or three-letter code. For example, the most congruent work environment for an E personality is an E work environment. On the other hand, an Investigative work environment would be the most incongruent work environment for an Enterprising personality. Holland suggests that individuals will search for and enter work environments congruent with their type in the hope that they will permit them to "exercise their skills and abilities, express their attitudes and values, and take on agreeable problem and roles" (Holland, 1997, p. 4). A good metaphor is "birds of a feather flock together." The next two concepts, consistency and differentiation, may also affect how individuals can make career choices or adapt to the work environment.

Consistency. The term **consistency** describes the internal harmony of personality types and work environments. It is represented by the proximity of types on the hexagon. The rule of thumb is the shorter the distance between any 2 types on the hexagon, the greater their similarity or psychological resemblance. Consistency is easy to confuse with congruence. Remember that consistency has to do with the relation between the first two letters within one code, and congruence has to do with the relation between two separate codes (Reardon and Lenz, 1998). For example, Social and Artistic personal or work setting types are close together on the hexagon model as seen in Figure 4.1 and, thus, similar. In contrast, Social and Realistic personal or work setting types are farther apart from each other on the hexagon and therefore different. The theory states that individuals with consistent interest types within their personal three-letter code should feel more at ease with their personality characteristics and encounter fewer difficulties in making career choices. Also, jobs with consistent codes may be easier to find. Consistency is not a primary goal when using the Holland model as is congruence and differentiation. So, an individual with an inconsistent type (SI) has not made a poorer career choice than a person who has a more consistent type (SAI) (Sharf, 2013).

Differentiation. The term **differentiation** explains the degree of certainty or strength of an individual's interests. In other words, is there a clear distinction between an individual's likes and dislikes? It also reflects how clearly a work environment belongs to one or two types. Typically, differentiation can be determined by looking at the three highest scores comprising the summary code. Scores that are close together are not well differentiated, whereas scores that are far apart are considered differentiated. For example, a person may have the following scores on the SDS: R=15, I=22, A=25, S=23, E=10 and C=2. Although the person's summary code is ASI, it is not well differentiated. The career practitioner would first approach interpreting this score by referring to the **rule of 8** which refers to RIASEC summary scale differences less than 8 on the SDS should be regarded as trivial because they are within the limits of the standard error of measure of the inventory. Meaning, the three letter codes are all equal to each other, and could be placed in any order. Next, career intervention would thus require exploring all SDS code combinations or permutations, called the **rule of full exploration**, to determine occupations that may be a good fit for the person. As such, the following three-letter codes would be explored with the client: ASI, AIS, SIA, SAI, IAS, ISA.

Differentiation can also be determined by looking at the general shape of the person's **profile** of scores on the six Holland types. A profile is a pattern or order indicating the degree of resemblance to the six ideal models or types. If all six scores are low or high, the profile is called flat or undifferentiated. Theoretically, low levels of differentiation lead to less clarity and more difficulty in making vocational choices. If scores are flat, it can mean that people do not really know their interests. A **high flat profile** indicates they could have many interests and may need to work on narrowing them down. A **low flat profile** may indicate minimal exposure to occupations and work activities, but could also show low self-esteem or symptoms of depression.

In this section, the Hexagonal model was used to explain the relationships among the six personality types and the six work environments. Holland's theory enjoys good reviews both from the perspective of research and of practice because it is useful and easily applied in practice while also being testable empirically. Rayman and Atanasoff (1999) stated that the key qualities that distinguish it from other career development theories are its simplicity, its face validity, its vocabulary, and the ease with which it translates to practice. As one can surmise, there are many nuances to the interpretation of Holland codes. Human service professionals should study the theory in depth, receive adequate training, and interpret codes under the supervision of an experienced career professional. Nevertheless, by simply teaching clients about the RIASEC model and concept of congruence, one can help them develop awareness for why a 'poor fit' may lead to being dissatisfied and unproductive in a work position, as well as to gain insight into how they may find the "best fit" possible for their choice of occupation.

Developmental Theories

Developmental theories, as compared to trait and type theories, are concerned with career issues over the entire life span. They view career development as a process as opposed to the trait and type theories, which deal with career issues at one given point in time. They emphasize the impact that biological, sociological, psychological, and cultural factors have on career choice and on life transitions. Because developmental theories cover extended periods of time, they tend to be more complex. A major developmental career theory is the one proposed by Donald Super.

Super's Theory

Probably no one has written as extensively about career development or influenced the study of the field as much as **Donald Super**. As early as the 1940s, Super was promoting the idea that career development is a process that unfolds gradually over the entire life span and involves multiple life roles. Human service professionals should be prepared to address client concerns over a lifetime of development during which individuals encounter situational and personal changes. In this section, we will discuss Super's approach to careers, which consists of three segments: self-concept, life span, and life space. Super's theory is also referred to as the Life-Span, Life-Space approach to careers.

Self-Concept

One of the most important contributions of Super's theory is his idea of how self-concept is applied in the career development process. At the heart of his theory, Super described vocational development as the process of developing and implementing a **self-concept** (Super, 1990). This self-concept consists of the individual's view of self and his or her view of the situation or condition in which he or she lives. This is a blend of how we see ourselves, how we would like to be seen, and how we think others view us. It is Super's contention that individuals seek out and implement their self-concepts into careers as a mean of self-expression (Super, 1990). People use this understanding of self when they identify their career goals and plans.

We form pictures of ourselves in many different areas of our lives. Sometimes these views are realistic and well-defined and other times they are unrealistic and poorly-defined. Super states that this vocational self-concept along with both personal (e.g., aptitude, values, and personality) and situational factors (e.g., community, economy, society, labor market) are major determinants of self-concept development. In identifying these determining factors, Super graphically depicted this concept as the **Archway Model** to clarify how biographical, psychological, and socioeconomic elements influence one's career development (see resources at end of this chapter for a diagram of the archway model). The point is that societal factors interact with personal and situational factors as a person lives and grows, and these lead to the development of the personality and to the accomplishments of the person.

Life-Span

Super identifies a series of developmental tasks one typically encounters in life and connects these tasks to stages and sub-stages of career development. Super defined five **life stages** of vocational development during a person's life-span: Growth, Exploration, Establishment, Maintenance, and Disengagement. These stages are motivated by developmental tasks. Tasks are related to the learning and planning that are necessary in order to move through these stages successfully and during the expected time range. These stages, substages, general tasks and typical age range are presented in Table 4.1.

Super and his colleagues originally described these five stages in the order in which the average person encounters them, but later recognized that individuals can reenter life stages that they have previously visited throughout their lives. Super called this **recycling**. Although stages are age-related in the sense that there are typical times when people go through them, individuals can experience a stage, with accompanying task, at almost any time during their lifetime. Many people reassess their career plans at various points during their lifetime and recycle through various stages for various reasons. When they do this, they revisit the exploration stage and may reassess their values, interests, and abilities.

Stage & Substage	Age Range	General Task
Table 4.1 *Super's Career Developmental Stages, Substages, and Tasks*		
Growth	4-14	
Fantasy		Using curiosity and occupational fantasies to explore environment
Interest		Acquiring information about work and own interests
Capacity		Acquiring information about own capacities
Exploration	14-25	
Crystallization		Developing and planning a tentative vocational goal
Specification		Firming the vocational goal
Implementation		Training for and obtaining employment
Establishment	25-45	
Stabilization		Working and confirming career choice
Consolidation		Gaining confidence and security in work
Advancing		Advancing in one's career
Maintenance	45-65	
Holding		Learning new things to adapt to changes in position
Updating		Continuing education, professional meetings, and networking to update knowledge
Innovating		Making new contribution to field, and developing new skills
Disengagement	65+	
Decelerating		Slowing down one's work responsibility
Retirement Planning		Financial planning, and planning activities during retirement
Retirement Living		Adjusting to changes in life roles

Note: At the time this theory was written, 65 was the expected age for retirement which is no longer accurate.

Life Space

Intertwined within Super's life-span segment are a variety of roles individuals take on at various ages in their **life space**. He graphically depicted this concept as the **rainbow model** (Super, 1980). Super described nine major life roles: Child, Student, Leisurite, Citizen, Worker, Spouse, Homemaker, Parent, and Pensioner. For example, the citizen role is described as the time and energy spent in nonpaid volunteer activities such as serving at a local hospital, school, charity, or community activity. All the roles together fill the life space.

According to Super, careers are the constellation of the interaction among these various roles, which are played out in different theaters: home, community, school, and the workplace. Various roles overlap and affect each other. Although some roles are played out in only one theater, most people play several roles simultaneously in several theaters. To the extent that a blend of roles can be successfully played and is satisfying to the individual, it is said that a person has a successful career. If the blend of roles does not bring satisfaction, it may be necessary to add, remove, or change the intensity or content of a role.

Career Decision-Making Theories

In addition to trait and factor and developmental theories, some theories have focused on the process of career decision making itself. This section discusses two categories of career decision-making models: descriptive and prescriptive. Descriptive theories describe or explain how career decisions are made. In contrast, prescriptive theories focus on an ideal approach to how career decisions ought to be made. The two approaches discussed are spirituality in career development, which is descriptive, and Cognitive Information Processing Theory, which is prescriptive.

Tiedeman's Lifecareer® Theory

A spiritual perspective of career choice emphasizes the influence that a person's spirit can have on his or her life, career choices, and the type of person he or she will become. Spiritual approaches to career development may or may not include a religious viewpoint.

Perhaps the best-known theory on making career decisions from a spiritual perspective is that of Anna Miller-Tiedeman. The central view of her **Lifecareer® theory** is that life is one's career. Miller-Tiedeman (1999) proposed that if one views career as a process, one can free up energy, gain a sense of balance and harmony, and focus on cooperating with approaching forces as opposed to worrying about finding a career. As Miller-Tiedeman (1999) stated,

> "If you do not look for the *life as process* theme in someone's' story, you'll miss it as it then takes on the character of separate happenings. However, when you look for the principles of process, you realize how

one experience followed another one, forming a pattern for the individual's life. Each experience carries an encryption useful in the next experience" (p. 52).

According to Miller-Tiedeman (2008), the key principles of Lifecareer® theory include the following:

- Career is viewed as life as opposed to a job;
- Each person is viewed as his or her own theorist with the ability to ask his or her own questions and derive personally acceptable answers rather than depending on answers from those perceived as authority;
- There is an emphasis on self-conceiving (a process or focus on giving meaning to self in experience);
- Individuals must cooperate with life as opposed to trying to control life;
- The whole of the person organizes the parts;
- Emphasis on making a life and a living as opposed to getting a job;
- One must respect decisions that work out as well as those that do not;
- An individual's personal experiences guide choice;
- Career is lived in the moment and becomes the path that one leaves behind.

Miller-Tiedeman has written extensively on the concept of life as a process. The model and counseling approach that applies the above features is referred to as *New Careering* and is based on the principle of flow. This model uses as its foundation a wide range of theories including quantum physics, Bohm's notion of wholeness, and Self-Organizing Systems Theory (Miller-Tiedeman, 1988) to encourage individuals to cooperate with the approaching forces in their lives.

Human service professionals who integrate the New-Careering model in their work with clients use a subjective approach as opposed to the more objective approaches found in traditional career models. For example, New-Careering does not emphasize the administration of inventories and assessments, nor does it focus on the helper offering advice and opinions. The goal of this approach is to support and encourage experience-based learning (Miller-Tiedeman, 1999).

Cognitive Information Processing Theory

A more recent theory for making career decisions focuses on understanding the process of career decision-making in terms of how individuals make a career decision and use information in career problem-solving and decision-making. In the early 1980s, a group of professors from Florida State University began to study how thought processes impact career decision-making (Peterson, Sampson, Lenz, & Reardon, 2002). **Cognitive information processing** (CIP) is an approach to career development that uses a pyramid to illustrate the essential areas of cognition or thoughts involved in career decision-making (see Figure 4.2 resources at end of this chapter for a diagram). There are three basic components of cognitive information processing theory: knowledge, decision-making skills, and executive processing. The base level of the pyramid contains the knowledge domains of self-knowledge on one side of the pyramid and occupational knowledge on the other side. According to Peterson et al. (2002), this level is the cornerstone of career planning.

The middle level of the pyramid is the decision-making skills domain. Career problem-solving is primarily a cognitive process that can be improved through a sequential procedure known as the **CASVE cycle** (Sampson, Reardon, Peterson, & Lenz, 2004). The cycle includes five phases: communication (identifying the problem or gap), analysis (understanding myself and my options), synthesis (formulating alternatives), valuing (judging each action in terms of the likelihood of success or failure and impact on others), and execution (implementing strategies to carry out plans).

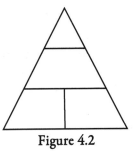

Figure 4.2
CIP Pyramid Model
Source: "A cognitive approach to career services: Translating concepts into practice" by J. P. Sampson, Jr., et. al., in *Career Development Quarterly, 41*, 67-74. 1992.

The apex of the pyramid is the executive processing domain. It involves metacognition, which is where the individual becomes aware of how he or she thinks, feels, and acts. This domain describes three key ways of thinking about decision-making: self-talk, self-awareness, and monitoring and control. Self-talk refers to the internal messages that we give ourselves about career choice and related issues and can be positive or negative. Self-awareness refers to being aware of one's career decision-making strategy and process. Monitoring and control refer to monitoring the way in which one goes through the CASVE cycle and one's ability to control how much time they give to each of the phases.

In general, a human services professional would first focus on the base of the pyramid, the knowledge domain, to help clients explore themselves and their options; then go to the decision-making domain to help clients explore how they make decisions; and finally arrive at the executive processing domain to help clients explore how they think about their decision-making. The authors of the model also provide a seven-step outline that can guide one's intervention:

1. Conduct an initial interview introducing the clients and identifying concerns.
2. Make a preliminary assessment of the client's career decision-making readiness.
3. Collaborate with the client to identify gaps in self and occupational knowledge.
4. Identify goals that will close the gaps.
5. Develop an individual plan.
6. Have the client execute the plan.
7. Review client progress.

Human service professionals who use the CIP can use each domain of the pyramid as a guide for delivering interventions. For example, the self-knowledge domain is addressed through the administration of various inventories. The occupational knowledge domain is attended to through informational interviewing and networking. Decision-making skills are taught by using the CASVE cycle. Finally, the executive processing domain serves as a model for challenging the individual's negative and unhealthy thinking related to their career choices.

Social Learning Theories

Social learning approaches are based on psychological research into the human learning process. A social-learning theory approach to career decision-making was first proposed by Krumboltz (1975) when he explained the origins of career choice. Krumboltz's career theory is based on Bandura's (1971) social learning theory, which emphasizes the influence of modeling and positive reinforcement. Later, Mitchell and Krumboltz (1996) extended the earlier social-learning theory approach to include Krumboltz's learning theory of career counseling, which explains how to help people with career concerns. They suggested that the entire theory be conceptualized as one theory with two parts and referred to it as a **learning theory of career counseling** (LTCC). LTCC focuses on how individuals make career decision and emphasize the importance of behavior (action) and cognitions (knowing or thinking) in making career decisions.

Krumboltz rejected the goal of career guidance in which career professionals find a suitable occupational match for clients based on interests, values, skill, and personality traits alone. He asserted that the goal is inappropriate for current American culture because matching requires that the occupation have a common and stable set of duties and expectations. Mitchell and Krumboltz (1996) stated that "the problems we face now are far larger than the problems trait-and-factor theory was designed to address" (p. 56). Thus, the second part of his theory proposes that people choosing careers in modern society must cope with trends within a constantly changing work environment, and it focuses on helping clients create a satisfying life where learning is the key.

The first part of Krumboltz's theory proposed that four categories of factors influence the career decision-making path for any individual. Each of these factors plays an important part in the eventual selection of a specific career choice:

- Genetic endowment and special abilities
- Environmental conditions and events
- Learning experiences
- Task approach skills

Although other career theories include inherited abilities and environmental events, social learning theory emphasizes the importance of learning experiences and task-approach skills. Therefore, career practitioners focus on learning experiences and task-approach skills to help people with their career problems.

One's career preferences are a result of her or his prior learning experiences. There are two significant kinds of learning: **instrumental learning** and **associative learning**. Instrumental learning occurs when positive outcomes (e.g., praise, money, positive emotions) follow a given behavior. Associative learning occurs when people observe outcomes that are experienced by others and then view these persons as role models after whom they want to pattern their own behavior. Examples of instrumental learning experiences that affect career choice include taking an exam, studying for an exam, reading about an occupation, or talking to someone about his or her work. Examples of associative learning experiences include observing a veterinarian, teacher, or a basketball player performing his or her job. Behavioral techniques include reinforcement, role-playing, role models, and simulation.

Learned cognitive and performance abilities that are used in the career decision-making process are called **task approach skills**. These skills include how one approaches setting goals, clarifying values, generating alternatives, and obtaining occupational information. According to LTCC, people form beliefs or make **self-observation generalizations** about their abilities, interests, values, and the world. For example, a person's cognitive response or self-talk (such as "used car salespeople are dishonest") is a generalization and can influence whether one approaches or avoids learning more about a career. Cognitive techniques include goal clarification, countering negative and troublesome beliefs, and rehearsing cognitive statements that are more positive. Techniques of learning theory can be applied in assisting individuals with their career issues.

Planned Happenstance

In addition to the dimensions of social learning theory, Krumboltz recognized the importance of chance events in people's lives. According to Krumboltz, individuals will be confronted with new, unanticipated problems and concerns that may come about while following through on their plan of action (Mitchell, Levin, & Krumboltz, 1999). Taking advantage of chance events is called **planned happenstance.** Examples involve unpredictable educational conditions, social factors, and occupational conditions. Mitchell et al. (1999) identified five **chance coping skills** that are helpful when coping with chance career opportunities; they are paraphrased here:

- *Curiosity.* exploring new learning opportunities
- *Persistence.* perseverance in the face of obstacles and setbacks
- *Flexibility.* avoiding rigidity in attitudes as events unfold
- *Optimism.* staying positive when pursuing new opportunities
- *Risk-Taking.* being open to new experiences and unexpected events

Because Krumboltz believes that it is difficult to have specific plan laid out well in advance, one should view oneself as open-minded instead of indecisive.

Human service professionals would assist clients by normalizing planned happenstance in the client's history, respond to chance events in a positive and open manner, and teach clients to produce desirable chance events (Mitchell et al., 1999). Krumboltz and Levin (2010) have written a book titled *Luck is No Accident* that illustrates through stories, cartoons, quotations, and exercises, how careers are built based in planned happenstance.

Postmodern Theories

Postmodern career counseling (PCC) is a philosophical and psychological framework from which to provide career counseling services. As such, career counseling becomes not so much a procedure as a philosophical framework for guiding the work of the practitioner and client. In contrast to the modernist tradition, which highlighted the notion of the self-contained individual with measurable traits, the postmodern conceptualization of career represents a unique interaction of self and social experience (Young & Collin, 2004). Career practitioners using PCC models and methods emphasize four main components: cultural context, relationship factors, narrative paradigm, and qualitative assessment. These four components are integrated throughout PCC and help clients adapt to the changing nature of work in the 21st century. Discussion of 21st century changes to work is found in Chapter 13 of this text.

Savickas's Career Construction Theory

Recently, **career construction theory** has emerged as a career counseling approach that helps conceptualize how people impose meaning on their vocational behavior. It complements the traditional trait-and-factor approach and challenges the notion that there are normative and predictable stages of career development. In this theory, Savickas (2001) incorporated Super's innovative ideas with a constructivist perspective to help counselors understand clients' career problems. We present here a brief overview of career construction theory as Chapter 13 of this book covers the theory in more detail.

Career construction theory views individuals from four perspectives: what people prefer to do, how individuals cope with vocational developmental tasks, occupational transitions and work traumas, and why individuals choose to fit work into their lives in specific ways. These perspectives enable practitioners to explore how individuals construct their careers and help them cope with feeling fragmented and confused in a precarious world-of-work. Practitioners strive to keep clients from losing their sense of self and social identity as they encounter evolving economic and work life changes in an unsettled economy (Savickas, 2005). Career construction theory, therefore, postulates that, regardless of one's socioeconomic status and reason for taking a job or position, work can become meaningful for most people.

Career construction theory helps practitioners uncover clients' unique approaches to meaning-making, purpose, and life direction. The theory is based in **constructivism**, which focuses on "meaning-making and the constructing of the social and psychological worlds through individual, cognitive processes" (Young & Collin, 2004, p. 375). Due to the massive changes taking place in the world of work, it has become increasingly difficult for career counselors to explain a person's career with only trait-factor and career developmental models (Savickas, 2005). For example, measuring a client's career indecision with inventories alone objectifies and decontextualizes indecision and thereby omits an individual's subjective experience of indecision (Savickas, 1995). Thus, a central question that has emerged from constructivist career counseling is: how can individuals negotiate a lifetime of job changes and transitions without losing their sense of self and social identity?

Conclusion

Career theories provide a conceptual framework designed to facilitate the understanding of the forces that influence a person's career choice, development, and behavior. Clients often seek career services when they are in a transition. The ways they think about their problems and the questions they have about resolving them can often come across to the helper as being disorganized. Thus, human service professionals need a map with which to identify and interpret clients' presenting problems. Of the various career theories, this chapter focused on five categories: Trait and factor, developmental, career decision-making, social learning, and postmodern theories. The theories and approaches selected are meant to provide a starting point for human service professional as they work with clients to understand their unique needs. We believe that the theories and models briefly described here will help you in working with clients as they explore, expand, and understand their own fascinating career journeys.

Key Chapter Terms

Theory	High Flat Profile
Epistemology	Low Flat Profile
Trait & Factor Theory	Archway Model
Trait	Life-Stages
Factor	Recycling
John Holland	Life-Space
Personality Types	Rainbow Model
Hexagonal Model	Lifecareer® Theory
RIASEC	Cognitive Information Processing
Model Environment	CASVE Cycle
Congruency	Learning Theory of Career Counseling
Summary Code	Instrumental Learning
Subtype	Associative Learning
Consistency	Task Approach Skills
Differentiation	Self-Observation Generalizations
Rule of 8	Planned Happenstance
Rule of Full Exploration	Chance Coping Skills
Donald Super	Postmodern Career Counseling
Self-Concept	Career Construction Theory
Profile	Constructivism

Web Resources

Note that website URLs may change over time.

The Development, Evolution, and Status of Holland's Theory of
Vocational Personalities: Reflections and Future Directions
for Counseling Psychology.
https://www.counseling.org/docs/david-kaplan's-files/nauta.pdf?sfvrsn=2

Super's Rife Rainbow, Self-Concept and Career Stages
https://www.careers.govt.nz/assets/pages/docs/career-theory-model-super.pdf

Surfing the Quantum: Notes of Lifecareer® Developing.
http://www.life-is-career.com/history.html

Trends in career development: *Cognitive information processing (CIP) approach to advising.* [Video File]
https://www.youtube.com/watch?v=Zv0PBYN8vC4

Practical Application of the CASVE Cycle of Career Problem Solving and Decision-Making.
www.career.fsu.edu/content/download/186387/1616623/Ex1casve.doc

Pacifica Community Television (2009). Steve Piazzale interviews John Krumboltz, *Luck is no accident* (part 1 of 3) [Video file].
https://www.youtube.com/watch?v=_3x9BN221FI

The Happenstance Learning Theory
https://web.stanford.edu/~jdk/HappenstanceLearningTheory2009.pdf

Savickas' Career Construction Theory
http://www.vocopher.com/pdfs/careerconstruction.pdf

Chapter 5

THE ROLE OF ASSESSMENT IN CAREER SERVICES

"It is better to sail with compass and chart than to drift into an occupation haphazard or by chance, proximity, or uninformed selection."
~Frank Parsons, 1909, p. 101

CHAPTER HIGHLIGHTS
Quantitative and Qualitative Assessment
Career Assessment Categories
Considerations for Administering Career Assessments
Methods of Administration
Multicultural Considerations in Assessment

Assessments are used to help clients learn more about their career needs and opportunities so that they can make well-informed decisions about work in their lives. Personal characteristics such as interests, values, personality, and skills are just some of the attributes that are measured and explored during the career assessment process. Career decision-making is seen as a continuous process in which all aspects of individuality receive consideration. Yet, assessment results are only one facet of individuality to be evaluated in the career helping process. Results can be used to help the human service professional understand a client's career problem, and as a stepping stone for further exploration to help the client gain awareness and insight into their concerns. Thus, assessment results constitute information that can provide the individual with an awareness of increased options and alternatives, and they can provide the human service professional with the information needed to provide the appropriate career interventions. Although Frank Parsons warned practitioners many years ago that they will need a chart to make their way through the proliferation of career assessments that are available, they will also need to consider what criteria or compass they should use for that navigation. This is often a "reflection of the career counselor's theoretical and philosophical position" (Arulmani, 2014, p. 609).

The purpose of this chapter is to provide an overview of several career-related inventories and assessments that can be administered by entry-level human service professionals. These assessments include quantitative instruments such as the traditional paper-and-pencil inventories, tests, and online inventories, as well as qualitative assessment tools. Some assessments work best in an individual setting, others in a group or classroom setting. This overview includes a description of several popular instruments, along with each instrument's purpose, intended population, and required reading levels. Multicultural considerations and cultural competence are discussed along with selection and use of assessment tools from a culturally sensitive perspective.

Quantitative and Qualitative Assessment

Assessment is a tool used by career service providers or by clients themselves to gather self-information that will be used in the career-planning process. Assessment can be defined as a broad array of evaluative procedures that yield information about a person (Neukrug & Fawcett, 2015). Human service professionals may engage in assessment under supervision as they conduct the career helping process, including administering and interpreting various types of quantitative and qualitative career assessments.

There are two main categories of assessments: quantitative and qualitative. In **quantitative career assessment**, the practitioner measures a person's objective resemblance to a select group of assessment-takers called a **norm group** in terms of categories such as abilities, interests, and personality traits. Some of these assessments are called **norm-referenced** because they provide scores that describe a client's results in relation to the results of others in a given population who have completed the assessment. In **qualitative career assessment**, the practitioner emphasizes the subjective meaning of personal traits and events within the context of a person's life circumstances.

Quantitative Career Assessment

Quantitative assessments use standardized tests that measure specific personal attributes or skills. It is an objective approach. Two types of quantitative instruments are tests and inventories. The term **test** refers generally to ability and achievement evaluations that have correct and incorrect answers and on which individuals attempt to perform as well as possible. The term **inventory** refers to instruments that solicit a preference or viewpoint from the client, such as their interests, personality, and values. Inventories have no right or wrong answers. Traditional career assessments use quantitative measures with standardized formats such as true/false questions, multiple-choice answer options, and short answer questions with a protocol for administration. There are several advantages of quantitative assessment:

- Tests hold predictive power that is of practical value in the selection of personnel and in education and training.
- They are relatively easy for a practitioner to administer and clients to self-administer.
- They do not generally take much time to complete.
- They can be used with individuals and groups.
- Some tests and inventories have the option to be scored and interpreted via computer.

Despite these advantages, quantitative assessment is not without criticism. A few limitations of this type of assessment include that they can be expensive to purchase, they may focus only on a client's immediate or single career choice rather than enhancing general career decision-making skills, they do not focus on uniqueness and personal meaning-making of the client, and they lack information on the client's cultural context. In addition, human service professionals should avoid administering too many assessment instruments to a client, as they can become confusing and counterproductive. Watson and McMahon (2014) noted that one reason quantitative career assessment has remained so dominant is that it lends itself more readily to practical application. Theorists and practitioners who have argued that traditional quantitative assessments are biased, mechanistic, and reductionistic have offered an alternative, qualitative approach to career assessment.

Qualitative Career Assessment

Qualitative assessments focus on the person as an individual with unique traits and aim to assess the client's perceptions about work and career. It is a subjective-based approach. In qualitative career assessment, personal meaning on the part of the client is more important than the practitioner's quantitative interpretation. Qualitative assessment may involve structured interviews rather than formal tests and inventories. For example, career practitioners may ask open-ended questions about current and/or future careers or ask the client to construct career timelines or genograms that look at career paths taken by members of their family in the past. They may also be asked to write an autobiography or describe their earliest recollections. These techniques create a narrative for a career practitioner based on the postmodern approach, which assumes that a person has their own subjective ideas about their lives based on their personal experience. There are several advantages of qualitative career assessment worth mentioning here:

- It focuses on personal meaning-making on part of the client.
- It is more holistic and systemic.
- It encourages a collaborative relationship between practitioner and client.
- It is suitable for groups focused on learning and growth.
- It is flexible when used with clients from diverse backgrounds.

This last point supports Lamprecht's (2002) assertion that the interpretation of quantitative career assessment remains largely decontextualized. This is primarily because quantitative career measures are used more as a static, point-in-time intervention in the career counselling process. Thus, they provide us with an isolated story that is not embedded in the client's culture and context. In contrast, qualitative approaches focus on social processes and the understanding that one's view of the world is not static and is concurrently influenced by historical and cultural contexts that are continually changing and developing (Whiston & Rahardja, 2005).

One disadvantage of qualitative career assessments is that they often take longer to administer than quantitative career assessments. Career practitioners may need to adjust the traditional hour of a session to allow enough time for a client to take full advantage of the benefits of qualitative career assessments and postmodern career counseling (Wood & Scully, 2017). In our view, quantitative and qualitative assessments may co-exist and provide a complementary process, where the strengths and limitations of each approach are counterbalanced by the strengths and limitations of the other (e.g., Watson & McMahon, 2014).

Purpose of Career Assessment

What do our clients need to gain from the career assessment process? Whichever career assessment perspective one takes (i.e., quantitative or qualitative), there are a variety of expected outcomes gained from the assessment process. In the broadest sense, most career practitioners would agree that the purpose of career assessment should be for the client to increase their ability to make a well-reasoned self-assessment and use the resulting knowledge in the decision-making process. Brown (2016, p. 189) suggests, however, that the outcomes of the career assessment process should cover at least six areas. Figure 5.1 is an adaption of Brown's outcomes:

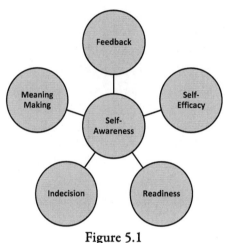

Figure 5.1

Six Purposes of Career Assessment

In the above figure, we see **six purposes of career assessment**: Self-awareness (interests, values, abilities, personality traits, etc.); Readiness to make a career decision (career maturity, future orientation, and planfulness); Self-efficacy (confidence); Decision-making approach (thoughts and indecision); Purpose and meaning making in cultural context; and Individual or group feedback about progress and change. It is important to remember that clients differ in the goals they bring with them (Brown & McPartland, 2005), and that effective career support may involve attaining different outcomes for different clients. Heppner and Heppner (2003) argued that the literature on career assistance outcomes is subject to what they called a **uniformity myth** or a tendency toward viewing career clients as homogenous or all the same. Thus, it is vital for the human service professional to not assume that the same type of treatment and the same type of outcomes are beneficial to all clients, regardless of their background, goals, or other attributes.

Career Assessment Categories

Assessment is often involved in career counseling and numerous instruments are routinely used to help individuals explore career directions and to assist in making effective career decisions. This section provides six different categories of career-related assessments that are used in the process of gathering client information. These measures consist of ability tests, interest inventories, personality and values inventories, career-development inventories, and qualitative assessment tools. Many of the tools listed below are described in *A Comprehensive Guide to Career Assessment* (Stoltz & Barclay, in press).

Abilities/Aptitude Tests

Ability refers to a person's maximum performance; tests of ability reveal the level of a person's present ability to perform a task. In a career counseling context, aptitude can be viewed as the "likelihood of learning or acquiring the skills required by the occupation" (Dawis, Goldman, & Sung, 1992, p. 457). Most measures used in career assessment are both ability and aptitude tests in that they provide scores to estimate a person's current level of performance (ability) as well as potential for future success in different occupations (aptitude) (Metz & Jones, 2013). The purpose of both types of test is to increase self-awareness, identify strengths along with areas that may need improvement, and for placement in a particular position.

Examples include Ability Explorer, Tests of Adult Basic Education, Career Key, Motivated Skills Card Sort, O*Net Ability Profiler, CAPS (abilities), and WorkKeys, as well as special tests in areas such as clerical, mechanical, artistic, and musical. The SAT, ACT, and GRE are considered aptitude tests.

Interest Inventories

At a fundamental level, interest are activities for which we have a liking or disliking and which we move toward or away from (or are indifferent to). Our level of interest in various activities relates to the extent to which we develop abilities in those areas (Strong, 1955). Interest inventories help to identify vocational interest patterns or themes as they pertain to the world of work. Items on interest inventories have no right or wrong answers. The purpose is to increase self-awareness and assist in identifying training, education, or career options that contain job duties that might interest an individual.

Examples include Self-Directed Search, STRONG Interest Inventory, Career Exploration Inventory 2, Guide for Occupational Exploration Interest Inventory, Leisure to Occupations Connection Search, Kuder Career Planning System, O*Net Career Interests Inventory, O*Net Interests Profiler, COPS (interests), and the Transition-To-Work Inventory.

Personality Inventories

Personality inventories identify an individual's personal style or traits in dealing with people, tasks, and events. A personality trait refers to the unique and relatively enduring internal and external aspects of a person's character. Traits are ways or styles of acting to meet a need in a given situation. Example of traits include openness, conscientiousness, extraversion, agreeableness, and neuroticism. Such inventories might help clients clarify how much contact they need or want with others, how they process information, or how much structure they would like. The purpose is to increase self-awareness, and thereby assist individuals in making decisions regarding training, education, and specific careers.

Examples include Myers-Briggs Type Indicator, Keirsey Temperament Sorter II, and the 16PF Career Development Profile.

Work Value Inventories

Values inventories allow individuals to identify and describe underlying needs that motivate their decision-making and lead to career satisfaction. There are general values (e.g., life and cultural values) and work values (e.g., achievement, prestige, security, creativity). Brown (2002) noted that cultural and work values are the most important variables in occupational choice, satisfaction, and success. The purpose of a work value inventory is to increase self-awareness and measure the values one seeks to express in the work environment to be successful and feel satisfied.

Examples include Super's Work Values Inventory, Work Orientation and Values Survey, Career Values Card Sort, O*Net Career Values Inventory, O*Net Work Importance Locator and Profiler, COPES (work values), Values-Driven Work Card Sort, and Life Values Inventory.

Levels of Decidedness/Career Beliefs & Thoughts

These inventories and scales measure those aspects that could interfere with an individual's personal growth, including faulty beliefs that interfere with decision-making, levels of dysfunctional thinking, and anxiety. The purpose of using these types of inventories is to increase self-awareness and help clients identify and understand intrapersonal barriers to the career exploration and decision-making process.

It is important to differentiate between an undecided client and a client who is indecisive. **Undecided** implies that not enough information has been gathered to allow for a sound and confident decision (Salomone, 1982). It is a *state* of being. Some individual's may not be particularly troubled about being undecided, while others may seek career services. **Indecisive** implies that even with more information, the individual has difficulty planning, and also has substantial anxiety that impedes such decision making (Salomone, 1982). It is an ongoing *trait*, and usually extends to other life domains as well. Different career counseling approaches are indicated based on whether the individual is undecided versus indecisive. With an indecisive client, personal and career counseling may be necessary before assisting them with career-decision making.

John Holland develop an inventory to help differentiate between the undecided and the indecisive client. The *My Vocational Situation* (MVS; Holland, Daiger, & Power, 1980) is a brief self-report screening tool to measure the clarity and stability of a person's vocational identity (see resource section for link to MVS). To score, the number of responses marked "false" is added to obtain the total Vocational Identity score, with higher scores indicating stronger vocational identity. Low scores on the Vocational Identity (VI) scale indicate confusion about a respondent's identity, indecision, and a lack of self-satisfaction (Hi VI = 13 to 18; Average VI = 6 to 1; Low VI = 0 to 5).

Examples include the Career Beliefs Inventory, Career Attitudes and Strategies Inventory, Career Decision Scale, Career Decision-Making Difficulties Questionnaire, My Vocational Situation, Career Transitions Inventory, and Career Thoughts Inventory.

Career Development Inventories

These instruments measure the degree to which an individual has completed specific activities or tasks considered to be important for a given stage of the career planning process. Many of these inventories are based on Super's life-span approach to career development discussed in Chapter 4 of this text.

Examples include the Career Maturity Inventory-Revised, Adult Career Concerns Inventory, Salience Inventory, Career Exploration Inventory, and the Leisure Work Search Inventory.

Qualitative Tools

Some instruments do not fit under any of the previously mentioned categories because they are non-standardized, non-normed-based tools used to help clients explore the subjective aspects to the career planning process. Qualitative assessment refers to instruments and activities that use methods such as open-ended questions to gather information. Many of these qualitative career tools are described in *Postmodern Career Counseling: A Handbook of Culture, Context, and Cases* (Busacca & Rehfuss, 2017).

Examples include the Career Construction Interview, My Career Story Workbook, My Career Chapter, Knowdell Card Sorts (values, occupational interests, leisure/retirement activities), Career Genograms, Life-Role Analysis, and Early Recollections.

Considerations for Administering Career Assessments

As a human service professional, you need to be aware of the concerns' clients may have with assessments. You may come across clients who react to formal assessments with apprehension and concern. This may be because it's their first time being exposed to testing and assessment or because they haven't been adequality prepared with regards to the assessment process. Some clients may feel intimidated by career assessments, particularly those who have had limited success in educational settings or who experience test anxiety. They may worry about their answers being right or wrong or be concerned about what the results may reveal about themselves. Other clients may wonder whether career instruments will reveal personal information such as if they are depressed or anxious. Also, assessments may lead clients to believe that the process of career planning is simplistic or that assessments can tell them definitively what to do.

Using assessments is one part of the career helping process with which to gather information about self and careers. It is valuable to remember that assessments are done *with* and *by* clients and not *to* them. The following section provides the human service professional with several factors to be aware of when administering career assessments to clients: which type of assessments to use, administration time, type of score report, level of difficulty, research properties (such as validity and reliability), and qualification level.

Type of Assessment to Use

Human service professionals do not need to administer every assessment to every client. Each career instrument or assessment tool has been developed for some specific purpose. When choosing an instrument to administer, the career practitioner should follow a three-step process:

1. Analyze the client's needs. This is generally determined by the intake interview, and the practitioner's conceptualization of the client's problem.
2. Establish a reason for the client to complete a formal instrument or assessment. Ask yourself, "what career service am I to provide?" For example, does the client require career guidance, career education, or career development? This comes with experience and is determined by the professional judgment of the practitioner.
3. Determine what instrument will be most useful for the individual. There are many instruments available on the market for career guidance, but there is no specific instrument that is the best. Once the career service needed is identified, selecting the right instrument for the client often concerns cost, administration time, type of score report, level of difficulty, research properties, and qualification level. Nevertheless, if one understands the purpose for using a career instrument or assessment, career interventions can be more efficient and effective.

Cost

Depending on the setting in which you work, some instruments may be too costly for the organization to purchase and make available for the practitioner. If you are in private practice, you may want to include the cost of the instrument in your fee.

Administration Time

Formal standardized instruments can take as little as 10 minutes or as much as one hour to complete. Informal qualitative assessments such as autobiographies and structured interviews by a practitioner can take longer. Some instruments, such as certain ability measures, may be timed; however, most are not. Estimated administration time is usually discussed in the manual or instrument itself.

Type of Score Report

The practitioner should be familiar with the type of **score report** or results provided for each instrument to be able to explain the assessment accurately and answer questions from clients. For many formal instruments, clients will need the help of a career practitioner in explaining and clarifying the meaning of the scores. Scoring can range from easy to difficult. Instruments can be manually scored or completed by the publisher or computer program if the instrument is administered online. Results typically come in print form from the website or computer from which the assessment was taken:

- *Raw Scores.* These provide a tally of responses in a specific category; examinee cannot compare personal scores with those of others.
- *Percentile Scores.* These compare the scores of an individual with those of a selected norm group.
- *Stanines.* This is a statistical way to divide percentiles into 9 ranges.
- *Standard Score.* This is a statistical way to indicate how far (in standard deviations) an individual's score is from the middle (50th percentile) of a distribution of scores.
- *Band of Confidence.* This is a range within which an individual score falls.

Level of Difficulty

Published formal assessments have been developed for clients at a specific reading or educational level. Thus, it is important to consider the client's reading level before selecting an instrument or assessment. Also, if you are working with clients whose primary language is not English, there may be a language barrier to consider. Further, visually impaired clients may need the practitioner to read the questions. When working with clients with any disability, it is important to review the literature on working with clients with disabilities and provide accommodations during the assessment process.

Research Properties

When using a formal standardized instrument, it is expected that human service professionals have basic knowledge of the psychometric properties of the instrument. This means being able to answer questions like, is the instrument reliable or consistent over time? Is the instrument valid? On what population is the instrument normed? Although you are not expected to become experts on psychometrics, human service professionals will need to understand some technical aspects of the instruments you use with clients. The following provides a brief description of several technical properties of instruments useful for the human service professional. The reader is referred to specialized texts on assessment for further information (e.g., Neukrug & Fawcett, 2015; Whiston, 2017).

Three technical properties of instruments discussed here will be validity, reliability, and bias. Human service professionals should have basic knowledge of these psychometric properties of instruments they use with clients. The **validity** of an instrument concerns how effectively the instrument measures what it has been designed to measure. There are numerous types of validity, but the one you will encounter most in your work is **face validity**. An instrument is said to have high face validity if it appears, to the practitioner and/or client, to measure what it is supposed to measure. The **reliability** of an instrument refers to the instrument's accurate and consistent measurement over time. There are numerous types of reliability, but the one you will encounter most in your work is called **test-retest reliability**, which refers to the consistency of scores obtained by the same individual each time the assessment is given. The manual or publisher's website will provide information on the validity and reliability of the career instruments.

In all assessment situations, human service professionals need to evaluate the assessment instruments for possible bias. An instrument is considered to have a **sample bias** if it favors or impedes a particular group. Bias can include cultural variables such as race/ethnicity, age, sex, disability, religion/spirituality, sexual orientation, and socioeconomic status, among others. Most bias in career instruments is unintentional and can be an artifact of the research design. A sample population cannot include all cultural variables or may want to focus only on specific cultural variables related to the purpose of the research study. It is important to have a clear definition of the norm group and consider if an assessment instrument is appropriate for a wide range of people, especially for your client. Be sure to know if the instrument is proper for the client population you work with and consult the manuals or publishers of the instruments for further information.

Specific validity issues have been investigated in the career assessment and counseling literature. Leong and Hartung (2000) analyzed the literature related to multicultural career assessment and discussed it in relation to the dimensions of cultural validity and cultural specificity. **Cultural validity** addresses the concept of whether instruments that have been developed from a Eurocentric perspective can be used with clients from other cultural backgrounds. **Cultural specificity** concerns the extent to which variables, such as worldview, cultural identity, communication style, and decision-making preferences, are addressed in the assessment process (Leong & Hartung, 2000). While Leong and Hartung advocated for more research on the cultural validity of various Western models of career development in general, they strongly advised that more research on culturally specific variables would help researchers and practitioners understand why Western models do not work well for culturally different clients when they are found to lack cultural validity. In the meantime, it is important that human service professionals be aware of the concepts of cultural validity and specificity in working with your clients.

Qualification Levels

Some instruments require more formal training to administer than others. In accordance with the Standards for Educational and Psychological Testing (American Educational Research Association, 2014), many assessments are sold only to professionals who are appropriately trained to administer, score, and interpret such tests and inventories. Many publishers of career instruments use qualification levels based on education, training, and experience. There are four qualification levels: Level A, B, C, and S. These levels are described below.

Level A: For assessments, inventories, and tests, no special qualifications are required. Assessments with this qualifications level have no educational requirements for administration. It is assumed that the career practitioner will complete the instrument themselves, observe an experienced person administering and interpreting the instrument, and will be supervised when first using the instrument.

Level B: For assessments, inventories, and tests, individuals must possess a bachelor's degree from an accredited 4-year college or university in counseling, psychology, social work, or a closely related field. In addition, the individual must have satisfactorily completed coursework in test interpretation, psychometrics and measurement theory, educational statistics, or a closely related area or have a license or certification from an agency that requires appropriate training and experience in the ethical and competent use of psychological tests.

Level C: For assessments, inventories, and tests, individuals must meet all qualifications for Qualification Level B plus they must possess an advanced professional degree (i.e., master's or doctoral degree) that provides appropriate training in the administration and interpretation of psychological tests; or they must possess a license or certification from an agency that requires appropriate training and experience in the ethical and competent use of psychological tests.

Level S: For assessments, inventories, and tests, individuals must possess a degree, certificate, or license to practice in a physical or mental health care profession or occupation, plus training and experience in the ethical administration, scoring, and interpretation of clinical behavioral assessment instruments.

Information about the level and credential required is typically included on the publisher's website, in their catalogues, or in the assessment manuals. It is the practitioner's responsibility and ethical obligation to research each instrument they intend to use and make sure they are qualified and have the necessary credentials to purchase, administer, and interpret.

Methods of Administration

Some inventories are available for clients to take as a paper-and-pencil format and others are administered with special computer software or over the internet. Before administering one of the formats to a client, make certain that you understand the instructions thoroughly so that you can explain them to clients and answer questions. Formats such as computer software or the internet may have specialized information on validity and reliability separate from print versions. Also, be sensitive to people who may not be comfortable with computers and who may prefer a paper-and-pencil version if available. Although the organization you work for may have specific procedures and policies to follow, the following are some considerations to think through with your colleagues when administering any career assessments to clients:

- *Determine Needs.* Determine what type of assessment would be helpful with your client. What career service are you providing? Will you use a quantitative and/or qualitative assessment?

- *Preparation for Assessment.* Explain the name and type of instrument that will be used, the type of questions asked, what information the instruments will and will not provide, how long the assessment will take, and when and where it will take place. How long will it take to get the results?

- *Testing Environment.* No matter what type of assessment you are giving, it is important that the client complete it in a quiet, well-lit room with as few distractions as possible.

- *Scoring.* Depending on the specific assessment you use, you may need to score the assessment yourself, rely on the computer program or an internet-based assessment, the publisher, or have the client self-score the instrument. If the client self-scores, make sure you double check for errors.

- *Transparency in Assessment Results.* The client should understand the assessment results before they leave the office. Make sure that you provide your clients with a copy of the test results. Encourage client feedback and ask open-ended questions such as, "How do the results compare with what you think about yourself?" Remember that results may become less clear for people over time and that they may have additional questions about the results. Make sure you offer clients follow-up sessions to correct any ambiguity or to further process assessment results.

- *Record-Keeping.* All assessment results that are kept at the office must be in a private and secure place as a part of the client's file. In addition to following the organization's policy on record keeping, make sure you also follow your professional organization's ethical standards for record-keeping and length of time to keep records.

Multicultural Considerations in Assessment

Diversity challenges human service professional to work with clients by embracing cultural competence and cross-cultural sensitivity. Career assessment can be more effective with clients if the human service professional is culturally competent and alert. **Culturally alert** helping can be defined as "a consistent readiness to identify the cultural dimensions of clients' lives and a subsequent integration of culture" into the helping process (McAuliffe, 2013, p. 6). In addition, career professionals have an ethical responsibility to understand and apply multicultural skills, including multicultural assessment skills.

There is excellent guidance in the selection and use of tests from a culturally sensitive perspective from various professional organizations. Organizations in the human service professions have provided standards addressing cultural diversity and the impact on assessment in counseling and education (e.g., Association for Assessment in Counseling and Education, 2012). One resource you may want to consider reviewing is the *Standards for Multicultural Assessment*, which includes a broad definition of multicultural assessment and addresses issues of social advocacy in assessment. The National Organization for Human Services (NOHS) Code of Ethics, for example, has an expectation that human service professionals will be culturally aware when conducting services to culturally diverse clients. We suggest that these standards can apply to the career assessment process. Specifically, Standard 11 and 26 of the NOHS Code of Ethics (NOHS, 2015) states the following:

STANDARD 11. Human service professionals are knowledgeable about their cultures and communities within which they practice. They are aware of multiculturalism in society and its impact on the community as well as individuals within the community. They respect the cultures and beliefs of individuals and groups.

STANDARD 26. Human service professionals seek the training, experience, education and supervision necessary to ensure their effectiveness in working with culturally diverse individuals based on age, ethnicity, culture, race, ability, gender, language preference, religion, sexual orientation, socioeconomic status, nationality, or other historically oppressive groups. In addition, they will strive to increase their competence in methods which are known to be the best fit for the population(s) with whom they work.

Career assessment can be a positive process when working with clients, but there are some concerns by scholars about the cultural suitability of traditional quantitative-based tests and inventories with diverse clients. It is important for human service professionals to be aware of whether the results of an instrument are applicable to a client because of his or her culture. For example, research has shown that some assessments have common problems regarding individuals from ethnic and sexual minority groups (Worthington, Flores, & Navarro, 2005):

- The normative populations for some assessments do not represent the percentage of ethnic minority groups in the United States.

- Using instruments available only in English are problematic for this whose English proficiency is limited and there is subsequently a language barrier.
- Translation of instruments is difficult given dialects, and idioms may be specific to some ethnic groups, region, and even within ethnic groups.
- Misuse of tests for specific ethnic groups and for sexual minorities is possible if the human service professional is not knowledgeable about the cultural incongruity that the test has for that group.

Although there has been progress in career research and practice and genuine steps have been taken to remedy the lack of cultural competence in career assessment, sensitivity to cultural differences should be displayed by human service professionals when suggesting, administering, and interpreting any career assessment tool. According to Flores, Spanierman and Obasi (2003), career assessment that is culturally appropriate has the following components, "it integrates culturally relevant information about the client; attempts to understand the client in his or her cultural, personal, and career contextual realities; and takes into account the limitation of traditional [quantitative] assessment and assessment tools" (p. 80). Presently, it is impossible to develop a culture-free instrument, but many professionals are committed to developing instruments that attempt to be more culturally fair (Whiston, 2017). Until that time, comes, it is incumbent on the human service professional to strive to provide culturally sensitive career assessment to clients. Cultural competence is discussed in greater detail in Chapter 8 of this text.

Conclusion

Human service professionals need to understand the method of using assessments to help their clients become more successful in the world of work. Assessment is an essential ingredient in career services aimed at increasing awareness and self-understanding. Human service professionals are responsible for knowing which assessments they are qualified to administer, which assessments are appropriate for use in various circumstances, and how the assessments are administered and interpreted. To be competent, professional needs to understand measurement concepts and different score reports. In this chapter, we contrasted quantitative and qualitative assessment approaches. Six types of traditional tests and inventories that are used in career services were presented: ability/aptitude tests, interests' inventories, personality, values inventories, level of decidedness, and career development. It was also explained that career assessment can be more effective with clients if the human service professional is culturally competent.

Key Chapter Terms

Assessment	Indecisive
Quantitative Assessment	Score Report
Norm Group	Validity
Norm-Referenced	Face-Validity
Qualitative Career Assessment	Reliability
Test	Test-Retest Reliability
Inventory	Sample Bias
Six Purposes of Career Assessment	Cultural Validity
Uniformity Myth	Cultural Specificity
Undecided	Culturally Alert

Web Resources
Note that website URLs may change over time.

Assessment Standards and Competencies
AACE, Standards for Multicultural Assessment
http://aarc-counseling.org/assets/cms/uploads/files/AACE-AMCD.pdf

Association for Assessment in Counseling, Responsibilities of Users of Standardized Tests (RUST) (3rd Edition)
http://aac.ncat.edu/Resources/documents/RUST2003%20v11%20Final.pdf

NCDA & AACE, Career Counselor Assessment and Evaluation Competencies
https://www.ncda.org/aws/NCDA/asset_manager/get_file/18143/aace-ncda_assmt_eval_competencies

Ability Assessments
O*NET Ability Profile
https://www.onetcenter.org/AP.html

Skills Matcher
https://www.careeronestop.org/toolkit/Skills/skills-matcher.aspx

Career Theory, Development, and Appraisal

COPS System
https://www.edits.net/support/eap-interpretation/

Interests Assessments
O*NET Interest Profiler
https://www.mynextmove.org/explore/ip

Career Cluster Interest Survey
https://careerwise.minnstate.edu/careers/clusterSurvey

IIP RIASEC Markers Scales
https://openpsychometrics.org/tests/RIASEC/

Personality Assessments
Keirsey Temperament Sorter
https://www.monster.com/career-advice/article/best-free-career-assessment-tools

IPIP Big-Five Factor Markers
https://openpsychometrics.org/tests/IPIP-BFFM/

NERIS Type Explorer
https://www.16personalities.com/free-personality-test

Values Assessments
My Plan Values Assessment
https://www.myplan.com/assess/values.php

Super's Work Values Inventory
https://humwork.uchri.org/wp-content/uploads/2015/01/Workvaluesinventory-3.pdf

InSight™ Values / Work Characteristics Inventory
https://www.careerperfect.com/services/free/insight-work-values/

Career Beliefs/Thoughts/Levels of Decidedness
Planned Happenstance
https://web.stanford.edu/~jdk/HappenstanceLearningTheory2009.pdf

My Vocational Situation
https://career.fsu.edu/sites/g/files/imported/storage/original/application/f3dd
4d17aeae2f581fb9837fd16381f5.pdf

Beliefs in Career Counseling
https://contactpoint.ca/wp-content/uploads/2013/01/pdf-02-03.pdf

Chapter 6

OCCUPATIONAL INFORMATION AND TECHNOLOGICAL RESOURCES

One of the best ways to generate career options is to cultivate a brainstorming mind-set."

~Sukiennik and Raufman, 2016, p. 125.

CHAPTER HIGHLIGHTS
Occupational, Career & Labor-Market Information: Definitions
Readiness for Career Information
Types and Sources of Information
U. S. Government Sources
Commercial/Private Sources
Evaluating Career Information and Technological Resources

Regardless of a person's career goal or stage of career development, information is needed each step of the way in the career helping process. When assisting clients with career development concerns, human service professionals often provide quality career information and resources to their clients. The amount of information and the resources that are available can be overwhelming. Helping professionals must not only be aware of occupational trends, for example, but they must also know where to acquire information and how to assess the quality of the information. The goal of career planning is to provide the career seeker with additional information to include in his or her decision-making process. In this chapter, we will focus on some of the most popular sources of career information, including print and online resources, web-based career guidance systems, informational interviews, job-shadowing experiences and One-Stop Career Centers. Because most career and occupational information is available online, we will cover tips and guidelines for evaluating the quality of web-sourced occupational information.

Occupational, Career & Labor-Market Information: Definitions

The terms career information, occupational information, labor market information, and work force information often overlap. It is, therefore, important to distinguish between them. First, **information** can be defined as data, knowledge, or intelligence that is either given or received. Information may be fact or opinion, valid or invalid, simple or complex, current or outdated, presented in or out of context, useful or not useful. Salomone (1989) suggested that occupational information is different from career information. In general, **occupational information** is that which is specific to given occupations while **career information** is a broader term that covers the career development process. In particular, Brown (2016) defined occupational information as educational, occupational, and psychosocial facts that are related to work. This type of information comes mostly from governmental sources. **Labor market information** includes data about the occupational structure and the trends that shape it for the purpose of informing both individuals and policymakers (Brown, 2016). Exposure to occupational, career, and labor market information is different from assessment and can be mediated by the human service professional.

Occupational information is an invaluable tool for facilitating the career development of children, adolescents, adults, and retirees. Whether clients are adolescents in the process of exploration, college students in the process of narrowing choices, adults involved in midcareer changes or preretirement programs, information about educational or occupational opportunities can help individuals accomplish their goals. The need for this information is lifelong, as the workplace changes and adults continue to make career choices throughout life. Having information, though, is just one part of the process of helping people with career concerns. As a human service professional providing career services, one of your roles is to help clients sort through the abundant information available to them and find that which best suits their particular needs.

Readiness for Career Information

Oftentimes, career and occupational information is only used when the helper is providing career guidance services. Referring to career theories discussed in Chapter 4, information is the second component of trait-and-factor career theory, and a necessary component of Super's career exploration and establishment stages of career development. Yet, information can be used during any career developmental stage to facilitate self-exploration, knowledge about the world-of-work, and the decision-making process. Most of the information provided in this chapter will be used to help prepare clients for the world-of-work and to gain self-awareness. Guidance works well with individuals who appear motivated to learn more about their subjective views of life, develop their personal and vocational identities, or crystallize occupational field and ability-level preferences (Savickas, 1996).

Motivation must be present in individuals in order for them to effectively benefit from occupational information. To become motivated, individuals must be assisted in seeing how their needs are met by whatever information is delivered (Herr, Cramer, & Niles, 2004). Readiness assumes that the individual is motivated to engage in some type and degree of information-seeking behavior. This is especially important when working with adolescents because they require a degree of readiness or **career adaptability** to engage in information-seeking behavior. To be career adaptable means to be future-oriented with planful attitudes and to be able to cope with career tasks such as exploring the world-of-work (Busacca, 2002). Thus, for a client to effectively use occupational information, it is important for the human service professional to first know if the client is ready to implement a choice and then to discuss how their needs can be met by seeking out career and occupational information.

Human service professionals should not assume that all clients need career information. Although they may present themselves as needing objective information, this could mask subjective concerns. Clients may believe that information will be the solution to their concerns, but during the initial interview, the human service professional may discover that other issues are more pressing and that information may in fact be useful later in the helping process (Gysbers, Heppner, & Johnston, 2014). For example, a recently-divorced 48-year-old woman states, "I don't know what to do next! I never thought I would have to work outside the home, but now without my husband's income, I need to find a career." It is important to assess whether or not the woman in this example is grieving with the loss of a long-term marriage, if there are children involved, and the details of her financial and living transition before she can look objectively at career information. It is important, therefore, to assess a client's total situation before deciding what career service would be most useful, and in some cases when mental health counseling is warranted.

Types and Sources of Information

A human service professional should be aware of the distinct types and sources of information so that they can provide the client with options that best meet their needs. Some types and sources of information include the following:

- Print materials such as books, pamphlets, or articles
- Web-based tools such as websites, blogs, or social networking sites
- Interpersonal interactions with someone who works in the field of interest
- Experiential activities in which one shadows, learns by observation, or hands-on activities
- Visual and audio presentations such as television, radio, or podcasts
- Career information delivery systems

The human service professional will use a variety of occupational information and technological resources to help clients with their career needs. Print materials are no longer the primary medium for career information delivery as the internet has become the vehicle for choice for assessing career information (Kirk, 2000). Human service professionals are now faced with an overwhelming amount of career information that must be organized in order to be useful. Much of our focus in this chapter will be on government-produced online and computer-based materials. In this section we begin with classification systems, career information resources, job search information, and social networking sites as well as other similar online tools.

Occupational Information Resources
Occupational information is compiled, published, and distributed by several organizations and companies. While a vast amount of career information exists in different formats, there are some specific tools that human service professionals should find valuable. Some of the most popular sources of print and online information can be grouped into the following categories: government sources, commercial publishers, professional societies/trade associations/labor unions, educational institutions, organizations for specific groups, and magazines. The web addresses for each of the following online sources are located at the end of this chapter.

U. S. Government Sources
Occupational Outlook Handbook: Maintained by the U.S. Bureau of Labor Statistics, the Occupational Outlook Handbook (OOH) provides comprehensive information on occupations and their requirements. The handbook provides profiles on over 325 occupations grouped into 25 clusters of related occupations. The clusters include: management, professional and related occupations, services, sales, administrative support, farming and related

occupations, construction, installation and related occupations, production, transportation, and jobs in the armed forces. Occupational information can be searched by several categories: nature of the work, working conditions, employment, training, other qualifications, advancement opportunities, job outlook, earnings, and related occupations. The OOH is updated every two years and is available online or in a print version.

Monthly Labor Review: The principal journal of fact, analysis, and research from the U.S. Bureau of Labor Statistics (BLS) is the **Monthly Labor Review** (MLR). Through *MLR* articles, economists, statisticians, and experts from BLS join with private-sector professionals and federal, state, and local government specialists to provide a wealth of research in a wide variety of fields. This is a good source for human service professionals to learn more about the labor force, the economy, employment, inflation, productivity, occupational injuries and illnesses, wages, prices, and more.

Career Outlook: A supplemental publication to the OOH, is **Career Outlook** (formally called Occupational Outlook Quarterly). Career Outlook is available online and provides an in-depth look at a range of career topics, explores unusual occupations through the work of someone in that occupation, describes a specific worker's career path, and provides a graphic presentation of data on employment and other topics.

O*NET

The **O*NET** system is a comprehensive system developed for the U. S. Department of Labor by the National Center for O*NET Development. The system contains the O*NET database, O*NET On-Line, and O*NET Career Exploration Tools. These three aspects of O*NET will be discussed in more detail below. O*NET replaced its predecessor, the Dictionary of Occupational Titles (DOT) which was the first comprehensive database of jobs in the United States published in 1939. O*NET is available both online and through several private- and public-sector publications.

*O*NET Database.* This online database contains both summary and detailed information on approximately 1000 occupations. The database is updated twice a year. Descriptors are given for tasks, knowledge, skills, abilities, work activities, work context, job zone, interests, work values, work needs, related occupations, wages, and employment. Occupational titles and codes are based on the Standard

Occupational Classification System (SOC) that allows the occupational information contained in the O*NET database to be linked to labor information.

*O*NET OnLine.* This online interface provides public access to O*NET information through a web-based viewer. It has a built-in screen reader capability, allowing readers to adjust the font size of text. In addition, it links directly to wage and occupational outlook information via America's Career InfoNet.

*The O*NET Career Exploration Tools.* Individuals using the O*NET Career Exploration Tools will find a variety of assessments to assist them in identifying interests, abilities, and values that will allow them to explore occupations matching their attributes.

CareerOneStop

Sponsored by the U.S. Department of Labor, Employment and Training Administration, **CareerOneStop** serves job seekers, businesses, students, and career advisors with a variety of free online tools, information, and resources. The site contains quality and up-to-date information as well as a searchable directory of American Job or One Stop Centers for clients seeking free local career development and employment assistance. CareerOneStop groups occupations into job families. CareerOneStop's job families are the same as the major occupation groups of the Standard Occupation Classification (SOC), excluding the military job family because there are no available wage and occupation trend data for this group. From exploration and self-assessment to educational options and information, and from occupational information to salary and economic trend data, CareerOneStop is a comprehensive website with resources and tools for any stage of the career development process.

My Next Move

The online site, **My Next Move**, was developed by the U.S. Department of Labor, Employment and Training Administration. It allows career seekers to explore potential occupations and opportunities. A link to the O*NET Interest Profiler, an informal career assessment, provides the job seeker with career and occupational alternatives based on their interests. There is also a My Next Move site designed to help Veterans in the transition to civilian life, as well as a Spanish-language version.

Information about the Military

Neither O*NET nor the OOH provides adequate information for clients considering the military as a career. Each of the armed services, however, publishes handbooks and brochures and maintains websites that describe career opportunities within each specific branch of service. In addition, the Department of Defense has developed a website that provides an overview of jobs available in all four branches of the military. These sources provide information regarding the relationship of each military specialty to civilian jobs. There are other useful websites that provide information about military careers, transitioning to civilian careers, and colleges and universities that accept the GI Bill at the end of this chapter.

Commercial/Private Sources

Careers.Org: An online source for employment, job search, and career education information around the world is Careers.Org. It includes detailed information about more than 1000 occupations, including wages, skills, corresponding college programs and careers, job and educational resources for states, cities, and counties in the United States, as well as Canada and other countries. Its unique feature is that it includes detailed profiles for thousands of colleges and universities in the United States and abroad, including academic programs, tuition and expenses, and admissions requirements. Additionally, college curriculum, industry reviews, career advice, and articles are available on the website's CareersToday and CareerGuides content forums.

ACT Profile: ACT is the private, non-profit organization most widely known for its national college-entrance testing program. ACT Profile is a free college and career planning platform built on more than 30 years of ACT research. It was previously known as the DISCOVER career guidance and information system. ACT Profile is a tool for students, counselors, and human service professionals. ACT Profile delivers self-assessments of Interests, Abilities, and Values, used together to suggest relevant occupations and majors. Based on respondents' answers, personalized results are populated onto interactive career and major maps. The Career Map is personalized based on the student's responses to the abilities and values inventories as well as their interest inventory.

To further clarify career choices, careers are divided into 26 different areas. When students click on a career area in the Career Map, they see a list of careers, and when they click on a career or occupation, they see extensive information about tasks, training, salaries, and more associated with that occupation. The personalized Major Map is based on the individual's interest inventory responses. The map contains groups of college majors and the student receives extensive information about typical required courses, attributes for success, and types of schools offering that major.

Although career information may now come to us in technologically sophisticated ways, there will be a significant amount of people who will access career and occupational information in other ways. There are many informal sources of information our clients will take advantage of such as family, community members, elders, ministers, peers, teachers, and others with whom we as human service professionals may never interact. For some clients of different ethnic, religious, or cultural backgrounds, the family, elders in the church or tribe, sage, prophet, shaman, spiritual advisor, or some other authority may be the preferred source of information.

Evaluating Career Information and Technological Resources

Helping people obtain, evaluate, and use career and occupational information is within the scope of a human service professional's role in facilitating career development. Online searches for career information will yield a vast array of results. Determining which are credible, reliable, and high-quality can be challenging, reflecting an ever-changing labor market. Today's sophisticated clientele expect up-to-date projections about the workforce. Helping client navigate and think critically about the information available online is one aspect of what human service professionals do in guiding clients to use technology and online resources. It should be remembered that caution must be taken because no guarantee is given that the information and assessments obtained from websites are accurate, up to date, and suitable for clients.

Before helping clients explore online career and occupational information, the National Career Development Association (2017) suggest that career providers should examine their own knowledge of evaluating occupational information and technological resources. Compare your current skills against the following career information competency checklist Table 6.1 by asking yourself, "Do I feel competent to...:" The items included in the checklist are not comprehensive. As information sources and tools evolve, skills that represent basic information competency must also progress. To help clients find quality information quickly and efficiently, a human service professional must stay current with the sources and tools available.

Table 6.1 *Self-Competencies for Using Online Career and Occupational Information*	
Self-Competencies	**Areas for Further Learning (✓)**
Locate career-related databases	
Perform a thorough search using relevant keywords	
Differentiate between primary and secondary sources of career information	
Evaluate information based on relevance, accuracy, timeliness, and validity	
Identify potential bias in information	
Identify unique resources specific to the career issue at hand	
Organize and synthesize information in a way that is useful to the client	
Differentiate between secure and insecure sites, especially when providing personal information	
Knowing and following copyright guidelines	
Adapted from: Jordan, A. L., & Marinaccio, J. N. (Eds.). (2017). *Facilitating career development: An instructional program for career development facilitators and other career development providers.* (4th ed.). Broken Arrow, OK: National Career Development Association.	

Evaluations checklists and guidelines created by professional organizations are available to help practitioners evaluate information contained in career software, information literature, and career media. Two organizations have prepared guides for developers of career information and for consumers to evaluate products and services:

The **Consumer Guide for Evaluating Career Information and Services** has been published by the Association of Computer-Based Systems of Career Information (ACSCI; 2009) for consumers to use in evaluating career products and services prior to purchase. ACSCI disseminates industry standards for developers of career information and services. They produced this publication to assist counselors, agency professionals, and government officials.

The **Alliance of Career Resource Professionals** (ACRP) promotes the worldwide development, delivery, and use of high-quality career information and resources among career professionals and consumers. They have created a product comparison tool which provides the career professional with the opportunity to evaluate and rate the importance one attributes to ACRP Content, Process, and Assessment Standards.

Although there are several guidelines from various organizations, they can be summed up with eight characteristics for evaluating quality career information. We find the criteria summarized by Duggan and Jurgens (2007) to be a helpful guide for students to use when evaluating career information. The acronym ACCURATE can be used to remember these characteristics:

- *Accurate.* Information is correct, real, reliable, valid, verifiable, and factual.
- *Comparable.* Information is organized in a consistent manner to help the reader compare and contrast the various types of information gathered.
- *Credited.* Information identifies who wrote it, who published it, who sponsored it. The information should answer these questions with clearly linked references.
- *Unbiased.* Information is objective. It neither encourages nor discourages individuals from selecting a specific field. Does the organization providing the information have a vested interest in the decisions of the individual?
- *Relevant.* Information specifies its intended audience. Is it relevant to the individuals who will use it? Information may be prepared for elementary schools, high schools, colleges and universities, rehabilitation agencies, libraries, or other audiences. It also should also be relevant to the geographical location of the individual.
- *Ample.* Information is comprehensive. It includes all types of information that are essential for evaluating occupational prospects. According to NCDA's (1991) content guidelines, it should include duties and nature of work, work setting and conditions, preparation required, special requirements or considerations, methods of entry, earning and other benefits, usual advancement possibilities, employment outlook, opportunities for experience and exploration, related occupations, and sources of additional information.
- *Timely.* Information is current, up-to-date, and applicable to the present time. According to NCDA (1991), the content should be revised at least every three to four years.

- *Explicable.* Information is understandable. It is user-friendly, easy to read and to comprehend. Information should be free from ambiguity and the data should be clearly explained and presented for a public audience.

Although it is not efficient to evaluate every career information resource extensively, having an awareness of these criteria will help you make sure you are using the most reliable tools and sources with your clients.

Conclusion

This chapter discussed some of the most popular sources of career information, including print and online resources, web-based career guidance systems, informational interviews, job-shadowing experiences and One-Stop Career Centers. We covered tips and guidelines for evaluating the quality of web-sourced occupational information. It was suggested that human service professionals defer to eight characteristics when evaluating the quality of career information.

Key Chapter Terms

Information	Career Outlook
Occupational Information	O*NET
Career Information	CareerOneStop
Labor-Market Information	My Next Move
Career Adaptability	Guide for Evaluating Career Info.
Occupational Outlook	Alliance of Career Resource
Handbook	Professionals
Monthly Labor Review	

Web Resources

Note that website URLs may change over time.

U. S. Government Sources

Occupational Outlook Handbook
https://www.bls.gov/ooh/

Monthly Labor Review
https://www.bls.gov/opub/mlr/

Career Outlook
https://www.bls.gov/careeroutlook/

O*NET Online
https://www.onetonline.org/

CareerOneStop
https://www.careeronestop.org/

My Next Move
https://www.mynextmove.org/

Military Occupational Information
Military.com
www.military.com/join-armed-forces/military-jobs

Online Military Education
http://www.onlinemilitaryeducation.org/

Today's Military
https://www.todaysmilitary.com/

Commercial/Private Publishers
ACT Profile
http://www.act.org/content/act/en/products-and-services/act-profile.html

ACT World-of-Work Map
http://www.act.org/content/dam/act/unsecured/documents/interest_invento
ry.pdf

Careers.org
https://www.careers.org/

Job Search Information
Career Builder
https://www.careerbuilder.com/

Monster.com
https://www.monster.com/

Career Theory, Development, and Appraisal

ExpatNetwork
https://www.expatnetwork.com/

Glassdoor
https://www.glassdoor.com/index.htm

HLoom Resume
https://www.hloom.com/

LinkedIn
https://www.linkedin.com/

LiveCareer
https://www.livecareer.com/career/advice/jobs/intvres

My Interview Simulator
http://myinterviewsimulator.com/

National Occupation Employment & Wage Estimates
https://www.bls.gov/oes/current/oes_nat.htm

PayScale's Salary Negotiation Guide
https://www.payscale.com/salary-negotiation-guide

Resume Writing Academy
https://resumewritingacademy.com/

Other Career-Related Websites
NCDA Internet Sites for Career Planning
https://www.ncda.org/aws/NCDA/pt/sp/resources

HigherEdJobs
https://www.higheredjobs.com/

Chapter 7

JOB-SEARCH COMPETENCIES

"Job-hunting is always mysterious. Sometimes mind-bogglingly mysterious. You may never understand why things sometimes work, and sometimes do not."

~Richard N. Bolles

CHAPTER HIGHLIGHTS
Job-Search Components
Job-Search Resources
Networking
Informational Interviewing
Job Shadowing
Social Media Competency
Resumes

For many people, the job-search process is far more than filling out applications and mailing resumes. It is a complicated undertaking that provokes anxiety for many job seekers, whether they are seeking their first jobs or are established workers looking for new ones. Because research tells us that people born in 1957 through 1964 held an average of 11.7 jobs between the ages 18 and 48 (U. S. Department of Labor, Bureau of Labor Statistics, 2015), having a strategic process along with proper planning and competencies can make a difference for people currently looking for a job and those who will seek one in the future. Although there are many books sold commercially that detail best practices for conducting a job search, many clients and students need the help of career service professionals. Being prepared to help them with the job-search process is essential for human service professionals. This chapter provides the human services professional with a primer on the many career resources available covering this topic while identifying competencies and guidelines for helping clients and students in their job-search process.

As discussed in Chapter 3, the job-search process fits into the career service of career placement. The primary objective of career placement today is to help people through the challenges related to obtaining a position. Placement activities relate minimally to theory, and involve practical interventions such as skill training, gathering information, networking, informational interviewing, job shadowing, resume preparation, searching for opportunities, social media competency, job interviewing, and refining self-presentation behavior. We will cover these areas in this chapter; others, such as marketing material, preparing for interviews, job applications, negotiating job offers, and placement agencies, are listed in the resources section.

Job Search Components

Because a job search should begin with a well-developed and carefully-executed plan of action, we will begin with the strategic job search. The effective **job search** involves searching for employment through developing, practicing, and improving a specific set of employability skills or competencies. The term **employability skills** refer to the development of a strategy for selling oneself to prospective employers and refining self-presentation behaviors. This includes using strategies and tools such as networking, personal branding, the use of social media, resume preparation, letter-writing, improving interviewing skills, job adjustment, and retention skills. There is no single approach for every person in a job search. Nevertheless, your clients will benefit from having a clear plan and strategy for their job searches. Duggan and Jurgens (2007) identified six **components of a job search** (see Figure 7.1). The following six components should be thought of as dynamic rather than linear:

Figure 7.1
Components of a Job Search

- *Know Thyself.* The job search process begins with a careful assessment of one's interests, values, personality, aptitudes, skills, and goals. A thorough assessment of these attributes, as discussed in Chapter 5, prepares the individual to make career decisions and market themselves to potential employers by identifying personal strengths.

- *Know the Position.* An essential element in determining whether a position is a good match with the candidate's attributes is to gather as much information about the position as possible. It is helpful to obtain a copy of specific job descriptions and information on the number of such positions filled annually and inquire about how the position became available. Information obtained about the typical career paths available within the organization, or minimal advancement opportunities, can help one decide if it is a good fit.

- *Know the Employer.* Information about an employer, company, or organization is usually available online to the public. It is recommended that job seekers gather information about the size and growth of the organization over past five years and about the potential for growth in the future, including plans for additional offices. A financial health profile, stock prices, and recent mergers or takeovers can be found by examining the websites listed in the resource section end of this chapter. It is also a good idea to collect information about organizational structure, whether it is for profit, nonprofit, public, or private. The job seeker should learn about the geographic location of the company along with the number of sites, the parent company, and relocation policies. In addition, organizational philosophy and personnel policies, training program, professional development opportunities, advancement policies, and diversity of the workplace along with policy statements on diversity are helpful pieces information to have on hand for interviews.

- *Know the Job Market.* The best source of current information on the job market is the U. S. Department of Labor, Bureau of Labor Statistics. The Bureau is the principal federal agency responsible for measuring labor market activity, working conditions, and price changes in the economy. More information on this topic is provided in Chapter 6 of this text.

- *Know Where to Find Information.* In addition to the internet, job seekers who want more information about companies can use libraries in their search. Public, university, and college libraries are all valuable resources that house a variety of business and government directories, basic reference books, financial reports, government indexes, workforce information, and industry- and state-specific directories. A librarian can assist not only clients but also human service professionals in locating these resources and gaining familiarity with the information available.

Career Resource Centers are located on the campuses of many universities and colleges as well as in some public libraries. They are a vital source of career and employment information, on-site recruiting, career fairs, and career libraries. Career Resource Centers or Career Services Centers, as they are sometimes called, are generally staffed with trained human service professionals who offer programs, placement, and career guidance services. Although some university and college programs and services are only available to students and alumni, many centers allow community members to access these resources, too.

- *Know Where to Look for Jobs.* Job seekers who want to consider all possibilities must be knowledgeable about two job markets: the visible and the hidden jobs markets. The **visible job market** includes those positions that are readily advertised to the public and through public media channels. These include information advertised in newspaper classified ads, employer hotlines, employer website listings, job banks including internet recruitment sites, classifies section of professional and trade journals, professional association placement services, public and private employment agencies, career fairs, and bulletin boards.

  The **hidden job market** includes those positions that are accessed primarily through building relationships with other professionals and organizations. These include networking contacts, alumni relations, mentors, newspaper articles, telephone books, temporary agencies, internships, job shadowing, informational interviews, professional trade journal articles, part-time and/or summer employment, freelance work, industry and professional websites, and chamber of commerce directories. The most effective approach when accessing the hidden job market is through network-building. Cold calling potential employers or emailing letters of introduction and interest are also effective ways of gaining entry or additional referrals. Human service professionals can help their clients by providing information on the visible job market and teaching clients about the advantages of the hidden job market and how to access this source for potential job opportunities.

Job Search Resources

The informational sources listed in Chapter 6 are useful for the job search or when providing a client with career placement services. Numerous websites provide online job boards which are available to the public and that provide individuals with career placement information. The National Career Development Association's (NCDA, 2018) website provides a listing of free, current, and credible resources that are available on the internet and are useful to career counselors, coaches, and human service professionals. The following categories contain a few sample resources that have been recommended by NCDA:

Resume Writing. **HLoom** site contains a step-by-step guide to crafting a resume. **Resume Writing Academy** contains resources on professional resume writing for job seekers and career professionals to include such tips as resume phrases, client questionnaire, verbs to use on a resume, etc.

Interviewing. **LiveCareer** offers articles and resources on the job interview. **My Interview Simulator** is a free online mock interview practice and rehearsal tool that provides basic interview questions (with response suggestions), behavior interview questions, and interview simulations with audible male and female voices.

Tools for Researching Employers. **Glassdoor** allows employees and former employees to anonymously review companies, give pros and cons, share information about the interview and job search process and report which company's employees rate the highest. **Crunchbase** is a private web platform for finding business information about private and public companies. It includes investments and funding information, founding members and individuals in leadership positions, mergers and acquisitions, news, and industry trends. Directories include **Dun's Million Dollar Directory, Standard & Poor's Register**, and the **Thomas Register of Manufacturers**, and the index to **The Wall Street Journal** and local **Chamber of Commerce** business directories.

Job Listing Sites. **CareerOneStop** is sponsored by the U. S. Department of Labor and a partner of the American Job Center network. This site offers a variety of resources for career exploration, training, and jobs. Specifically, the site links job seekers to state job banks, employment agencies, military options, and job fairs. **CareerBuilder** is a job search community that allows a job seeker to store a resume online without posting it in the database. It offers the option to sign up for job alerts and provides online job search tips. Registered users can create up to five personal search profiles to track new jobs added to the database, and an e-mail message can be generated to a user when a match is discovered. **Monster.com** is one of the most recognized names in the online job search community. It offers a variety of job and career resources for everyone from college students to contractors to chief executives. It also offers several industry/job field communities, including healthcare, human resources, and finance and plenty of job search extras: networking boards, job search alerts, and online resume posting.

International Job Search. **ExpatNetwork** is a free membership-based site provides current information, products, services, jobs, and CV-hosting for individuals seeking overseas employment – regardless of home country. Members may access the quarterly Expat Living Magazine and 17 destination guides (updated daily by expat experts) free of charge, though additional destination guides are available for a fee.

Salary Information & Negotiation. **National Occupational Employment & Wage Estimates** provides data collected from employers in all industry sectors in metropolitan and nonmetropolitan areas in every state in the U.S. **PayScale Salary Negotiation Guide** contains information on salary research, negotiation strategy, and the negotiation process. Scripts, templates, benefits to consider, and facts about salary negotiation are included.

Social Media. **LinkedIn** allows users to create a profile that acts as an online resume with options to describe experiences, skills, qualities, and showcase work samples. Users can follow organization pages, connect with professional networking contacts, search for jobs (there is a student job database in addition to the primary job database), find university alumni, join groups or discussion boards, and read articles authored by industry professionals.

Strategies for Identifying Job Opportunities

In addition to helping clients assess job-search information, human service professionals can teach clients about key strategies for identifying job opportunities. Career and occupational information can also be found by engaging in structured interviews, direct observation, and direct exploration with individuals who work within the field of interest. These opportunities help increase awareness of self and one's potential fit to work in a particular field or job.

Networking

Connecting with people who are doing the kind of work you want to do is referred to as **networking**. The process includes meeting, socializing, and talking with as many people as you can about career fields, industries, and companies that interest you. Among career professionals, networking is considered the most effective method of job searching. In a 2008-2012 survey of people who started a new job (Right Management, 2013), *46 percent* of individuals in the 2012 cohort obtained their jobs through networking, consistently making it the most preferred job-search strategy across the 2008-2012 cohort results. Listed below are the most significant types of networks:

- Personal Relationships
- Professional Relationships
- Associations (National and Local)
- Job/Career Fairs
- Opportunistic or Chance Networks

Building a network can feel very natural for people who are sociable, but for those who are shy or introverted, network building can be intimidating. Referring to the Holland code E (Enterprising), networking requires adequate verbal skills to persuade other people to reach personal goals. According to Holland, people with high E in their RIASEC code like to use verbal skills to persuade and tend to be assertive and self-assured. Regardless of whether or not a client is low on E personality characteristics, enterprising behaviors can be learned. Thus, the human services professional may find that they need to provide some clients with encouragement, assertiveness training, and help build self-esteem to increase their enterprising skills.

It is important to instruct clients on how to conduct networking with a plan. The job seeker needs to define what they want to learn and be sure to ask relevant questions. Have clients make a list of questions they would want to ask people they encounter. Questions may contain identifying an employer with whom they can conduct an informational interview, getting feedback on a resume, or gathering specific information about a company or organization. Whatever the goal, it is important to stress that the aim of networking is building relationships. Networking is an activity that builds on itself as each contact is likely to generate several more (Asher, 2011; Yate, 2017). Because networking relies on enterprising personality attributes, it is an essential skill that can continue to have a positive impact throughout one's employment and not just while job seeking.

Informational Interviewing

An excellent networking tool that uses a structured interview format is the **Informational interview**. This method involves spending time with a professional in an occupation of interest to learn useful information that can help the individual validate or modify their career direction. Where the purpose of a job interview is to land a new job, informational interviewing allows the client to conduct a screening process of the career and setting before applying for a specific job (Duggan & Jurgens, 2007). Human service professionals should share the many benefits of informational interviewing with their clients. Informational interviewing can help clients in the following ways:

- *Network Building.* Helps clients gain important visibility and establish or enhance professional networks that will provide the support needed to enter the field.
- *Perspective Taking.* Helps clients learn about the pros and cons of a field as well as specific skills needed to be successful in a given occupation. Allows clients to see firsthand how they will fit into a particular job.
- *Hidden Job Market Revelations.* Allows clients to become aware of job opportunities not advertised.
- *Professional Development.* Helps clients learn about the important skills needed for particular jobs which may require further education, qualifications, certifications, or licenses to position themselves as a better candidate.
- *Confidence Building.* This can serve as a dress rehearsal for self-presentation behavior and the real interview, decreasing anxiety that some people may have about going into a job interview.

Job Shadowing

Clients can discover whether they might enjoy certain jobs by observing the work environment, occupational skills, duties, projects, and potential career options that come along with the job. **Job shadowing** experiences can help clients gather information through direct observation of the day-to-day activities involved in a certain job. The experience is temporary and unpaid, but job shadowing provides exposure to the work setting and networking opportunities. At times, informational interviews can lead to job shadowing experiences.

Human service professionals can find job-shadowing opportunities by contacting businesses and organizations directly. Human services organizations and educational institutions have departments and professionals that often help clients and students connect to job shadowing opportunities. There are also virtual job shadowing opportunities available on the internet. Human service professionals should provide job-shadowing guidelines to their clients to help make the experiences a positive one for all involved.

Direct exploration of work environments is another source of gaining knowledge about an occupation. Volunteer work, cooperative education, internships, work-study programs, or part-time employment offer excellent experiences for clients and students and help increase awareness of self and validation of one's potential fit in a field or job.

Social Media

Social media has changed the job search process by expanding opportunities for networking. Where searching for a job was once primarily a face to face process, people are now able to reach out to others across broader geographic and industrial ranges. Stollak, Vandenberg, Felhofer, and Sutherland (2014) reported that, over the past eight years, social media has continuously grown into a major aspect of life. A recent survey released by Jobvite showed that 94 percent of employers use or plan to use social media for hiring (Quigley, 2013). Certainly, the impact of social media on the job search process has increased and is influencing the behaviors of today's job seeker and the ways in which employers' source candidates and make hiring decisions. As such, human service professionals should be well-versed in the use of social media in their client's job-search process.

Davis, Deil-Amen, Rios-Aguilar, and Gonzalez Canche (2012) defined **social media** as "web-based and mobile applications that allow individuals and organizations to create, engage, and share new user-generated or existing content, in digital environments through multi-way communication" (p.1). The Pew Research Center Survey of U. S. Adults (Smith & Anderson, 2018) found that younger Americans (ages 18 to 24) stand out for embracing a variety of social media platforms and using them frequently. At the same time, there are pronounced differences in the use of various social media platforms. For example, Americans ages 18 to 24 are more likely to use platforms such as Snapchat, Instagram and Twitter even when compared with those in their mid- to late-20s. LinkedIn remains especially popular among college graduates and those in high-income households. Some 50% of Americans with a college degree use LinkedIn, compared with just 9% of those with a high school diploma or less.

Social Media Competency

While social media provides new opportunities for job seekers, it also presents challenges. While it has the potential to bring access to many clients by removing potential barriers for distance seekers, clients with disabilities, nontraditional clients, and other underserved populations (Nell, 2014) using social media may feel very isolated.

Human service professionals who provide career services have a responsibility to educate clients on the basics of social media use. Clients who fail to use social networking are at a disadvantage when compared to their peers who make use of it for occupational and company research, networking, and job search leads (Nell, 2014). We recommend, as suggested by Nell (2014), that practitioners foster basic **social-media knowledge competencies** for the three most popular social media platforms: Facebook, Twitter, and LinkedIn.

- *Create an Online Presence.* Clients should be encouraged to create a LinkedIn profile as it is used to build more professional rather than social relationships. Some clients may use social media, but not for professional networking. It is important to consider when a client should be involved in social media and on what platform. For example, LinkedIn may not be appropriate for career-undecided clients, but is a good platform on which to begin promoting oneself when the desired career path is known.

- *Clean up Digital Art.* If clients already have social media accounts, they likely need to review the sites for inappropriate pictures, content, and links. Inform clients that according to a Harris Poll survey, 70 percent of employers use social media to screen candidates before hiring, up significantly from 60 percent last year and 11 percent in 2006 (CareerBuilder, 2017). In addition, 54 percent have decided not to hire a candidate based on their social media profiles, as research suggests that social media activity can be a predictor of future job performance (Kluemper, Rosen, & Mossholder, 2012).

- *Create Employer-Friendly Sites.* Encourage clients to promote a positive, professional online presence. This can be done by highlighting career-related posts and key accomplishments on Facebook timelines; retweeting positive stories or topics related to a field of study or occupation; placing career goals and interests in the headlines of LinkedIn accounts (Rutledge, 2012); and uploading a professional headshot and making sure that one's social media sites have a link to a resume or e-portfolio. Like networking, the key to success when using social media is to establish clear goals and concrete objectives for achieving those goals.

Resumes

When applying for a position, one needs a strategic marketing tool to gain an interview with an employer. A **resume** is a document that a candidate composes to communicate their background and value to an employer (Sukiennik & Raufman, 2016). A resume serves two important functions: it helps clarify goals and most marketable attributes, and it identifies selected accomplishments and presents them in a way that relates them to the type of work that one is seeking. Because there are a lot of details that go into preparing a resume, we will only address basic information on the types and preparation of resumes. The reader is encouraged to consult with the resources at the end of this chapter for further information.

Before we describe the different types of resumes, there are a few details about preparation that need to be considered. First, resumes should include your full name, address, and contact information. This text is commonly placed in a header and centered and bolded with larger font on top of each page. In addition, a resume should begin with the applicant's specific job objective. A **job objective** is a concise and precise statement about the position that the candidate is seeking (Sukiennik & Raufman, 2016). The job objective is also referred to as a goal, professional objective, position desired, or summary. The more specific the objective statement, the better your ability to focus your resume directly on the target. The information that comes after the objective should support the objective statement. Ideally, one should design a distinct resume for each job objective.

To effectively communicate the work activity in which the applicant has been involved, keywords and phrases are used. In a resume, keywords are referred to as *action words* or *action verbs*. They are words or short clear phrases chosen for the purpose of involving the reader and making the resume active. Words such as implemented, coordinated, developed, directed, planned, organized, evaluated, and managed are examples of action verbs. Avoid general comments such as "My duties were..." or "I worked for..." Applicants should begin phrases with action verbs that concisely describe the tasks they were involved in. In addition, **transferable skills** are those that a person carries from one job to another and can be used in a variety of occupations and life situations. Transferable skills should be identified before preparing resumes and emphasized in a resume. They are also articulated during the interview process. One method for identifying transferable skills is to look up the given occupations on O*NET and compare how well the skills listed match your own or the client's skills.

Resumes can be submitted to employers as a hard copy, via online as a plain text or pdf file, or through an online/web-based system. The three general resume types are functional, chronological, and hybrid. A **functional resume** presents the candidate's experience, skills, and job history in terms of the functions they have performed. Like any resume, it should be tailored to fit the main tasks and competencies for the job you are seeking. Select and emphasize activities from previous employment that relate to the specific job being applied for and deemphasize or omit irrelevant background information. Functional resumes are useful for people who have limited work experience, breaks in employment history, or are changing fields.

The **chronological resume** is the traditional and most frequently used resume style today. This type of resume lists the candidates work history in reverse chronological order, starting with his or her current or most recent position or occupation. The work history should include dates employed, job title, job duties, and employers' names, addresses, and telephone numbers or email addresses. This type of resume format is useful for people with no or minimal breaks in their employment record and for whom each new position indicates continuous advancement and growth. If your present position is not related to the job you are applying for, employers may feel that your current experience is the most important consideration and eliminate you from competition. However, if you emphasize skills in your present job that will be important in the new position in your resume, as well as in your cover letter, you can address the issue logically.

The **hybrid resume** is considered a double advantage with a combination of the functional and chronological resume styles. This style of resume is suitable for people who have major skills that are relevant to the desired position in addition to an impressive record of continuous job experience with reputable employers. The hybrid style usually lists functions followed by years employed, with a list of employers. This can satisfy employers who also want to see dates.

Usually, if references are requested of an employer, one will need to submit their names and contact information on a separate form. As such, you don't have to list reference information on the resume unless specifically instructed to do so. Before you apply for a position, have three people in mind who can endorse your work habits, skills, and accomplishment. Most often these individuals should be supervisors who can speak directly to the clients work in previous positions. Let clients know that they should ask the people in advance if they may list them as a reference as that will prevent any surprises down the road.

There are specific resume types such as the curriculum vitae that are used for higher education positions, federal positions, military veterans, and internationally focused resume. The reader is referred to the resource section at the end of this chapter for further information on resume types, cover letters, transferable skills, and the interview process.

Conclusion

Successful job seekers must have excellent information and job search competencies. Human service professionals can assist their clients by becoming competent in job search strategies, networking, informational interviewing, job shadowing, the effective use of social media, and resume preparation. Promoting oneself involves a lot of challenging work, and the client may become discouraged at times. Helpers can provide support, knowledge, and the necessary expertise to alleviate feelings of frustration and to increase client confidence. By helping clients remain focused, flexible, open-minded, and persistent, human service professional can make the job-search process an effective and positive experience.

Key Chapter Terms

Job Search	Social Media
Employability Skills	Social-Media Knowledge Competencies
Components of a Job Search	Resume
Visible Job Market	Job Objective
Hidden Job Market	Transferable Skills
Networking	Functional Resume
Informational Interviewing	Chronological Resume
Job Shadowing	Hybrid Resume

Web Resources
Note that website URLs may change over time.

Job Search Resources
Career Builder
https://www.careerbuilder.com/

CareerOneStop
https://www.careeronestop.org/

Monster.com
https://www.monster.com/

ExpatNetwork
https://www.expatnetwork.com/

Glassdoor
https://www.glassdoor.com/index.htm

Crunchbase
https://www.crunchbase.com/

HLoom Resume
https://www.hloom.com/

LiveCareer
https://www.livecareer.com/career/advice/jobs/intvres

Interviewing
My Interview Simulator
http://myinterviewsimulator.com/

ODU-Interviewing
https://www.odu.edu/success/careers/tools/interviewing

Salary Negotiation
National Occupation Employment & Wage Estimates
https://www.bls.gov/oes/current/oes_nat.htm

PayScale's Salary Negotiation Guide
https://www.payscale.com/salary-negotiation-guide

Career and Occupational Evaluation Guidelines
ACRP Comparison Tool
http://www.acrpro.org/aws/ACRP/asset_manager/get_file/78905?ver=9759

Consumer Guide for Evaluating Career Information and Services
https://ncda.org/aws/ACRP/asset_manager/get_file/37672

Social Media
Social Media and Employability
https://www.youtube.com/watch?v=zpOyQk_H7QM

LinkedIn
https://www.linkedin.com/

Resume Preparation
ODU-Resumes and Professional Communication
https://www.odu.edu/success/careers/tools/resume

Transferable Skills
https://www.odu.edu/content/dam/odu/offices/cmc/docs/TransferableSkills.pdf

Resume Writing Academy
https://resumewritingacademy.com/

Chapter 8

MULTICULTURAL CONCEPTS AND STRATEGIES FOR CAREER SERVICES

"Dreams and expectations about work and career are very much shaped by individuals' cultural expectations and by the society in which they live."
~Fouad and Kantamneni, 2013, p. 215

CHAPTER HIGHLIGHTS
Multiculturalism
Cultural Competence
Cultural Awareness
A Career Framework for Helping Diverse Clients
Cultural Limitations of Traditional Career Theory
A Postmodern Perspective of Career and Culture

Culture has been a powerful force within the evolution of society. As suggested by Chudek, Muthukrishna, and Henrich (2016), cultural information spreads horizontally and needs to not be limited to genetic transmission in offspring. It is a commonly held belief that human life evolved out of Africa millions of years ago. Many indigenous African tribes are direct descendants of the earliest modern human (Homo sapiens) groups. These tribes have been able to preserve their cultural traditions for thousands of years despite European colonization in nearby regions. Remarkably, some tribes such as the Hadza are still around and practicing their ancient traditions. Anthropologists have described how these tribes have maintained a distinctive cultural character for over 10,000–years.

The Hadza tribe of northern Tanzania rely extensively on hunting and gathering or foraging for their survival. Woodburn (1970) noted the importance of sharing, minimal politics, egalitarianism, and an intimacy to social relations wherein most individuals act towards others like kin. Many Hadza overtly reject the noise, crowds, dangers, and discrimination that life in neighboring villages would entail. An important gender ritual expressed by the Hadza tribe is the epeme dance. In camps with enough adults, this takes place after dark on moonless nights. Men wear bells on their legs, a feather headdress, a cape, and shake a maraca as they sing and dance one at a time in a call-and-shout manner, inspiring the women to sing and dance around them. The performance aims for reconciliation between the sexes, healing and successful hunting (Power, 2015). Although many cultures change and interact with other cultural groups, the Hadza tribe is amazing in that they still maintain many of the same patterns of cultural behavior as they did in earlier times. Cultural evolutionary theorists attribute this to cultural explanations rather than solely biological (e.g., Marlowe, 2010).

Anthropologist have a variety of reasons for the stasis in the Hadza's cultural evolution. Marlow (2002) discusses such phenomena stemming from genetics to cultural encapsulation (e.g., insulation from agriculture and trade). If we try to understand this from a cultural perspective, the knowledge, practices, and behaviors expressed through common values, habits, norms, symbols, artifacts, language, and customs, are in part the reason why the Hadza have resisted dominant culture for all those years. For the Hadza, and other indigenous tribes, **agency** or the ability to make choices and exercise free will even within dominant structures (Schultz & Lavenda, 2017) served to help them hold on to their way of life. Like the Hadza, many cultures today hold on to their beliefs.

In this chapter, we will help you learn the basics of multicultural career services related to working with clients from diverse backgrounds. We first examine the multicultural movement and the need for culturally competent services. We then define some key terms related to diversity that you will often encounter in the literature. Next, we address the importance of multicultural awareness as a foundation for cultural competence for human service professionals. Self-reflection exercises for several core competencies are provided, along with a practical model for working with diverse clients during the career helping process. This chapter concludes with a look at the cultural limitations of traditional career theories, and the postmodern view of career and culture.

Multiculturalism

America's population consists of an abundantly rich multiracial, multiethnic, and multilingual mix. In fact, more than one third of Americans are members of racial and ethnic minorities, and such minorities are expected to account for the majority of the U. S. population by the year 2043 (U. S. Census Bureau, 2018). Tremendous demographic and cultural shifts that occurred between 2000-2015 have reshaped the structure of the labor force, and this cultural pluralism is increasingly reflected within our society at large (Niles & Harris-Bowlsbey, 2017). All these changes in demographics, in addition to cultural plurality, influence the career helping process. Thus, there is a need for human service professionals to have the proper awareness, knowledge, and skills to work with an increasingly diverse clientele. For the human service professional, issues related to diversity and being a culturally competent helper are critical (Neukrug, 2017).

Multiculturalism has been referred to as the fourth force in mental health. It is a relatively new paradigm following the first three forces in our profession: psychoanalysis, behaviorism, and humanistic psychology. **Multiculturalism** is a pervasive force in modern society that "seeks to provide a conceptual framework that recognizes the complex diversity of a plural society while, at the same time, suggesting bridges of shared concern that bind culturally different persons to one another" (Pedersen, 1991, p. 7). The movement developed in large part due to a major criticism that existing psychological theories were based on European American culture and values (Katz, 1985), and, thus failed to adequately address the intricacies of a diverse client population. Its roots were embedded in helping poor and marginalized groups. However, scholars have argued that subsequent theoretical developments and research in the field have resulted in a practice that is geared toward a small, privileged segment of society: middle-class, educated, white-collar workers (e.g., Blustein, 2006; Pope, 2012). Thus, multicultural counseling (previously used terms include pluralistic counseling and cross-cultural counseling) is often used to refer to a specialized aspect or subfield of clinical practice, although Speight, Myers, Cox, and Highlen (1991) argued that, "all counseling is multicultural in nature" (p. 31). Nevertheless, there has been a strong and growing movement in the career helping profession to address the problems of applying career development principles to other cultures.

Embracing cultural competence and sensitivity can challenge human service professionals. Such contact with differing cultural backgrounds can initially lead to questioning, confusion, guilt, and anxiety about topics of diversity (Baruth &

Manning, 2016). When helping professionals lack cultural skills, it can result in clients from diverse backgrounds being misunderstood, misdiagnosed, having the impact of negative social forces minimized, finding relationships less helpful, seeking mental health services at lower rates, and terminating helping relationships earlier (Neukrug & Milliken, 2008; Sewell, 2009). In addition, because human service professionals are often people from diverse backgrounds, it is incumbent upon them to develop their own cultural awareness, evaluate their personal views, and understand that other people's perspectives may be as legitimate as their own. Before we discuss cultural awareness more specifically, we will define some important terms you will encounter in the literature related to diversity. These terms are important to human service professionals and will be revisited throughout the book.

Terminology

Acculturation. The term **acculturation** has been defined as a socialization process that occurs when members of two or more cultures encounter one another (Berry, 2002). When this occurs, many individuals from each group learn the cultural values and practices of a new culture while maintaining some degree of cultural affiliation with their traditional culture (Berry). Some of the aspects of culture that are affected by acculturation include language, friendship patterns and social affiliations, customs, music, and food preferences. This is especially relevant when immigrants arrive in a new country (e.g., international students), and when people migrate within a country or region that consists of multiple cultures (e.g., relocating for employment).

Culture. The literature generally defines **culture** as a body of knowledge, practices, and behavior that is expressed through common values, habits, norms of behavior, symbols, artifacts, language, and customs (McAuliffe, 2008). Typically, when we think of culture, we usually think of race or ethnicity. Yet, there are many more dimensions (i.e., socio-identity groups) of diversity that contribute to a multicultural environment. For example, age, sex, sexual orientation and gender identity, social class, disability status, citizenship, tribal or indigenous affiliation, and religion/spirituality are the most discussed dimensions.

Context. The contextual influences and interactions that make and remake the individual can be described as the **context** or cultural context. It is through contextual variables, that act as socializing agents, that individuals not only acquire in part their cultural identity (Cushner, McClelland, & Safford, 2015), but also knowledge, attitudes, skills, and values about work and occupations. There are generally 12 socializing agents: electronic media, peer group, neighborhood, community, house of worship, school, family, technology, workplace, print media, the arts, and sports. Each of the agents have a slightly different interpretation of work and occupations, thus an individual's understanding of work, occupations, and having a career is interpreted or mediated by a socializing agent or a combination.

Cultural Pluralism. The term **cultural pluralism** denotes when smaller groups within a larger society maintain their unique cultural identities, characteristics, and mores (American Psychological Association, 2015). Their values and practices may be accepted by the wider culture provided they are consistent with the laws and values of the wider society. Cultural pluralism is also referred to as multiculturalism.

Discrimination. A major issue in career development for members of minority groups, **discrimination** involves active, harmful, and conscious and unconscious behaviors toward an individual of a minority or marginalized group (Neukrug, 2017; Fassinger, 2008). It is particularly damaging when one is in the establishment or maintenance stage of one's career development. Direct experiences of discrimination have been related to emotional distress among African Americans, Latinos, Latinas, Asian Americans, and American Indians (Carter & Forsyth, 2010). Also, immigrants may face discrimination when they move to a new culture by being denied promotions, attractive assignments, raises, or other advantages because of racism. According to McAuliffe (2013a), scholars call discrimination a crisis because of the notion of **compound discrimination**. This term refers to overlapping oppressions for members of multiple nondominant cultural groups. For example, oppressions such as racism, sexism, classism, and homophobia, can occur simultaneously in any one person. This is discussed further under the term intersectionality.

Ethnicity. The term **ethnicity** refers to a shared unique sociogeographical and cultural heritage. The sociogeographical customs (e.g., language, religion, food, dance, values, ceremonies) commonly associated with specific ethnic groups are passed down from one generation to the next.

Intersectionality. Drawing on feminist and multicultural perspectives, **intersectionality** refers to the assumption that an individual's cultural identities must be considered in combination and not in isolation (Cole, 2009). Cultural variables such as age, gender, race, class, sexual orientation, religion/spirituality, and disability simultaneously affect their perceptions, experiences, and opportunities. For example, one can be a lesbian who has a minority ethnic background. One can be gay and living in poverty. One can be transgender with a disability. The intersections are complex and cannot be considered independently from one another, since they constantly interact with each other. Intersecting identities can reinforce social inequality, injustice, and discrimination.

Race. The social science literature has generally defined **race** in two ways: Natural/biological race and social race. Natural race refers to shared genotype or physiology that often is outwardly manifested in a group's' physical characteristics. Biologist and social scientists have challenged the use of natural race. One reason is because race is socially constructed and is very much related to the society in which one lives (Smedley & Smedley, 2005). Social race encompasses the shared sociohistorical experiences of a group of people; shared experiences and social relationships between races significantly affect one's beliefs, behaviors, and sociopolitical and economic conditions (Flores, 2014).

Social Class. The term **social class** has been defined in relation to socioeconomic status and includes education level and occupational, and financial status. Some researchers have gone beyond socioeconomic status, however, to include issues such as lifestyle, power, and prestige (e.g., Diemer & Ali, 2009). Social class has been demonstrated to affect a host of career-related variables, including perceptions of work, career development progress, and vocational expectations. Social class is regarded as a critical aspect in understanding the career development process of all clients, regardless of their racial or ethnic group affiliations (Flores, 2014).

Worldview. The term **worldview** refers to a frame of reference that a person uses to interpret and define events and to make decisions, and can be said to comprise their attitudes and values (Sue & Sue, 2016). Worldview is typically acquired through the process of a person learning how to perceive his or her relation to self, community, and the world during their cultural socialization into a racial, ethnic or social class community.

It is important to think of diversity beyond the typical labels and stereotypes we are exposed to. To be diverse means to be inclusive and curious about differences. According to Flores (2014), "when career counselors view their clients broadly as members of a specific cultural group, they risk relying on group stereotypes and may overlook the variables that make each client unique" (p. 61). This is, in part, because culture is a learned behavior. That is, just because a client may belong to one or more of the diverse groups, he or she has unique worldview, beliefs, values and histories that are embedded in context and should not be overlooked. When working with diverse clients, consider that a focus only on the differences between cultural groups limits recognizing the variations among individuals within groups (McAuliffe, 2013a).

Multicultural effectiveness requires that the human services professional has awareness of the diversity that exists between different cultural groups in addition to the diversity that exists within cultural groups. This is relevant for human service professionals providing any type of service for any client.

Cultural Competence

Before providing any career service to clients, we suggest that human service professionals begin by exploring what it means to be culturally competent. A basic definition of **culturally competent helping** has been offered by McAuliffe (2013b), who suggested that culturally competent helping is "a consistent readiness to identify the cultural dimensions of clients' lives and a subsequent integration of culture into counseling work" (p. 6). This definition is relevant for human service professionals as well. Various competency frameworks have been developed by scholars and professional organizations to guide helpers when providing career services to culturally diverse clients (e.g., NCDA). Human service students and professionals should first be familiar with the National Organization for Human Services (NOHS) ethical standards as they relate to working with culturally diverse clients (see Appendix E). Although these frameworks are beyond the scope of this chapter, competency frameworks such as those focus on oppression and racism (Arredondo, 1999) and [a general model explicated by Neukrug (2017) may be helpful for any human service professional to gain familiarity. But first, the foundation for working competently with culturally diverse clients is the awareness of our biases, stereotypes, and beliefs, as well as those held by society.

Cultural Awareness

As a human services professional helping people with their career issues, you will not be expected to be an expert in all areas of multicultural awareness. But you may regularly be required to step outside of your own worldview to work effectively with the clients you serve. You will strive to work with your clients with as much understanding of and empathy for their worldview and all the cultural variables they bring with them. Today, training focuses more on helper self-awareness.

The most important foundation for human service professionals to work effectively with culturally diverse clients is self-awareness. The National Organization for Human Services (NOHS) Ethical Standards for Human service professionals (2015) states the following regarding working with culturally diverse clients:

> Human service professionals are aware of their own cultural backgrounds, beliefs, values, and biases. They recognize the potential impact of their backgrounds on their relationships with others and work diligently to provide culturally competent service to all of their clients (Standard 34, Responsibility to Self).

Multicultural awareness starts with personal reflection. Strive to frame your work within a cultural context, helping clients set goals from their worldview rather than the helper's worldview. Without understanding of the self, there is limited chance that an individual will be open to learning about different cultures (Neukrug, 2012). We first suggest reflecting on the following questions to create a frame of reference for understanding how culture can impact an individual's career development:

- What role has cultural context played in my own career decisions?
- How have I been affected by mainstream cultural expectations about work?
- Do I believe that I am limited by my cultural/ethnic background? Have I limited my occupational choices based on this belief?
- How is my cultural context framing the way I view other people's career or work problems?
- Has my gender or sexual orientation ever limited the occupational choices I have considered?
- If you have a chronic mental health problem or physical disability, has it influenced your thinking about work or jobs?

Cultural Awareness Competencies

As a human services student or professional, you will need to explore your own awareness for working with clients from a multicultural perspective. Padilla and Borsato (2008) suggested that practitioners may not be aware of how their linguistic, social class, and other cultural experiences influence their construction of knowledge, selection of instruments, and interpretation derived from assessment procedures. Three competency domains, each with several core competencies, have been proposed by Collins and Arthur (2007), and we believe they provide a useful framework for learning to become culturally competent. We will focus here on Domain I, **Cultural Awareness of Self**, which involves the active awareness of your personal assumptions, values, and biases and serves as a good vehicle for self-reflection. Discuss with a fellow student or write a journal entry on how you would demonstrate your awareness of the four core competencies below:

- What are your own cultural identities? Your cultural identities (or socio-identity groups) include your race/ethnicity, sex, sexual orientation, gender identity, age, disability status, religion/spirituality, socioeconomic status, citizenship, and tribal or indigenous affiliation. The first step toward multicultural competence is to acknowledge that you are a cultural being.

- What are the differences between your own cultural identities and those of individuals from other dominant or non-dominant groups? Acknowledgement of difference is critical to culturally sensitive practice.

- What is the personal and professional impact of the inconsistency between dominant and non-dominant cultural groups in the United States? A step beyond simply recognizing and valuing the differences that exist across cultural groups is acknowledgment of the degree to which resources, opportunities, and options are differentially available based on group membership (Kiselica, 1999). When a person has a distinct advantage by virtue of her of his membership in a dominant cultural group (i.e., it is not earned) it is referred to as **privilege** (Grothaus, McAuliffe, Danner, & Doyle, 2013).

- What is your current level of multicultural competence? Human service professionals should focus their attention in terms of their own self-awareness in honest reflection about their level of multicultural competence. How do you believe that enhancing multicultural competence is a priority?

Being culturally competent requires continuous professional reflection, study, and development as human service professionals move through their careers. Because a client's cultural background plays a role in shaping their view of reality, human service practitioners must develop a repertoire of multicultural competencies that address how these factors may influence conceptualization of the client's career needs, and the identification of appropriate career interventions. Human service professionals, therefore, need to work in ways that promote the career development and functioning of individuals of all backgrounds.

A Career Framework for Helping Diverse Clients

Researchers and practitioners have provided guidelines to consider when working with clients from diverse backgrounds, and several models have been developed for use in the career counseling process. In Figure 8.1, we present a culturally appropriate career model (Gysbers, Heppner, & Johnston, 2014) that can organize the work of the human services professional in the career helping process. Embedded in this model, Flores (2014) described some of the culturally salient aspects of the career planning process and offered suggestions for working with diverse clients. Summarized below is the **two-phase cultural career model** with corresponding objectives:

Phase 1: Problem Identification

- *Opening and Forming the Working Alliance.* Establishing a rapport and early connection with a client can set the stage for the collaboration necessary for effective goal formulation and following career services. Helpers may assess the client's level of "racial salience" or "class salience" to explore the extent to which the client perceives race or class to be influential in the career process, including in perceived work options, level of occupational stereotyping, and career decision-making (Helms & Piper, 1994). Gently asking a client to teach you about aspects of their culture that you do not fully understand can be a way to build a therapeutic relationship.
- *Gathering Client Information.* This includes assessing culture-specific variables and individual differences, so the helper can filter the information through a cultural context. In addition, assessment should extend beyond the traditional quantitative use of interest, abilities, and values inventories to include qualitative assessments and interviews such as the *My Career Story* interview (Savickas & Hartung, 2012).

- *Understanding and Hypothesizing about Client Information & Behavior.* The helper may explore the role and impact that poverty, sexism, racism, or discrimination have had on the client's self-efficacy. That is, the client's belief in their probability of succeeding in the traditional labor market and the outcomes he or she perceives to be possible. Also, the helper can explore the gendered, racialized, and classist nature of the client's self-concept (i.e., how they view or evaluate themselves in relation to work) and how it may influence job options). According to Brown (2002), for people with **individualistic values**, where self-actualization and an autonomous way of living is the goal, highly prioritized work values are the most important determinants of career choice. For people with **collectivistic values**, however, the career decision-making process will be heavily influenced by the wishes of the family, group, or community. The culturally competent helper would determine which value the client relies on more.

Phase 2: Problem Resolution

- *Taking Action.* During this phase, it is important to help clients identify those aspects of the issue that are within or beyond their personal control. This may be very helpful for clients who are living in poverty. It is also helpful to encourage clients to take part in group interventions such as career exploration groups or job clubs which reinforces their worldview and allow individuals to connect with others from similar backgrounds or who face similar challenges. Such interventions can provide opportunities to connect clients to culturally-similar role models.
- *Developing Career Goals and Plans of Action.* An individual career plan is developed in this phase to serve as a roadmap for the client. Here the helper may suggest action steps to overcome potential obstacles and even serve as an advocate for the client if needed. The helper may role-play responses to situations of racism, classism, and discrimination that the client could face in the workplace.
- *Evaluating Results and Closing the Relationship.* This phase concerns evaluating the sessions from both a content (what we did) and a process (how we did it) perspective. During this phase, the helper emphasizes the client's strengths and their progress made toward various aspects of the career-planning process. Welcoming clients to return to session for further assistance after termination is offered, but it must be noted that

this has important implications for diverse populations. Fouad and Bingham (1995) asserted that individuals from some racial and ethnic minorities may ascribe expert or even familial status to the human services professional. Also, returning to session after termination may be perceived as a failure or shameful, especially for some Asian Americans.

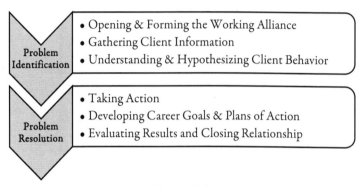

Figure 8.1
Two-Phase Cultural Career Model

The development of cultural competence involves a process of life-long learning and personal self-reflection. As each of us increases our multicultural competence, we become a force for change at the professional level and are in a better position to help clients who need career services. Today, many career scholars and practitioners are committed to developing career services objectives and strategies that will assist individuals of various cultural groups to overcome a multitude of barriers. Regardless of the client or setting you are working in, as a human service professional you should strive to develop the attitudes, beliefs, knowledge, and skills to work effectively with diverse populations.

Cultural Limitations of Traditional Career Theory

Much of the traditional research examining the effectiveness of specific career interventions or general career counseling services seemed to treat all clients not only as if they were alike but also as if the clients' gender, race/ethnicity, and sexual orientation for example had minimal, unimportant influences on their receptiveness to counseling or the positive outcomes that they might achieve (Miller & Brown, 2005). This is because many of the traditional career theories were developed in the early to mid-20th century and reflected the culturally encapsulated and paternalistic view of that time. The focus was on middle-to upper class Caucasian males and had at its core the assumption that individuals have the economic means to pursue their career interests and goals (Flores, 2014). This approach to career counseling is no longer supported in a postmodern society, as career theories and interventions have become more inclusive and are based in the assumption that every client has a unique background embedded in and influenced by their cultural context (Busacca & Rehfuss, 2017).

A Postmodern Perspective of Career, Culture, and Context

There are five primary features of the postmodern approach to working with diverse clients that distinguish it from traditional career approaches. We provide only a brief overview of career and culture from a postmodern perspective here; for a more comprehensive discussion refer to Chapter 13 of this book. Following are five features that underly the focus of a postmodern approach to career counseling:

1. *Meaning-making in the career helping process.* As McAuliffe and Emmett (2017) noted, postmodern human service professionals emphasize the role of clients as meaning-makers who design (not discover) their own realities through continuous reflection on their unique life experiences and social contexts. Thus, a focus of helping from a postmodern approach is on the personal meaning and interpretations individuals ascribe to their experience, and includes cultural attributes such as race, ethnicity, age, sex, disability, spirituality/religion, and sexual orientation.

2. *The embrace of all expressions of diversity.* Cultural identity includes not only race and ethnicity, but also gender, sexual orientation, disability, age, religion, spirituality, and factors in the intersectionality of these identities. The postmodern approach looks beyond group membership and draws attention to diversity within groups. Thus, intersections of culture can affect one's career and work by reinforcing social inequality, injustice, and discrimination.

3. *Viewing individual career behavior as related to the context in which it occurs.* Context involves a focus on the individual's interaction with and within their social and environmental contexts. Contextual variables such as socioeconomic status, electronic media, peer group, neighborhood, community, house of worship, school, family, technology, workplace, print media, the arts, and sports can have an influence on how clients perceive their career issues.

4. *Examining the linkages between culture and social justice.* This underscores how language is ruled by the hierarchies of discourse,

including structures of power, ideology, and knowledge (Stead & Bakker, 2010). That is, human service professionals shift the focus from society's story for how people should live and work in the United States to the client's individual story. The social justice perspective requires that counselors encourage clients to give voice to their experiences of oppression and to examine how dominant discourses have framed their career experiences (Blustein, Schultheiss, & Flum, 2004).

5. *Exploring the ways in which work is rooted in a relational context.* Relational theory proposes that people learn about themselves, their social world, and their culture through relationships (Blustein, 2011). The relational understanding of work and career enriches traditional career counseling practice by acknowledging the potential adaptive function of interpersonal connection when helping individuals with career transitions and in making a career choice. Yet some multicultural theories have persisted in their use of models which are entrenched in individualistic dominant discourses.

From the discussion above, one can see that a postmodern approach to helping culturally diverse individuals with their career issues is more of a philosophical orientation than the use of tools and techniques. As suggested by Busacca and Rehfuss (2017), professionals who provide career counseling should first locate the client's interactions and experiences within their contextual environment that shaped their career problem or personal narrative, and then help the client use their own culturally-embedded stories to revise their narrative. It is important to keep in mind that traditional career theories, and those discussed in Chapter 4 of this text, can be useful in helping people with career issues if applied from a culturally competent stance or integrated with postmodern approaches.

Conclusion

This chapter covered the basics of culture as related to working with clients with career issues. We examined the multicultural movement and then defined some relevant terms related to diversity. Next, we addressed the importance for the helper in developing self-awareness, the need for culturally competent services, and provided a self-reflection exercise on several core cultural competencies. A practical career model for working with diverse clients was presented. We concluded this chapter with a look at the cultural limitations of traditional career theories, and an explanation of the postmodern perspective of career and culture.

Key Chapter Terms

Agency	Race
Multiculturalism	Social Class
Acculturation	Worldview
Culture	Culturally Competent Helping
Context	Cultural Awareness of Self
Cultural Pluralism	Privilege
Discrimination	Two-Phase Cultural Career Model
Compound Discrimination	Individualistic Values
Ethnicity	Collectivist Values
Intersectionality	

Web Resources

Note that website URLs may change over time.

Counseling in Challenging Contexts by Michael Ungar [Video]
https://sapibg.org/en/book/counseling-in-challenging-contexts-by-michael-ungar-video

Diversity in Career, Individual and Group Counseling [Video]
https://www.youtube.com/watch?v=8ohrjU0vXAw

Diversity Resources Provided by University of California, Berkeley
https://career.berkeley.edu/Infolab/Diversity

Chapter 9

ADULT-CAREER TRANSITION AND SPECIAL POPULATIONS

"Every transition begins with an ending. We have to let go of the old thing before we can pick up the new one—not just outwardly, but inwardly, where we keep our connections to people and places that act as definitions of who we are."
~William Bridges, 2004, p. 11.

CHAPTER HIGHLIGHTS
Adult Career Transition
A Model of Transition
Displaced or Dislocated Workers
Offender/Ex-Offenders
The Veteran Population
People with Chemical Dependency

Career transitions are influential events in people's working lives. In the United States, occupational and economic changes are challenging adult workers to adjust to more frequent career transitions. Many adults can no longer expect a lifetime of employment within a single organization or steady movement up a predetermined career ladder. Working today, which is shaped by a global economy and propelled by information technology, is characterized by uncertain, unpredictable, and risky employment opportunities (Kalleberg, 2009). Because career planning in the future will include circular as well as linear moves, human service professionals will need to emphasize adaptation and flexibility in the work role. There are also current social issues that are related to career transitions and require an array of human services to meet the needs of clients.

There are many diverse populations that have unique characteristics and needs, including single parents and displaced homemakers, welfare-to-work clients, the working poor and homeless population, older workers, and the newly immigrated. Sometimes these groups are referred to as underserved or hard-to-serve populations. These special populations have a unique set of obstacles that impede successful career development and they are increasingly in need of work adjustment assistance. Because these diverse clients are frequently seen by entry-level professionals, human service professionals need to be prepared for the complex task of addressing barriers to career success and self-sufficiency that they face.

This chapter introduces adult career transition and looks at several special populations that human service professionals will typically serve in any setting. We begin with a discussion of the nature of transitions and explore the types of career transitions typically experienced over the course of the life-span. There are several models of career transitions; the two that will be presented in this chapter are Schlossberg's transitional model and Hopson and Adams's stage model. Next, we will present several special populations that have unique barriers to transition. The populations covered in this section will be displaced or dislocated workers, offender/ex-offenders, the veteran population, and people with chemical dependency. The primary objective of the discussion in this chapter is to develop increased sensitivity to the special needs that clients bring to the career helping process. The second objective is to raise the reader's awareness of the distinct characteristics that influence the career development process. We hope that this chapter stimulates more study to work with clients from different backgrounds and with unique concerns.

Adult Career Transition

Changes in the economic and employment landscape are challenging adult workers to adjust to more frequent career transitions and changes to the length of time they are likely to spend with a given employer. Many workers spend five years or less in each job, so they devote more time and energy transitioning from one job to another. Individuals born from 1957 to 1964 held an average of 12 jobs from ages 18 to 50 (BLS; Bureau of Labor Statistics, 2017). The BLS (2018a) reported the median employee tenure (i.e., how long wage and salary workers had been with their current employer) of the civilian noninstitutional population age 16 and over was 4.3 years for men and 4.0 years for women. The uncertainty of employment coupled with the needs and expectations of adults has resulted in progressive loss of stable employment.

A high percentage of younger workers are also experiencing shorter durations of time spent at successive jobs. In 2018, median employee tenure was higher among older workers than younger ones (Bureau of Labor Statistics, 2018a). Among jobs held by workers 25 to 34 years old, the median tenure was 2.8 years. For those 35 to 44 years old, the median job duration was 4.9 years, and among 45- to 54-year-olds, the median tenure at a job was 7.6 years. Regardless of whether personal choice or an unpredictable world of work drives adult career transition, multiple career changes seem to be the rule and not the exception (Ebberwein, Krieshok, Ulven, & Prosser, 2004). Transitions occur more frequently than ever, leading to discontinuities and fragmented careers. Thus, it is important that human service professionals be prepared to help people who experience issues adjusting to career transition.

Nature of Adult Transitions

Theorists have viewed transitions as developmental turning points. Louis (1981) stated that a **transition** is the "period during which an individual is either changing roles (taking on a different objective role) or changing orientation to a role already held (altering a subjective state)" (p. 57). Transitions occur in social, cultural, and political contexts and have the potential to affect an individual's relationships, assumptions, routines, and roles (Anderson, Goodman, & Schlossberg, 2012). Moving through a transition can be distressing for some people because it involves loss or requires letting go of aspects of the self, letting go of former roles, and learning new roles (Anderson et al., 2012). Multiple transitions can produce a cumulative decrease in well-being if an individual is unable to recover before another transition occurs (Williams, 1999). Whether viewed as a time of crisis or as a developmental adjustment, some theorists view transitions as an opportunity for growth and transformation (e.g., Bridges, 2004; Hudson, 1999).

Types of Adult Career Transitions

There are a variety of adult career transitions that people experience over the course of a lifetime. According to Gunz, Peiperl, and Tzabbar (2007), a **career transition** can be defined as a move across different types of boundaries that can create both minor discontinuities and major interruptions in an individual career. The following types of career transition are prevalent and have a wide range of potential consequences for the individuals affected:

- Adults who have graduated high school and are unprepared for work

- Employed adults who are choosing to shift career direction (e.g., midlife career transition, calling)
- Individuals who have focused their time and energy on roles other than that of paid worker in the civilian workforce (e.g., homemakers caring for children, veterans in transition).
- Welfare to work transition
- Job loss due to termination, illness, downsizing, restructuring, or relocation

A Model of Transition

The transition process is complex and involves many variables and, as a result, a variety of transition models have been developed. Models focus on development as well as psychological, cultural, and political determinants that can be useful in helping people cope with transitions. To understand transition, it is first important to identity the type of transition the client is facing. We will focus on the transition model proposed by Schlossberg (1984), which focuses on life events entailing change and is helpful in working with clients who are dealing with career or other life transitions.

There are primarily four types of transitions. **Schlossberg's transitional model** identified the following transitions: anticipated, unanticipated, chronic hassles, and nonevents (events that do not happen). Anticipated events are ones that will happen in the life span of most individuals, such as graduating high school, getting married, starting a job, and retiring. Unanticipated events are those that are not expected. Examples include the death of a family member or being fired or laid off from a job. Chronic hassles are situational such as a long commute to work, an unreasonable supervisor, concern with deadline pressures, or unnecessary unpleasant physical working conditions. A nonevent is something that an individual wants to happen but that never occurs. For some, this may be a promotion or a transfer to a desired department or community. A common nonevent for women is the ability to enter or leave the workforce. Some women want to leave and spend more time with family but cannot do so because of financial conditions.

Factors That Influence Transitions

The ways in which people cope with transitions can be an asset or liability. **Coping** can be defined as the behavior's individuals use to prevent, alleviate, or respond to stressful situations (George & Siegler, 1981). According to Goodman, Schlossberg, and Anderson (2006), the **4S system of coping** includes four major factors that influence how individuals handle transitions: situation, self, support, and strategies. Human service professionals should assess these factors, which are defined as follows:

The Situation. What is happening? The relevant characteristics surrounding the transition include: Trigger (what initiated the transition?), timing (does the transition relate to the social clock?), source (where does individual control come in?), role change (does the transition involve a role change?), duration (is it permanent or temporary?), and previous experience with similar transitions and concurrent stress.

The Self. To whom is it happening? Everyone is different in terms of life issues, personality, and ways of coping. To understand how the person is coping with the transition, the personal and demographic variables that need to be considered include socioeconomic status, culture/race/ethnicity, gender role, age, stage of life, and state of health.

The Support. What help is available? Although options vary for everyone, social supports may include intimate relationships, family, friends, and institutions such as church, community, and social service organizations. The type of support may be emotional, affirmational, financial, or some form of advocacy or advice.

The Strategies. How does the person cope? The individual may try to control or modify the source of strain, control the meaning of the situation to think more neutrally about the event, or control the stress associated with the transition before and during it (Pearling & Schooler, 1978). Assessing how the person copes can reveal strengths and opportunities to teach clients about various coping strategies and determine the most effective option.

This approach partially addresses the question of why different individuals react differently to the same type of transition and why the same person reacts differently at different times. Although Schlossberg's 4S model was designed to help retirees through transition, it can also be applied to individuals faced with other transitions because it is a systematic method of coping with changes in life (Scharf, 2013). Exploring the 4S's can help the human service professional understand how the client is coping with a transition.

How Career Transitions Affect Diverse Populations

Discrimination is well-documented as a major issue in career development for members of minority groups (e.g., Fassinger, 2008). Discrimination can be particularly damaging when one is in the establishment or maintenance stage of one's career, as work is important to one's self-esteem. Direct experiences of discrimination have been related to emotional distress among African Americans, Latinos, Latinas, Asian Americans, and Native American (Carter & Forsyth, 2010). Also, immigrants may face discrimination when they move to a new culture by being denied promotions, attractive assignments, raises, or other advantages because of racism.

According to Sharf (2013), scholars call discrimination a crisis because of the notion of double jeopardy. **Double jeopardy** refers to the situation in which a person from a minority group faces occupational barriers both because they are a minority and because they are culturally different from the dominant culture. It is vital therefore, that human service professionals who work with clients respond appropriately with empathy and seek to empower individuals in a wide variety of career-related transitions.

Displaced or Dislocated Workers

Displaced workers, also known as dislocated workers, are those who have worked in their chosen field for a period and lost their jobs due to a company shutdown, workplace relocation, or organizational restructuring. Job displacement is usually beyond the person's control and often comes as a complete surprise to those affected.

According to the Workforce Investment Act of 1998, a displaced or dislocated worker is one who falls into one or more of the following categories (U. S. Department of Labor, 2018a):

- Has been terminated or laid off, or has received a notice of termination or layoff from employment;
- Is eligible for or has exhausted unemployment insurance;
- Has demonstrated an appropriate attachment to the workforce, but is not eligible for unemployment insurance and unlikely to return to a previous industry or occupation;

- Has been terminated, laid off or received notification of termination or layoff from employment because of a permanent closure or substantial layoff;
- Is employed at a facility where the employer has made the general announcement that the facility will close within 180 days;
- Was self-employed (including employment as a farmer, a rancher, or a fisherman) but is unemployed because of general economic conditions in the community or because of a natural disaster; or
- Is a displaced homemaker who is no longer supported by a family member.

Population Statistics

The Bureau of Labor Statistics (2019) reported that in 2018, 6.3 million Americans were unemployed, resulting in an unemployment rate of 3.9% (down from 4.1% the previous year). The number of people considered to be long-term unemployed (those jobless for 27 weeks or more) was at 1.3 million and accounted for 20.5% of the total unemployed population. From January 2015 through December 2017, there were 3.0 million workers displaced from jobs they had held for at least 3 years (Bureau of Labor Statistics, 2018). This was down slightly from 3.2 million workers for the prior survey period covering January 2013 to December 2015.

Employment Characteristics

Dislocated workers come from a variety of occupations, including sales and office occupations; service occupations; production, transportation, and material moving occupations; and management, professional, and related occupations; and natural resources, construction, and maintenance occupations. 37% percent of long-tenured displaced workers from the 2015-2017 period reported that they lost their job because their plant or company closed or moved; an additional 37% said that their position or shift was abolished, and 26% cited insufficient work. In January 2018, 66% of the 3.0 million long-tenured displaced workers were reemployed, similar to the number in January 2016.

During the 2015-17 period, 479,000 long-tenured manufacturing workers were displaced from their jobs—16% of all long-tenured displaced workers. Manufacturing displacements occurred mostly in the durable goods industry (313,000). Workers in professional and business services accounted for 15% of all long-tenured displacements, while those in retail trade accounted for 12% of displacements, as did workers in education and health services.

Nature of Job Loss

Displaced and dislocated workers usually experience the unanticipated type of transition. Schlossberg (2009) emphasized the importance of **mattering**, or finding people and purposes in life that matter to you. Although there are several good models of transition, mattering underlies models of career transition in areas of life that involve work.

Losing a job is a devastating experience for some people. Psychological ramifications of unplanned unemployment can lead one to experience depression, anxiety, reduced self-esteem, and a sense of hopelessness and helplessness. People in this situation often begin to believe their job skills no longer have value. In addition to job loss contributing to feeling of depression, job loss can affect sense of confidence, physical health, coping skills, and alcohol usage (Sharf, 2013). Although positive growth may occur after involuntary work changes, negative maladjustment is often what happens, and individuals may seek the help of a human service professional.

Hopson and Adams' (1977) **stage model of transition** describes the relationship of seven phases of a crisis or transition to mood and to time (Figure 9.1). The phases include immobilization, minimization, self-doubt, letting go, testing out, search for meaning, and internalization. Although the model was developed years ago, it is still useful for human service professionals who work with adults who have been fired, forced to resign, downsized, or laid off. The seven-phase model of stages accompanying transition is summarized as follows:

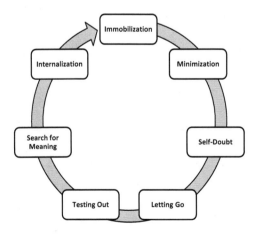

Figure 9.1
Hopson and Adams' Stage Model of Transition

- *Immobilization.* This is the initial shock of finding out that one has been fired or laid off. The person may experience elation or despair, depending on the nature of the transition. In the later, the person is overwhelmed, depressed, and unable to make plans. This period can last from a few moments to a few months.

- *Minimization.* The person can deny that the change is happening or have the desire to make the change appear smaller than it is, or even state that things will be perfectly fine regardless of the transition.

- *Self-Doubt.* Many different feelings and emotions can occur at this phase. An individual may doubt their skills and ability to provide for self and others. Other common reactions are anger, anxiety, sadness, frustration, resentment, fear of future, and negative self-talk.

- *Letting Go.* As the individual lets go of negative feelings, they start to accept what is really happening. The individual detaches from the original situation and starts to look toward the future with more positive thinking.

- *Testing Out.* At this point, individual may develop a burst of energy to take control of the situation. They may begin planning and envisioning the future. For example, an individual may have thought about how he or she is going to network.

- *Search for Meaning.* In this phase, an individual seeks to understand how events are different and why. This process can include existential and spiritual components. The search for meaning and purpose is a process through which individuals try to understand not only the feelings of others but also their own.

- *Internalization.* In the final phase of transition, the person has changed values and lifestyle. They may have developed new coping skills and grown emotionally, spiritually, or cognitively because of the crisis.

Offender/Ex-Offenders

The number of adults in the correctional population has increased. According to the U.S. Department of Justice (2018), 6.6 million people were under some form of correctional supervision as of 2016, including persons in the community on probation or parole and those incarcerated in prisons or local jails. State and federal correctional authorities held an estimated 1.51 million prisoners at year-end 2016. The majority (97%) of prisoners in 2016 were sentenced to more than 1 year. Overall, there were 450 prisoners per 100,000 U.S. residents of all ages and 582 per 100,000 residents age 18 or older in 2016.

Demographic and Offense Characteristics

The majority (93%) of prisoners were male at year-end 2016. Among the female prison population, there were more than twice as many white females (48,900 prisoners) as African American (20,300) or Hispanic (19,300) females in state and federal prison in 2016. However, the imprisonment rate among the general population for black females (96 per 100,000 black female residents) was almost double the rate for white females (49 per 100,000 white female residents). Black-to-white racial disparity was also observed among males. Black males ages 18 to 19 were 11.8 times more likely to be imprisoned than white males of the same age. More than a tenth (11%) of prisoners sentenced to more than 1 year in state or federal prison at year-end 2016 were age 55 or older. In December of 2106, states held fewer than 1,000 prisoners age 17 or younger in adult facilities.

More than half (54%) of state prisoners sentenced to more than 1 year were serving time for a violent offense at year-end 2015 (the most recent year for which data are available). Overall, 15% of state prisoners at year-end 2015 had been convicted of a drug offense as their most serious crime. However, a higher percentage of females (25%) than males (14%) had a drug crime as their most serious offense. In comparison, nearly half (47%) of federal prisoners serving time in September 2016 (the most recent date for which data are available) were convicted of a drug offense. As in state prisons, more females (56%) than males (47%) were serving time in federal prison for drug crimes. In addition, more than a third (38%) of federal prisoners were imprisoned for a public order offense, including 17% for a weapons offense and 8% for an adjudicated immigration offense.

As a human service professional, it's important to learn as much as possible about the special needs of clients who are justice-involved. The Bureau of Justice Statistics website found in the resource section of this chapter provides a plethora of information and reports related to corrections and the justice-involved populations nationally.

Criminogenic Factors

Employment of the justice-involved includes assessing the clients criminogenic or recidivism needs. **Criminogenic needs** relate to the characteristics, traits, or problems that directly influence an individual's **recidivism** or probability of reoffending or committing another crime and can be changed and/or addressed through interventions (Bonta & Andrews, 2017). When working with individuals who are justice-involved, it's important to know that the risk of recidivism is the highest within the first 90 days of release. Over two-thirds of ex-offenders are re-arrested within three months after release. Many of these re-arrests are due to new crimes or technical violations of their release. Many ex-offenders were unemployed before entering the corrections system and remain unemployed after their release. To help an individual sustain employment, you may be required to address a client's criminogenic needs.

Offenders high in prisonization (i.e., accepting the ways and culture of prison life) have lower career maturity and lack a job planning attitude. Homant and Dean (1988) determined that securing employment for ex-offenders without improving their overall psychological adjustment does not lessen recidivism rates. Recidivism is also defined as a person's relapse into criminal behavior after undergoing some type of interventions for a crime (e.g., jail, prison). Recidivism is an important aspect of post-incarceration behavior and is closely measured. Varghese and Cumming (2013) posit that stable employment is the greatest predictor of reduced recidivism, and they emphasize the importance of providing career development programs for ex-offenders. Present career interventions lack adequate focus on offender attitudes, and Varghese (2013) highlighted the necessity of understanding offender characteristics such as negative attitudes toward work.

Without addressing these negative attitudes and thoughts concerning work, only slight improvement is expected in recidivism rates. Andrews, Bonta, and Hoge (1990) identified eight risk factors of criminal behavior and recidivism. These predictors include antisocial history, personality pattern, associating with peers who have antisocial beliefs and values, poor problem-solving, family and marital dysfunction, lack of employment and job skills, leisure interests, and substance abuse. In addition, poverty is a significant risk factor for many recently released individuals; they may return to the same neighborhoods and the same situations after release. According to Morgan (2013), offender counseling interventions cannot be successful without exploring these criminal risk factors. Morgan also noted that work attitudes are an important dimension in these risk factors.

With the increase in arrest rates and the high recidivism rates reported for offenders, human service professionals may prove to be a valuable resource in helping to reverse these cultural trends. One critical contribution that we can provide is service focused on career transition and development. As researchers have pointed out (e.g., Morgan, 2013; Varghese, 2013), career interventions for offenders are not well understood and are not commonly provided to offenders. Current programs often lack the centrality of career development and focus on educational instruction and training (Stoltz, 2017). Once a person encounters the legal system at post-release, life may become challenging due to various legal restrictions, stigma, discrimination and other barriers, making reintegration into the community and work role difficult.

When developing a career plan and goals for a client who is justice-involved, one of the first areas a human service professional should evaluate is their criminogenic needs that may impact employment. This initial information includes identifying barriers that require immediate intervention. Keep in mind that assessing a client's criminogenic needs may require the assistance of someone who is qualified to provide the appropriate treatment, such as a licensed counselor, social worker, or psychologist. Duggan and Jurgens (2007) have identified several key barriers to success for the justice-involved. The potential areas to assess include structural, individual, physical, and mental health barriers.

Barriers to Career Success
Structural Barriers
Offenders and ex-offenders face several structural barriers. Structural barriers can be regarded as external obstacles that collectively and disproportionately affect a group and perpetuate or maintain disparities in outcomes. Eight common structural barriers are:

- *Geographic Location Upon Release.* Ex-offenders often congregate in major metropolitan areas that are poorly equipped to handle the influx of ex-offenders.
- *Employer Attitudes.* Many employers are reluctant to hire ex-offenders because they are concerned that ex-offenders will not make good employees and that they, the employers, can be held legally liable for the actions of their employees.
- *Lack of Suitable Employment Opportunities.* Some jobs are viewed as a better fit for ex-offenders than others. Such industries often have a high number of unskilled jobs with high turnover. Thus, ex-offenders would add to their already unstable work history.
- *Restrictions on Prison-Based Work Programs.* Prison work in industries has been successful in reducing recidivism, but only about 7 percent of state and federal inmates work in prison-industry programs.

- *Legal Barriers.* Ex-offenders face legal barriers to reentry including their criminal records, public assistance, and housing.
- *Lack of Resources in the Prison.* Prisons have relatively few resources to address educational, vocational, physical health, and mental health needs.
- *Parole Supervision Issues.* An increasing number of ex-offenders are reentering the community without supervision.
- *Lack of Juvenile-Appropriate Services.* Juveniles have different incarceration and post-release needs than their adult counterparts. Multiple agencies and institutions lack systematic reintegration services.

Individual Barriers

There are several individual barriers that offenders and ex-offenders face. Individual barriers are regarded as intra-and interpersonal issues that impede one's wellness and success in the educational, family, and work roles. Three major individual barrier categories are:

- *Lack of Education, Cognitive Skills, and Work Experience.* The poor skills and work experience of many ex-offenders often conflict with the credentials and skills that are required by most employers.
- *Family Issues and Peers.* Offenders are spending longer time in prison, which results in declining frequency of contact with family members. Reintegrating into peer networks is particularly important for juveniles but peers can have a positive or negative influence.
- *Lack of Employability Skills.* Ex-offenders often lack the employability or life skills they need to obtain and maintain a job.

Physical Health Barriers

Offenders and ex-offenders are prone to several physical health barriers. Three physical barrier categories are:

- *Communicable Diseases.* A high number of inmates suffer from infectious diseases such as AIDS, HIV, hepatitis C, and tuberculosis.
- *Chronic Diseases.* Inmates often suffer from a variety of chronic diseases such as asthma, diabetes, cancer, and cardiovascular disease.
- *Disabilities.* 10% of inmates reported having a learning disability, which is over three times the prevalence in the general population. Many

juveniles in the criminal justice system also have undiagnosed and untreated learning disabilities.

Mental Health Barriers

Offenders and ex-offenders face several mental health barriers. Mental health barriers addressed by Duggan and Jurgens (2007) include:

- *Mental Illness.* Over 89% of the nation's private and public adult correctional facilities reported that they provided mental health services to their inmates. Mental health problems may contribute to the prevalence and frequency of illegal behaviors among some youth. It has been reported that the prevalence rates of many mental illnesses are higher in the criminal justice populations than in the general population.
- *Substance Abuse.* Substance abuse is a problem for both adults and young offenders or ex-offenders. More than two-thirds of adult prisoners have histories of substance use, and almost one-third have served time for drug possession or sales. 57% of adolescent offenders reported consuming alcohol at least once a week for the past month, and 32% reported being under the influence of alcohol when they committed their most recent crime.

Pre-Employment Retention

Individuals who have been incarcerated for a period of time may have difficulty managing realistic expectations about work. Helpers can address issues of work retention through pre-employment retention strategies designed to identify potential job loss risks and needs that must be addressed to improve a client's long-term reintegration success. **Employment retention** among justice-involved populations can be defined as continued attachment to the workforce regardless of whether it is with a single employer or a series of employers (Houston, 2006). According to the National Institute of Corrections, job retention rates gradually decline once employed with approximately 40% of clients quitting or leaving their job after 40 days. Due to an individual's criminal record, lack of work skills, or recent work history, most jobs available to someone recently released are typically entry level and low-paying. This may mean a loss of social status among family or peers, which has been identified as a cause of recidivism.

Some other areas for the human service provider to consider for discussion are triggers for negative thoughts and emotions, peer pressure, testing control, or any other activity that can lead to a choice that results in a negative consequence. The client's social skills should also be considered. Because a survival mentality was essential while incarcerated, additional education on how to deal with authority figures and coworkers in the workplace may be needed. Creating a retention agreement with the client, connection to job clubs or a support group, mentoring, and proving incentives and recognition for employment behaviors can also be helpful in increasing retention.

Many changes are occurring for an individual who was recently released from incarceration. There are very few organizations or human service providers that can meet all the diverse needs of individuals who are justice involved on their own. Collaboration and the formation of partnerships is encouraged and essential. Having a plan in place to deal with workplace stress or anxiety, along with identifying a positive support system, should be addressed prior to the client's reentry into the work role.

The Veteran Population

A **civilian veteran** is a person 18 years or older who has served in the armed forces (i.e., U. S. Army, Navy, Air Force, Marine Corps, or Coast Guard) or in the Merchant Marine in World War II. Those who have served in the Reserves or in the National Guard are only classified as veterans if they have been called or ordered to active duty (in addition to their initial training and yearly summer camps). There were around 20.4 million U.S. veterans in 2016, according to data from the Department of Veterans Affairs, representing about 7% of the total U.S. adult population. According to Veterans Affairs' 2016 population model estimates, Gulf War-era veterans now account for the largest share of all U.S. veterans, surpassing Vietnam-era veterans in 2016, according to Veterans Affairs' 2016 population model estimates (Bialik, 2017).

According to the VA's 2016 population model estimates, 9% of veterans are female. By 2045, the share of female veterans is expected to double to 18%. In 2016, the number of veterans 50 years old and younger was 27%, those aged 50-69 accounted for 39%, and those aged 70 years and over was 34%. The overall profile of race/ethnicity of the U. S. veteran population in 2016 estimates non-Hispanic whites accounting for 77%, Blacks 12%, Hispanics 7%, and Asians 2%. The racial and ethnic diversity in the veteran population is predicted to increase in the future reflecting increased diversity in current personnel (Bialik, 2017).

The U. S. Department of Housing and Urban Development (2017) is one federal entity responsible for estimating the number Veterans without safe, stable housing. About 11% of the adult homeless population are veterans. On a single night in January 2018, just over 37,800 Veterans were experiencing homelessness, and just over 23,300 of the Veterans counted were unsheltered or living on the street due to poverty, lack of support from friends and family, and living in substandard housing or in cheap hotels. The nation's homeless veterans are predominantly male, with an estimated 9% being female. Roughly 45% of all homeless veterans are African American or Hispanic. Nearly half of homeless veterans served during the Vietnam era. Legislation is continuously being passed and updated to decrease the number of homeless veterans, and to help transition them back to work.

Employment Characteristics
According to the Bureau of Labor Statistics (2018b), the unemployment rate for veterans who served on active duty in the U.S. Armed Forces at any time since September 2001, a group referred to as Gulf War-era II veterans, was 4.5% in 2017. The unemployment rate for male veterans (3.6%) declined over the year, and the rate for female veterans (4.1%) changed little in 2017. Among the 370,000 unemployed veterans in 2017, 59% were age 25 to 54, 37% were age 55 and over, and 4% were age 18 to 24. About 41% of Gulf War-era II veterans had a service-connected disability in August 2017, compared with 24% of all veterans.

The New Generation of Veterans
People who have been members of the U. S. military since October 2001 constitute the **post-9/11 veterans**. They are now, or will become, veterans of the United States' post 9/11 armed conflicts—military operations which have an increasingly complex set of official titles: in Afghanistan, Operation Enduring Freedom (OEF) and Operation Freedom's Sentinel (OFS); in Iraq, Operation Iraqi Freedom (OIF), Operation New Dawn (OND), and beginning in August 2014, Operation Inherent Resolve (OIR). Between 2002 and 2015, 1.9 million veterans who served in these wars became eligible for VA medical and/or mental health services (U. S. Department of Veterans Affairs, 2017a).

In general, members of this population of young veterans are simultaneously finding new jobs, establishing new daily routines, and taking on new challenges like earning college degrees. Exiting the military can also mean relocating, living independently for the first time, becoming a parent, or reuniting with a partner and children after long periods overseas.

When service members exit the military, many need new jobs. Due to the difficulty some veterans have transferring military trained skills to civilian employment, finding suitable work can be challenging. For example, in a study of the veteran population of Chicago and surrounding areas, between 2014 and 2016, 65% to 80% of veterans left the military without a job, expecting to find meaningful employment quickly (Kintzle, Rasheed, & Castro, 2016).

Military Culture

Military members operate within a unique context involving experiences specific to their way of life. **Military culture** has the components of any recognized cultural group – a unique "language, a code of manners, norms of behavior, belief systems, dress, and rituals" (Reger, Etherage, Reger, & Gahm, 2008, p. 22). Strom et al. (2012) outlined examples of military-specific cultural components for human service professionals to learn, such as the importance of rank, unique terminology, and a focus on the value of teamwork. It is incumbent upon practitioners intending to work with the military population to learn relevant terminology in order to understand service members' issues within their own cultural context. (See resource section at end of this chapter for some common military terms and lingo.)

The environment of the military plays a large role in constructing the organization of meaning, perspective, and information for service members (Rausch, 2014). The context offers significant benefits to military service members who confront challenges that may arise. The amount and nature of the time spent in the military is also an important consideration related to the experience of veterans (Black, Westwood, & Sorsdal, 2007). The defined structure, a prominent aspect of military life, may be antithetical to the individualistic and materialistic culture that constitutes several aspects of North American society (Black et al., 2007).

Career Needs of Military Members

Eventually, when veterans are ready to look for new work, they may be unprepared for a variety of reasons. Because working in the military happens in a disciplined, rigid, high-stakes environment with a relatively transparent salary structure and authority hierarchy, a veterans' job preparedness can be diminished in unexpected ways (Zogas, 2017). For example, interviews with case managers showed that veterans have unrealistic expectations of how their skills will transfer to the civilian job market. Although they are highly motivated to work hard and move up corporate hierarchies, veterans were frustrated by having to start in low paying entry-level positions and felt as if they were starting over (Kintzle, et. al., 201).

Because of these and other challenges, career development and employment are often significantly affected. Specific skills such as resume preparation, interviewing, networking, and negotiating a job offer have been identified as key areas for counselors to focus on when addressing the career needs of military veterans (Hayden, Ledwith, Dong, & Buzzetta, 2014). This includes helping veterans with their non-technical skills or soft skills that they bring with them from their military experience. These can be barriers to successful civilian work transition. **Military soft skills** include leadership, persistence, reliability, conscientiousness, and attention to detail, and can be difficult to translate to civilian job skills (Hardison & Shanley, 2016). The skills that veterans have gained through military experience must be translated into terms that are understood by civilian employers. For service members in certain career fields and for officers, this translation is straightforward. The skills of an Army medic, for example, are readily matched to those of a civilian EMT. Yet for enlisted members in other career fields, particularly infantry and similar specialties that are more operationally-focused, the skills acquired in the military may not be as apparently relevant to civilian employers (Hall, 2016). Related to soft-skills is military identity.

Service members are familiar with their work identity as a member of the military. **Veteran identity** is "that part of the self-concept that reflects past military experience in the present civilian space and time" (Atuel & Castro, 2018, p. 488). Transitioning to a new, public-sector workplace, without the same type of recognition previously received as a military person, can feel foreign and leave members unsure of their status or identity in the public sector (Robertson, 2013). In a survey by Kintzle et al., (2016), veterans noted that their military identity (in this study characterized by the imperative to be punctual, professional, and respectful to people in authority) makes it difficult to adapt to civilian workplaces, where they perceive these behaviors to be undervalued. At the same time, veterans rejected civilians' lateness and lack of deference to authority, and reported feeling rejected by civilian employers, whom they perceive as dismissive of military skills and experience, or unaware of and insensitive to the needs of veterans. More extreme still, when surveyed, over a third of post-9/11 veterans said they thought prospective employers believe that veterans are dangerous or "broken" (Kintzle et al., 2016).

For many veterans, their career journey will include entering higher education. Understanding the uniqueness of student veterans and their families is of utmost importance. Student veterans encounter a vast array of transition issues as they arrive on the college campus. Issues range from role incongruities, maturity issues, relationships, and identity renegotiation (Rumann & Hamrick, 2010). Members of campus communities, such as counselors, administration, and educators, have an obligation to understand the specific needs of this diverse population so that they can ease veterans' adjustment to the college environment and classroom (e.g., Jenner, 2017; Kirchner, 2015).

In addition to the barriers discussed above, there are additional barriers to consider when working with veterans. Areas to assess include structural, individual, physical, and mental health barriers. Several key barriers for military veterans are discussed below.

Barriers to Career Success

Structural Barriers

Veterans face a variety of structural barriers. Three categories include the following:

- *Communication Problems Associated with Military Jargon.* Veterans have spent their time in the military using military jargon and talking in acronyms. This does not transfer easily into civilian communication.
- *Societal View of Veterans.* Sometimes employers have unrealistic expectations of veterans including expecting them to be rigid and lacking the knowledge of how to succeed in a civilian world.
- *Difficulties Transferring Military Credentials to Civilian Work Settings.* Credentials earned in the military do not readily transfer into civilian credentials.

Individual Barriers

Some of the individual barriers that veterans may face include:

- *Less Than Honorable Discharge.* Veterans who receive a bad conduct or other than honorable discharge may find it more difficult to obtain civilian employment.
- *Issues Related to the Military Culture.* Veterans develop habits that meet their needs and help them adjust to their transition into the military.

These habits may need to be changed as they transition out of the military.

- *Family Adjustments.* Families that needed time to adjust to a family member's frequent absences due to deployment must now adjust very quickly to having the family member at home.

Physical Health Barriers

Veterans are susceptible to several physical health barriers. Apart from difficulties with overall adjustment to civilian life for some veterans, military veterans may return with significant physical and psychological injuries (Tanielian & Jaycox, 2008). Former POWs (prisoners of war), for example, may suffer from frostbite, related organic conditions, post-traumatic osteoarthritis, heart disease, stroke, type II diabetes, a variety of nutritional deficiencies, irritable bowel syndrome, and/or cirrhosis of the liver. Exposure of military members to Agent Orange and other herbicides has been linked to such illnesses as type 2 diabetes, non-Hodgkin's lymphoma, and prostate cancer. Gulf War veterans may suffer from chronic fatigue syndrome, fibromyalgia, irritable bowel syndrome, skin disorders, headaches, muscle pain, joint pain, abnormal weight loss, and cardiovascular symptoms. Still other veterans may have lost their limbs, eyesight, or hearing while in the military.

Mental Health Barriers

There are instances in which military veterans may confront issues in their transition back into civilian life related to mental health issues. Often, we hear in the media and literature the term **invisible wounds.** This term refers to the psychological struggles, unlike the physical wounds of war, that are often invisible to the eye, remaining invisible to other service members, family members, and society in general. Although many military veterans reintegrate into society without a diagnosable or debilitating condition (Bonar & Domenici, 2011), mental health barriers exist for a substantial number of veterans who were in combat or in a combat zone. These conditions include anxiety disorders, dysthymic disorder, sleep disturbances, depression, PTSD, psychoses, traumatic brain injury, substance abuse/chemical dependency, and gambling addiction. Mental health issues such as posttraumatic-stress disorder and traumatic brain injury have significant implications for the career needs of veterans (Hayden et al., 2014). Unfortunately, stigma surrounding mental health issues is present in the military and can serve not only as a barrier to effective treatment (Eckart & Dufrene, 2015), but to one's career advancement as a service member and as a civilian. Zinzow et al. (2013) indicated that the primary reason military members give for not seeking mental health services is the concern that therapy will have a negative impact on their careers.

People with Chemical Dependency

In 2013, an estimated 21.6 million persons aged 12 or older were classified with substance abuse or dependence in the past year (8.2 percent of the population aged 12 or older) (National Institute on Drug Abuse, 2015). Individuals are described as engaging in **abuse** of a substance when they continue to use the substance despite experiencing negative consequences for their use. **Dependency** on a substance is when, in addition to the negative consequences, individuals build tolerance and experience withdrawal if they stop using the drug (Martin, 2014). Of the people classified with abuse and dependency, 2.6 million were classified with dependence or abuse of both alcohol and illicit drugs, 4.3 million had dependence or abuse of illicit drugs but not alcohol, and 14.7 million had dependence or abuse of alcohol but not illicit drugs. Illicit drugs include marijuana/hashish, cocaine (including crack), heroin, hallucinogens, inhalants, or prescription-type psychotherapeutics (pain relievers, tranquilizers, stimulants, and sedatives) used for non-medical reasons.

Drug use is highest among people in their late teens and twenties, with 22.6% of 18- to 20-year-olds reported using an illicit drug in the past month. Drug use is increasing among people in their fifties and early sixties, and for adults aged 50 to 64, the rate of current illicit drug use increased from 2.7% in 2002 to 6.0% in 2013. In 2013, the rate of current illicit drug use among persons aged 12 or older was higher for males (11.5 percent) than for females (7.3 percent) (National Institute on Drug Abuse, 2015). In 2013, among persons aged 12 or older, the rate of current illicit drug use was 3.1% among Asians, 8.8% among Hispanics, 9.5% among whites, 10.5% among blacks, 12.3% among American Indians or Alaska Natives, 14.0% among Native Hawaiians or Other Pacific Islanders, and 17.4% among persons reporting two or more races (National Institute on Drug Abuse, 2015).

In 2013, illicit drug use varied by the educational status of adults aged 18 or older. The rate of current illicit drug use was lower among college graduates (6.7 percent) than those with some college education but no degree (10.8 percent), high school graduates with no further education (9.9 percent), and those who had not graduated from high school (11.8 percent) (National Institute on Drug Abuse, 2015).

In 2013, 4.1 million persons aged 12 or older (1.5 percent of the population) received treatment for a problem related to the use of alcohol or illicit drugs. Of these, 1.3 million received treatment for the use of both alcohol and illicit drugs, 0.9 million received treatment for the use of illicit drugs but not alcohol, and 1.4 million received treatment for the use of alcohol but not illicit drugs (National Institute on Drug Abuse, 2015).

Employment Characteristics

Illicit drug use differed by employment status in 2013. The majority of individuals who abuse drugs and/or alcohol are employed and bring their drug abuse problems to work. Among unemployed adults aged 18 or older in 2013, 18.2% were current illicit drug users, which was higher than the rates of 9.1% for those who were employed full time and 13.7% for those who were employed part time. People who use substances are far more likely to be unemployed or underemployed than people who do not use substances. Nevertheless, of the 22.4 million current illicit drug users aged 18 or older, 15.4 million (68.9 percent) were employed either full or part time. Additionally, 1/3 of all employees are aware of illegal sale of drugs in their workplace. Substance abuse is more likely to be prevalent in industries dominated by males and those work environments with large numbers of young workers (National Institute on Drug Abuse, 2015).

The highest rates of heavy drinking and illicit drug use are reported by food preparation workers, wait staff, and bartenders; construction workers; those in other service occupations; and transportation and material moving workers. A Hazelden Betty Ford Foundation survey of over 300 human resources professionals found that 67% of respondents believe substance use is one of the most serious issues they face among those in the workforce, with consequences related to absenteeism, reduced productivity, and a negative impact on their company's reputation (Levy Merrick, Volpe-Vartanian, Horgan, & McCann, 2007). Abuse of tobacco, alcohol, and illicit drugs (not including misuse of prescription drugs) cost the United States more than $740 billion annually through crime, lost work productivity, and related health care (National Institute on Drug Abuse, 2017a). Substance abuse leads to accidents as well as low morale and high illness rates in the workplace. Alcohol and drug abuse have a devastating impact on the economy and businesses, resulting in high costs for both employers and employees.

Barriers to Career Success

Structural Barriers

People with chemical dependency encounter various structural barriers, such as:

- *Social Stigma.* Although both men and women with substance-abuse problems experience social stigma, it should be noted that society in general views women who abuse drugs more harshly than men.
- *Lack of Reliable and Low-Cost Childcare.* Parents are likely to worry about finding appropriate childcare while they are in treatment.
- *Costs Associated with Substance-Abuse Treatment.* Costs associated with treatment can make participation difficult for many clients.
- *Lack of Flexible Services.* Many treatment services lack the flexibility that is necessary to meet the need of clients. For example, some treatment programs may prohibit individuals from entering treatment because of the amount of time they require a person to be clean prior to entering the treatment program.
- *Insufficient and Inaccessible Program Information.* Some programs lack effective outreach and, as such, people may not be aware of the treatment options available.

Individual Barriers

People with chemical dependency face several individual barriers. These include feelings of shame, guilt, and poor motivation; problems acknowledging the impact of use; fear of losing love and support or of being isolated; and the fear of losing custody of their children. The fear of losing their children can prohibit clients from entering residential treatment because of the concern of giving their children up and never getting them back. Lack of positive modeling (e.g., peer group, familial/parental, societal), and negative attitudes toward vocational rehabilitation and toward disability can be further client obstacles to employment (Center for Substance Abuse Treatment, 2000).

Physical Health Barriers

People with chemical dependency are prone to several physical health barriers. Drug abuse can weaken the immune system and can also lead to risky behaviors like unsafe sex and needle-sharing. Substance abuse can also lead to cardiovascular problems, respiratory problems, adverse effects on the gastrointestinal and musculoskeletal systems, disruptions in the normal production of hormones, kidney and liver damage, brain damage, cancer, and drug-related deaths.

Substance abuse can also have serious consequences on the unborn child (National Institute on Drug Abuse, 2017b).

Mental Health Barriers

Chronic abuse of drugs can lead to long-lasting changes in the brain. These changes may cause depression, paranoia, aggression, and hallucinations (National Institute on Drug Abuse, 2017b). Adults with substance abuse concerns were more than twice as likely to have serious mental illness when compared to adults without substance abuse problems. Individuals with major depressive episodes were more likely than people without major depressive episodes to have used an illicit drug in the past year. A link has also been found between suicide and substance use disorders.

Intervention

Because substance abuse disorders can be a barrier to employment, it is imperative that vocational services be incorporated into substance abuse treatment. Unemployment and substance abuse may become intertwined long before an individual seeks treatment (Center for Substance Abuse Treatment, 2000). Individuals with histories of substance abuse will have varying work histories, ranging from being chronically or permanently unemployed to being continuously employed. Employed clients who have a strong work history usually respond well to substance abuse treatment. Other variables that measure functioning and stability can also influence treatment success, such as education and a positive marital relationship. Years of research show that the best predictors of successful substance abuse treatment are gainful employment, adequate family support, and lack of coexisting mental illness (Center for Substance Abuse Treatment, 2000). Employment helps moderate the occurrence and severity of relapse to addiction (Wolkstein & Spiller, 1998). In addition, employment can offer the opportunity for clients to develop new social skills and make new, sober friends who can help clients maintain sobriety.

Although the literature provides a variety of strategies for promoting employment for individuals with substance abuse issues, Nightingale and Holcomb (1997) provide useful strategies that human service professionals can use throughout the employment continuum:

Job Placement Strategies

- Job search assistance, either in a group setting or through one-on-one counseling or coaching, sometimes through "job clubs" with workshops, access to phone banks, and peer support.
- Self-directed job search, where individuals search and apply for jobs on their own. Sometimes individuals must submit a log of their job contacts.
- Job development and placement, where program staff members identify or develop job openings for participants.

Job Training Strategies

- Classroom occupational training, by training or educational institutions such as community colleges or vocational schools, community-based organizations, or nonprofit or for-profit training centers.
- On-the-job training with public or private sector employers, who usually receive a subsidy to cover a portion of the wages paid during the training period.
- Use of a mentor, who provides support to the client within the work setting. A mentor could be someone who went through substance abuse treatment and is now working.

Broad Education Strategies

- Remedial education, such as preparation for the general equivalency diploma (GED), basic skills instruction in reading and mathematics, or English-language classes for persons whose primary language is not English, and computer-skills building.
- Postsecondary degree programs (e.g., associate's or bachelor's degree), generally financed by grants, federal loans, or scholarships.

Mixed Strategies

- Supported work experience, with pre-employment preparation, assignment to public jobs, and gradually increasing hours and work responsibility combined with ongoing counseling, education, and peer support.

While the entry-level human service professional and even alcohol or drug counselors are not expected to be a specialist in vocational rehabilitation services, she or he must acquire at least rudimentary skills in the area of vocational services provision, as well as be prepared to function as a case manager who advocates for the needs of the client and calls on other expert professionals as needed to provide the services that support the treatment process. Initial vocational screening can be done by an alcohol and drug counselor, and more in-depth assessment should be conducted by a VR counselor or vocational evaluator.

Human service professionals who work with clients with chemical dependency must be knowledgeable about common issues and barriers members of this population encounter. Clients who are abusing substances or may have an addiction should be referred to clinical treatment program prior to focusing on their career development needs. This may start with an employee reaching out to the organization's employee assistance program.

Conclusion

This chapter introduced you to adult career transition and looks at several special populations that human service professionals will typically serve. We reviewed the nature of transitions and explored typical types of career transitions individuals experience over the life-span. Two models of career transition were highlighted: Schlossberg's transitional model and Hopson and Adams's stage model. Then we looked at a few special populations that have unique barriers to employment transition including displaced or dislocated workers, offender/ex-offenders, veterans, and people with chemical dependency. This overview hopefully has increased your sensitivity to the needs that clients bring to the career helping process and made you more aware of the ways in which you can assist them in their career development challenges.

Key Chapter Terms

Schlossberg's Transitional Model	Recidivism
Coping	Employment Retention
4S System of Coping	Civilian Veteran
Transition	Post-9/11 Veterans
Career Transition	Military Culture
Double Jeopardy	Military Soft Skills
Displaced Workers	Veteran Identity
Mattering	Invisible Wounds
Hopson & Adams' Stage Model	Abuse
10 Criminogenic needs	Dependency

Web Resources
Note that website URLs may change over time.

Displaced/Dislocated Workers
Department of Labor's Rapid Response Services for Laid off Workers
https://www.doleta.gov/layoff/workers.cfm

Meyers, L. (2014, December). *The lingering crisis of the Great Recession.*
Counseling Today. Retrieved from https://ct.counseling.org/tag/career-employment-counseling/

Single Parents Network
http://singleparentsnetwork.com/

Offenders/Ex-Offenders
Bureau of Justice Statistics
http://www.bjs.gov

BJS-Definitions of Probation and Parole
https://www.bjs.gov/index.cfm?ty=tdtp&tid=15

EEOC Green Factors-Legal Guidelines Related to Hiring
www.clarifacts.com/resources/employment-screening-faqs/green-factors

Military Veterans
National Coalition for Homeless Veterans
http://nchv.org/

U.S. Chamber of Commerce Foundation. (n.d.). *Hiring our heroes.*
https://www.uschamberfoundation.org/hiring-our-heroes

U.S. Department of Veterans Affairs/Department of Defense. *Veterans employment center.*
https://www.ebenefits.va.gov/ebenefits/jobs

Common Military Terms and Lingo, Department of Veterans Affairs
https://www.mentalhealth.va.gov/communityproviders/docs/terms_lingo.pdf

Career Theory, Development, and Appraisal

Military Culture: Core Competencies for Healthcare Professionals Course
https://deploymentpsych.org/military-culture

Substance Abuse/Dependency
Association for Addiction Professionals
https://www.naadac.org/

National Institute on Drug Abuse
https://www.drugabuse.gov/

Substance Abuse and Mental Health Services Administration (SAMHSA)
https://www.samhsa.gov/

Substance Use in the Workplace-Butler Center for Research
https://www.hazelden.org/web/public/document/substance-use-in-workplace.pdf

Chapter 10

CAREER ISSUES OF PERSONS WITH DISABILITIES

"Individuals with disabilities must have the independent desire to bring about change and be empowered to be change agents in their own lives."

~David R. Strauser, 2014, p. 2

CHAPTER HIGHLIGHTS
Nature of Work for the Disabled
Social Model of Disability
Brief History of Vocational Rehabilitation
Employment Barriers for Disabled
Psychosocial Reactions to Disability
Vocational Counseling Process for Disabled
Reasonable Accommodation Process
Empowerment Model of Disability

For hundreds of years, people with disabilities have been among the most disenfranchised, impoverished, and unemployed individuals in society (Barnes, 2000). In 2017, the unemployment rate for persons with a disability was 9.2%—more than twice that of those with no disability (4.2 percent) (Bureau of Labor Statistics, 2018). Despite these figures, more than 60% of respondents on surveys by the National Council on Disability indicated their willingness to work (Bertoni, 2010). The decision to enter or return to work among people with disabilities is influenced by political, social, and environmental forces. Even when people with disabilities do work, their opportunities are more limited than those of their nondisabled peers in terms of pay, full-time employment, and re-employment after layoff (Houtenville & Burkhauser, 2004). Certainly, the issues and needs associated with disability can be wide-ranging and pervasive, and people with disabilities require professionals who are able to help empower and assist them in their employment needs.

In this chapter, we present an introduction to providing human services to people who have disabilities. We begin with terminology and a conceptual look at the social model of disability. Next, we cover general and employment statistics for the disabled, followed by a look at employment barriers and psychosocial reactions to disability and chronic illness. Typical phases in the vocational rehabilitation process when assisting chronically ill and disabled people with employment issues are presented. Finally, a brief view of reasonable accommodations and the empowerment perspective for working with people with disabilities will be addressed.

Nature of Work for the Disabled

Human service professionals working with people who have disabilities must understand the complex nature of employment to assist individuals in attaining and maintaining work and in interacting effectively and appropriately with coworkers. Getting and keeping a job can be challenging in terms of dealing with social attitudes, having to disclose or reveal personal information to obtain necessary accommodations, and coping with a chronic illness or disabling condition (Baron & Salzer, 2002). From a socioeconomic perspective, the nature of work and the meaning of career have been restructured and reinvented over the last three decades. Shaped by a global economy and propelled by information technology, the new social arrangement is characterized by uncertain, unpredictable, and risky employment opportunities (Kalleberg, 2009). This not only affects the nondisabled population but confounds issues for people with disability.

Disability is multilayered and requires comprehensive strategies to address self-concept, life roles, social status, adaptation, and especially the work role. Helping clients with disabilities calls for special assessments, interventions, materials, and programs. The overarching goal for a human service professional working with people with disabilities is to maximize everyone's potential for life and work. Some clarification of terminology frequently encountered when providing services to people with disabilities will be provided before we go further.

Terminology

There is no universally accepted definition of disability, and which definition is used in a given situation makes a tremendous difference regarding how many people are counted or left out. Mashaw and Reno (1996) documented over 20 definitions of disability that were used for purposes of entitlement to public or private income support programs, government services, or statistical analysis. Nevertheless, the definition of **disability** commonly used in the U. S. has been defined by the Americans with Disabilities Act (ADA). The ADA identifies an individual with disabilities as a person who has a physical or mental impairment that substantially limits one or more "major life activities," or has a record of such impairment, or is regarded as having such impairment (ADA, 1990). Impairment can be the result of a physical, sensory, cognitive, intellectual, mental, or chronic disabling disease. Major life activities include caring for oneself, performing manual tasks, walking, seeing, hearing, speaking, breathing, learning, and working.

Population Statistics

According to a 2012 population survey report (Bureau of Labor Statistics, 2013), the U. S. workforce totaled about 135 million workers, of whom approximately 5.2 million people were classified as disabled. The American Community Survey 2017 annual report (Kraus, Lauer, Coleman, & Houtenville, 2018) estimated that the overall rate of people with disabilities in the U. S. population in 2016 was 12.8%. Nearly 80% of disabled people were not in the labor force (i.e., neither working nor looking for work) (U. S. Bureau of Labor Statistics, 2018). In contrast, only about 30% of people without a disability did not participate in the labor force. Although older people in general are less likely to participate in the labor force, even among younger people, those with a disability have markedly lower rates of work participation than people with no disability. Overall, women were more likely to have a disability than men, partly reflected by the greater life expectancy of women. In 2017, the prevalence of disability continued to be higher for Blacks and Whites than for Hispanics and Asians.

In 2016, an estimated 25.1% of non-institutionalized civilian veterans aged 21 to 64 reported having a service-connected disability (a disease or injury determined to have occurred during military service) (Erickson, Lee, & von Schrader, 2017).

Level of education is another factor in the difference between groups. Persons with a disability are less likely to have completed a bachelor's degree or higher education than those with no disability. Among both groups, those who have completed higher levels of education are more likely to be employed than those with less education. Across all levels of education, persons with a disability in 2017 were much less likely to be employed than their counterparts with no disability.

Employment Statistics

Employment rates are much lower for people with disabilities. The unemployment rate for persons with a disability was 9.2% in 2017, which was more than twice that of those with no disability. Unemployed persons are defined here as those who did not have a job, were available for work, and were actively looking for a job in the 4 weeks preceding the survey. Unemployment among people with disabilities hovers at 70%, although nearly half of the people with disabilities are of an employable age (Kraus, Lauer, Coleman, & Houtenville, 2018). However, across all age groups, persons with a disability were much less likely to be employed than those with no disability. Workers with a disability were more likely to be employed part-time than those with no disability. A large proportion of persons with a disability—about 8 in 10—were not in the labor force in 2017, compared with about 3 in 10 of those with no disability (U. S. Bureau of Labor Statistics, 2018). In part, this reflects the older age profile of persons with a disability.

In 2017, the unemployment rate for men with a disability (9.0%) was about the same as the rate for women (9.5%). The unemployment rates for both men and women declined from 2016 to 2017. Although jobless rates for persons with a disability declined among all major race and ethnicity groups in 2017; Blacks (13.8%) continued to have a higher unemployment rate than Hispanics (10.2%), Whites (8.5%), and Asians (6.6%) (U. S. Bureau of Labor Statistics, 2018).

A significant number of persons with a disability live in poverty. The poverty percentage gap, or the difference between the percentages of those with and without disabilities, has been between 7.4 and 8.3 percentage points over the past 8 years (Kraus, Lauer, Coleman, & Houtenville, 2018). For people with disabilities the percentage of people living in poverty was 21% in 2016, and for people without disability the percentage in 2016 was 13.1%.

Employment is more precarious for people with disabilities. Data suggests that workers with disabilities are much more likely than workers without disabilities to have temporary or part-time, low-skill, low-wage jobs or work as contingent workers, and to perceive their jobs as less secure, and to experience job losses and periods of unemployment (Jordan & Marinaccio, 2017).

Social Model of Disability

The World Health Organization's (WHO; 2001) **International Classification of Functioning, Disability, and Health** (ICF) adopted the more conceptual definition of disability, as "an umbrella term for impairments, activity limitations, and participation restrictions. It denotes the negative aspects of the interaction between an individual (with a health condition) and that individual's contextual factors (environmental and personal factors)" (p. 212). Changes to any of these factors over time can have an impact on a person's ability to function and participate in activities (Burkhauser & Houtenville, 2010). The **ICF model of disability** focuses on the experience of disability as an interaction between the impairment itself and the person's environment, and thus can be considered a social model of disability. It recognizes that a person's impairment can become much more disabling in an unresponsive and insensitive environment and much less disabling in an accessible and accommodating space (Anctil, 2017).

Although the ICF disability concepts may seem to follow a linear progression, this is not necessarily the case for everyone. Because there is often overlap across impairment, activity limitation, and participation restriction, it is possible for one of them to occur without any relation to the others (see Figure 10.1). For instance, a person can have a participation restriction without an activity limitation or impairment; or a person with a history of mental illness, but who is coping well and no longer has a loss in capacity or activity limitation, may also be unable to find employment due to discrimination resulting from his or her health condition.

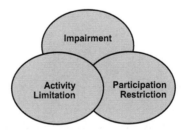

Figure 10.1
Social Model of Disability using ICF

The roles of the human services professional in providing career services to persons with disability, therefore, is to maximize opportunities for accommodation and accessibility to employment.

Rehabilitation is the process by which people with disabilities are prepared for work and for life in general. According to the Commission on Rehabilitation Counselor Certification (CRC), **rehabilitation counseling** is a systematic process which assists persons with physical, mental, developmental, cognitive, and emotional disabilities to achieve their personal, career, and independent living goals in the most integrated setting possible through the application of the counseling process (CRC, 2019). People who have disabilities are often seen by rehabilitation counselors because of the type of training required and specialized services provided. The field of rehabilitation counseling is a specialty within the rehabilitation profession, with counseling at its core, and is differentiated from other related counseling fields. Yet, various rehabilitation services may be provided by various professions such as human services, psychology, counseling, social work, medicine, and nursing.

One of the job functions central to the professional practice of rehabilitation counseling is vocational counseling and consultation. **Vocational rehabilitation** has traditionally been referred to as the process of returning a disabled worker to a state of employability (Brown, 2016). Today, vocational rehabilitation is most frequently provided by rehabilitation counselors whose training and experience usually includes familiarity with the medical and social aspects of various disabilities and their relationship to work (Brown, 2016). The job role of a vocational rehabilitation counselor calls for a broad base of knowledge and skills related to emotion-centered counseling, vocational assessment, vocational counseling, case management, job development, and placement counseling (Rubin, Roessler & Rumrill Jr., 2016).

Brief History of Vocational Rehabilitation

Prior to the 20th century, precursors to vocational rehabilitation (VR) services were generally provided in some fashion by charitable organizations (e.g., the Salvation Army and the American Red Cross). By the end of the 19th century, the industrialization of the American workforce prompted a greater recognition of the complexity of social issues relevant to the welfare and economy of the United States (Elliott & Leung, 2005). Many workers often lacked skills or possessed skills that were rendered obsolete by new technology and industry. The Smith–Hughes Act of 1917 provided matching funds to states to develop vocation education programs, and the Federal Board of Vocation Education was created as a part of the legislation to administer VR programs. World War I required the unprecedented infusion of vocational assessment to classify enlisted personnel; increased need for VR efforts was required for many veterans returning from the war with acquired physical disabilities (Elliott & Leung, 2005). The Soldiers Rehabilitation Act (1918) provided funds to rehabilitate disabled veterans, and the Federal Board of Vocational Education was to administer these services. Beginning with Public Law 236 (the Smith-Fess Act of 1920) the federal government initiated a series of acts that expanded VR services to citizens who were not affiliated with the government. **Public Law 236** essentially ensured vocational education to persons with physical disabilities who were unable to work.

Vocational rehabilitation agencies provide individualized coordination of counseling, career planning, training, support services, and job placement appropriate to the employment and life goals of persons with disabilities. The public VR service system in the United States grew out of Public Law 236 which was designed to assist people with disabilities return to work, and is the central goal and rationale for the existence of the public VR program (Patterson, Bruyere, Szymanski, & Jenkins, 2011). To receive services, an individual must be disabled and require VR services "to prepare for, secure, retain or regain employment" (Vocational Rehabilitation Act, 1973). Therefore, any service an individual is to receive from the VR system must be connected to an ultimate employment goal.

Individuals with disabilities may receive services through other settings as well. School counselors, college counselors, clinical counselors, chemical dependency counselors, social workers, and psychologists are likely to encounter disabled persons in settings such as private practice, community mental health and social service agencies, veterans' hospitals, K-12 schools, and colleges and universities.

Employment Barriers for the Disabled

Persons with disabilities find great meaning in work. Researchers have found that working allows person with disabilities to increase their activity levels and gain self-esteem (Freedman, 1996). Nevertheless, people with disabilities often encounter physical, psychological, social, educational, financial, and vocational barriers that greatly interfere with their quality of life, impede employment, and decrease work participation. For the disabled, an **employment barrier** is something that prevents them from gaining access, maintaining, or returning to employment or other useful occupation. Human service professionals will address employment barriers through assessment, interventions, and other rehabilitation services. Yet, because some barriers may involve the client's broader system and have social justice implications, advocacy with the client, community, or public may be necessary. As Fabian (2014) noted,

> "One of the major obstacles to achieving work participation among people with disabilities remains the prevailing medical model assumption in disability policy and service; in other words, the emphasis is still on the problem within the individual, rather than focusing efforts on remediating policy, cultural, or systemic issues that depress employment entry for people with disabilities" (p. 190).

According to the 2012 Current Population Survey (Bureau of Labor Statistics, 2013), half of those with a disability who were not employed (i.e., those who were either unemployed or not in the labor force) in May 2012 reported at least one barrier to employment. When asked to identify barriers they had encountered, most reported that their own disability was a barrier to employment (80.5%). Other barriers cited included lack of education or training (14.1%), lack of transportation (11.7%), and the need for accommodations at the job (10.3%).

A distinct set of ten employment challenges encountered by a substantial amount of people with disabilities can be used as a reference point for the human services professional. These barriers can be organized into structural, individual, and systemic.

Structural Barriers
- A changing workforce economy and precarious work
- Inadequate or absent workplace accommodations
- Employer and others' attitudes and misconceptions

Individual Barriers
- Social and personal stigma or shame
- Attitudes about work, discouragement, and lack of self-awareness
- Functional limitations or restrictions in major life activities
- Low education, job skills, limited early vocational and social experiences

Systemic Barriers
- Inadequate workforce or career services
- Insufficient financial resources and transportation issues
- Lack of social support system

These barriers are not exclusively employment barriers. Many factors related to disability and non-disability can interact and have a profound effect on the lives of individuals with chronic illness and disabilities (Livneh & Antonak, 2005). Among these, some of the most commonly recognized factors include uncertain prognosis, the prolonged course of medical treatment and rehabilitation interventions, and the psychosocial stress associated with the incurred trauma or disease process itself.

As a human services professional providing career services to clients with disabilities, you will need to consider three broad questions:

1. What barriers will the client experience during the job search process?
2. What barriers might the client experience in the workplace?
3. What barriers will the client experience while obtaining services?

One of the first steps in helping clients with disabilities gain employment is gathering all the facts. While you are not a medical professional, increasing your knowledge about the cause, symptoms, and treatment of a disability can help you determine how the disability will impact the client's ability to access career services and adjust in the workplace. The information will also be useful in educating your client, other service providers, and potential employers. Nevertheless, human service professionals should balance information about the disability and using client-centered helping skills as discussed in Chapter 1. As Dr. Amos Sales noted, "One can become more preoccupied in understanding the disability than in understanding the person" (see Shallcross, 2011).

Psychosocial Reactions to Disability

When providing career services to individuals with disabilities, human service professionals will need to draw on their expertise in the areas of (a) stress, crisis, and coping with loss and grief; (b) the impact of traumatic events on self-concept, body image, and quality of life; and (c) the effects of uncertainty, unpredictability, stigma, and prejudice on an individual's adaptation to disability. Human service professionals must also be familiar with clients' psychological reactions to their conditions and the external environment. In this section, we focus on the six most frequently experienced **psychosocial reactions to disability:** shock, anxiety, denial, depression, anger, and adjustment noted by (Livneh & Antonak, 2005):

- *Shock.* This reaction marks the initial experience following the onset of a traumatic and sudden injury or the diagnosis of a life-threatening or chronic and debilitating disease. The reaction is usually brief and characterized by psychic numbness, cognitive disorganization, and dramatically decreased or disrupted mobility and speech.

- *Anxiety.* This reaction is characterized by a panic-like feature on initial sensing of the nature and magnitude of the traumatic event. It is accompanied by confused thinking, negative thinking, and a multitude of physiological symptoms including headache, rapid heart rate, hyperventilation, excess perspiration, and gastrointestinal discomfort.

- *Denial.* This reaction involves the minimization and even complete negation of the chronicity, extent, and future implications associated with the condition. It includes wishful thinking, unrealistic expectations of (full or immediate) recovery, and at times, blatant neglect of medical advice and therapeutic or rehabilitation recommendations.

- *Depression.* This reaction is considered to reflect the realization of the permanency, magnitude, and future implications associated with the loss of body integrity, chronicity of condition, or impending death. Feelings of despair, helplessness, hopelessness, guilt, and isolation, as well as sleep issues, appetite disturbance, and distress are frequently reported during this time.

- *Anger/hostility.* The reaction of anger/hostility is frequently divided into internalized anger (i.e., self-directed feelings and behaviors of resentment, bitterness, guilt, and self-blame) and externalized hostility (i.e., other- or environment-directed retaliatory feelings and behaviors; Livneh & Antonak, 2005). Behaviors commonly observed during this time include aggressive acts, abusive accusations, antagonism, and passive-aggressive modes of obstructing treatment.

- *Adjustment.* This reaction comprises several components: (a) less negative thinking, understanding of and compromise about the condition, its impact, and its chronic nature; (b) an affective acceptance of oneself as a person with a disability, and a continued search for new meanings; and (c) an active (i.e., behavioral) pursuit of personal, social, and/or vocational goals.

Vocational Counseling Process for People with Disabilities

The issues and needs associated with disability can be wide-ranging and multilayered, and different theoretical orientations and strategies can be used depending on the training and expertise of the human services professional. Unless you are assessing a client for an impairment, the individual may already have a record of physical or mental impairment documented or may be regarded as having an impairment as defined by the Americans with Disabilities Act of 1990.

In general, there are **five phases in the vocational rehabilitation process** that typically occur when assisting chronically ill and disabled people with employment issues. These are interview and assessment, creating an individual service plan, determine needs, referrals, and employment placement. These phases are discussed below:

Phase 1: Interview & Assessment

Employment services with rehabilitation counseling clients usually begins with the intake interview and initial assessment. Here the human services professional is working collaboratively with the client to investigate the nature of their concerns, psychosocial needs, and what they want to do with a former or current job or to obtain new employment. Part of your role is to assist the client in identifying a career goal or aspiration to work toward.

During phase 1, career assessments are often administered using some of the assessment tools discussed in Chapter 5 (e.g., interest, ability, values inventories) along with other instruments that may be more specific and normed to the disabled population for matching a client to a job. Career assessments may be administered and interpreted by a counselor or other human service professional, depending on the scope of practice in the provider's workplace. In addition, the human service professional should assess and address the client's physical and mental health, and their self-confidence, self-acceptance, and self-advocacy skills.

The provider, along with the client, can then interpret the assessment results and formulate achievable and measurable goals and objectives for a long-term employment plan.

Phase 2: The Individual Service Plan

Based on the information gained from the intake process and from the administration of the career-related assessments, the helper provides an employment plan called an Individual Service Plan (ISP), also called **Individual Plan for Employment** (IPE) by Vocational Rehabilitation agencies. The goal of the ISP or IPE is the long-term employment of the client with a disability. It is a collaborative effort between the human services professional and the client to identify needs. The needs include identifying and reducing barriers to employment, matching skills or the individual with the skills needed for a position, making reasonable workplace accommodations, and providing support, training, and education, and other referrals the client may need for life and work success. Services may be provided directly by the VR counselor, coordinated with other services, or purchased by the VR agency on the client's behalf.

Phase 3: Determine Training, Educational, and Other Needs

Individuals with disabilities can often enhance their employment prospects through rehabilitation, training, and education. The largest program to assist such clients is through the **Workforce Innovation and Opportunity Act** (WIOA), an amendment to the Rehabilitation Act of 1973. WIOA provides leadership, resources, and funding to state and other agencies that provide vocational rehabilitation (VR) and other services to individuals with disabilities. WIOA's goal is to maximize an individual's employment, independence and integration into the community and the workforce. For example, services might include employment services, such as working on interview skills, and matching clients to employment positions. If it becomes evident the client needs retraining or additional education to obtain employment, services can be provided through the state or federal VR services program. Thus, the human services professional must be aware of the types of assistance and range of services available to individuals with disabilities.

Phase 4: Referrals to Professionals and Agencies

Each client will have a unique set of circumstance and needs that will require the human services professional to work collaboratively with a variety of agencies, systems, programs, and other human service professionals to provide the most comprehensive services to the client. You may find that your training and expertise has prepared you to work with employment issues, but requires additional professionals to work with medical, psychiatric, or even severe psychological issues that complicate career services with chronically ill and disabled clients. It is incumbent upon the service provider to make referrals when services are outside the scope of practice of the professional or organization the client works in.

In addition, human service professionals must be familiar with various funding sources and the eligibility requirements for each source. A variety of funding sources are available for individuals with disabilities. These programs include Supplemental Security Income (SSI), Social Security Disability (DI), Workers' Compensation (WC), and Veterans Administration programs. Due to the dysfunction and negative impact of trauma and its symptoms in the lives of service members, the VA has recognized and developed the VA disability rating system. The disability rating system considers both physical and mental health-related conditions. The more areas of a veteran's life that are impacted (i.e. social and occupational difficulty or physical limitation and/or pain), the more financial compensation the veteran could potentially receive. If the client became disabled because of a work-related or military service-connected injury, they may qualify for rehabilitation services through Workers Compensation or via the Veterans Administration. All these programs provide cash payments to individuals based on program-specific criteria.

Phase 5: Employment Placement

Once the client has received the needed interventions, the human service professional assists him or her in initiating career placement services. The role of the helper varies, depending on the needs of each client. Some of the roles include serving as mentors, coaches, career specialists, and advocates for their clients. Human service professionals should also work with their clients in anticipating reactions from employers and dealing with such reactions in a confident, positive manner. Components of the employment campaign include assisting clients with the strategic job search, completing job applications, writing job search correspondence, formatting resumes, and assisting with interviewing skills.

Human service professionals who work with disabled people often work with potential employers or the client's coworkers as well, helping to set up accommodations for the client in the workplace. In working with an employer, the human services professional's goal is to find out what can be changed in the client's environment or support system to allow the individual to work. For example, if an employee was injured and can no longer handle heavy lifting, a human service professional might work with the employer to modify the person's job description.

Lastly, program evaluation is an essential element of career services. Program evaluation should be integrated within every phase of the career development program, from development to termination. It provides accountability for programs and serves as a means of determining whether the programs are meeting the needs of the clients and agency.

Reasonable Accommodation Process

During the placement process an important question to consider is whether your client will need an accommodation. The following provides the basics of the accommodation process when working with disability. The American with Disabilities Act requires **reasonable accommodation** for an individual with a disability and is enforced by the Equal Employment Opportunity Commission (EEOC). Reasonable accommodation is any change to a job, the work environment, or the way things are usually done that allows an individual with a disability to apply for a job, perform a job function, or enjoy equal access to benefits available to other individuals in the workplace (EEOC, 2002). A reasonable accommodation is a tool provided by employers to enable employees to accomplish their jobs. For example, an employee who is visually impaired might need a computer that operates by voice command or has a screen or other tolls that enlarges print.

An **undue hardship** is a legal term defined in the ADA as an action entailing significant difficulty or expense for the employer in providing an accommodation (EEOC, 2002). Some factors to consider include the nature and cost of the proposed accommodation, the overall financial resources of the business, the effect of the accommodation on resources, and the impact of the accommodation on the operation of the employer's facility. An employer is obligated to make an accommodation. Nevertheless, it is the responsibility for the applicant or employee with a disability to inform the employer that an accommodation is needed. The employer is responsible, however, for notifying job applicants and employees of its obligation to provide accommodations for otherwise qualified individuals with disabilities.

Reasonable accommodation varies based on an individual's needs. However, one of the most commonly requested accommodation is a flexible work schedule. Usually sought out by older workers after retirement age. Other requested accommodation relates to accessible communications, reduction in environmental distractions, and physical space changes.

The employer may request from the applicant or employee documentation of the individual's functional limitation and its impact on the job or job functions to support the request. According to ADA policy, the employer may require an employee to provide documentation, but cannot ask unrelated questions or request complete medical records. Additionally, the documentation does not need to contain the actual name or type of disability. An employer may ask for written documentation from a physician, psychologist, rehabilitation counselor, physical therapist, independent living specialist, or other professional with knowledge of the person's functional limitation. A useful resource to learn more about reasonable accommodations is the **Job Accommodation Network** (JAN). JAN is a service of the Department of Labor, Office of Disability Employment Policy. Free information is available for employers, individuals with disabilities, and practitioners and is listed in the resource section of this chapter.

Empowerment Model of Disability

Regardless of where a person with a chronic illness or disability receives career services, it is incumbent upon human service professionals to be aware of disability empowerment and develop a framework for providing career services from an empowerment perspective (Kosciulek, 2014). **Empowerment** of individuals with disabilities may be viewed as ensuring that they possess the same degree of control over their own lives and the conditions that affect their lives as is generally possessed by people without disabilities (Harp, 1994). Because people with disabilities can be viewed as an oppressed minority group—a group that experiences a need to feel more power in their lives—Sales (2011) eloquently asserted,

> "They have been denied power throughout their lives. They have dealt with the medical model all their lives where they've been told what they can do and cannot do. Because of mobility issues, they've been denied access. All of those things feed into being in a lower power position. They come to counseling with a need to be more empowered" (p. 31).

During the career helping process for people with disabilities, the important behavior changes that occur involve the client's movement from discouragement to encouragement and their movement from lack of determination to self-determination. Whether changes are big or small, this involves empowerment—a transfer of power and control, of values, decisions, choices, and directions of human services from external entities to the individuals themselves (Bolton & Brookings, 1996). Active client involvement is the key. In an empowerment approach, clients are actively involved in (a) gathering information, including self-assessment and learning about occupations and the labor market; (b) generating alternative courses of action and weighing these alternatives; and (c) formulating a plan of action (Kosciulek, 2014). Empowerment does not mean that the human services professional plays a passive role in the helping process, but it is a facilitator of client change. As Williams (2001) reminds us, we need to "acknowledge the near universality of disability," because this "minority group can include any of us—today, tomorrow, or the day after" (p. 139).

Conclusion

This chapter introduced the human services professional to the employment concerns of people who have disabilities. Terminology and a conceptual look at the social model of disability were presented. Next, we covered general and employment statistics of the disabled, followed by employment barriers and common psychosocial reactions to disability and chronic illness. Typical phases in the vocational rehabilitation process when assisting chronically ill and disabled people with employment issues were presented. Finally, a brief view of reasonable accommodations and the empowerment perspective for working with people with disabilities was addressed.

Key Chapter Terms

Disability	Psychosocial Reactions to Disability
ICF	Phases in Vocational Rehabilitation
ICF Model of Disability	Individual Plan for Employment
Rehabilitation Counseling	Workforce Innovation/Opportunity Act
Vocational Rehabilitation	Reasonable Accommodation
Public Law 236	Undue Hardship
Vocational Rehab. Agencies	Job Accommodation Network
Employment Barriers	Empowerment

Web Resources
Note that website URLs may change over time.

Advocacy and Legislation
Association of Persons in Supported Employment
https://apse.org

ADA Update: A Primer for State and Local Governments
https://www.ada.gov/regs2010/titleII_2010/titleII_primer.pdf

Americans with Disabilities Act of 1990
https://www.ada.gov

Employers' Practical Guide to Reasonable Accommodation Under the
Americans with Disabilities Act
https://askjan.org/publications/employers/employers-guide.cfm

Job Accommodation Network
https://askjan.org

State Vocational Rehabilitation (VR) Agencies
https://askjan.org/concerns/State-Vocational-Rehabilitation-Agencies.cfm

U. S. Department of Education Client Assistance Program
https://www2.ed.gov/programs/rsacap/index.html

Journal and Newsletters
American Rehabilitation Counseling Association Newsletter
http://www.arcaweb.org/newsletter

Rehabilitation Counseling Bulletin
https://journals.sagepub.com/home/rcb

Population Statistics
Disability Statistics Cornell University
http://www.disabilitystatistics.org

Career Theory, Development, and Appraisal

BLS–Labor Force Characteristics of People with a Disability
https://www.bls.gov/spotlight/2018/labor-force-characteristics-of-people-with-a-disability/home.htm

Professional Organizations
American Rehabilitation Counseling Association
http://www.arcaweb.org

National Rehabilitation Counseling Association
https://www.nationalrehab.org

Chapter 11

CAREER EDUCATION AND GUIDANCE IN HIGH SCHOOL

"Students of today and tomorrow will require an education that provides them with the academic, career and technical, and guidance and counseling knowledge, skills, and dispositions to be career ready upon graduation from high school."
~Norman C. Gysbers, 2013, p. 283

CHAPTER HIGHLIGHTS
Preparation and Role of the School Counselor
History of Career Education & Guidance in Schools
Career and College Readiness
Career Theory and Assessment for Schools
Developmental Concerns and Career Readiness

C hanges in population, economics, and technology in the past few decades have increased the need for professionals in the schools to emphasize educational planning and career development for students. The preparation of students for college and the world-of-work through career and educational planning must keep up with the pace of the 21st century (Niles & Erford, 2019). America's students are facing increasing competition for meaningful employment from candidates around the world as more people in other countries are becoming highly educated. At the same time, employers' expectations for the level of education and training needed for entry level jobs have increased. Consequently, workforce projections call for graduating secondary students to have at the least some postsecondary education in order to fulfill the demands of work (Carnevale, Smith, & Strohl, 2013). "If young people's impressions of the labor market and their own career journeys develop during their time at school, it is reasonable to suggest that schools have some responsibility to provide a context within which these ideas can be formed in positive and constructive ways" (Sampson, Hooley, & Marriot, 2011, p. 1). To ensure student readiness, young adults entering the workforce would benefit from being flexible, adaptable, and committed to lifelong learning as they approach postsecondary education or the job market (Johnson, 2000). To be successful in college and a career in the 21st century, students need academic, employability, and technical skills as well as adaptable interpersonal factors and dispositions.

This chapter begins with the role of the school counselor in helping students develop relevant skills and knowledge. This is followed by a brief landscape of the history of career and college readiness in schools. We will review some of the prominent initiatives that impact career and college readiness for students, and then distinguish between career and college readiness. Next, we will cover several career theories and assessment tools that are relevant for use with a high school population. Last, some developmental issues involving identity and self-efficacy will be examined, along with approaches for helping adolescents become college and career ready. Although career readiness begins in elementary grades, this chapter will focus on career and college readiness for grades 9 through 12.

Preparation and Role of the School Counselor

Professionals that are in the best position to support students' career and postsecondary planning and create truly comprehensive career and postsecondary programs are the professional school counselors. To become a school counselor, one must have a master's degree in school counseling. Such degrees are often similar to master's degrees in other counseling specialty areas or are housed in the same department as mental health counseling programs. The program requirements range from having a few courses in school counseling (along with practicum and/or internship experiences in the schools) to having the majority of the classes geared specifically to school counseling. In many programs, students who are on the school counseling "track" are asked to focus their projects on school counseling as they take all the program courses. While it is notable that some school counselors were teachers before venturing into school counseling, more than three decades of research on the importance and efficacy of being a teacher before being a school counselor appears to indicate that school counselors both with and without teaching background are equally capable and competent (Baker & Gerler, 2008).

The school counselor's roles are many and varied and sometimes much more involved than people think. The American School Counselor Association's (ASCA) **school counselors' role statement** defines professional school counselors as, "uniquely qualified to address all students' academic, personal/social and career development needs by designing, implementing, evaluating, and enhancing a comprehensive school counseling program that promotes and enhances student success" (ASCA, n.d.). Through leadership, advocacy, prevention programming, and individual and group counseling, school counselors promote equity and access to rigorous educational experiences for all students. In addition, school counselor's duties include scheduling, registering, test coordination, and preparing individual educational plans. Yet, the role of school counselor often varies between districts and even between schools within the same district. Many schools today also have school social workers as members of the counseling department. School counselors and social workers are employed at the elementary, middle, and high school levels, in direct supervisory positions, and as educators. An important part of school counselors' work will be to help students and their families to become aware of the pathways they could take to achieve their long-term career goals.

School counselors play many roles in the lives of students, but one that might be the most influential is the one that helps students see themselves within the context of their future (Kolbert, Williams, Morgan, Crothers, & Hughes, 2017). School counselors understand that the academic, personal/social, and career development needs of students are not considered separate but are intertwined, each affecting the other (Schenck, Anctil, Smith-Klose, & Dahir, 2012). Today's school counseling is developmental and preventative, and services are interwoven throughout the school's total educational program. To create postsecondary opportunities for students, school counselors need to create a sustained culture of career and college readiness that includes parents, students, teachers, administrators, and community partners (Curry & Milsom, 2017).

History of Career Education & Guidance in Schools

With the inception of comprehensive school guidance and counseling programs in the 1970's, interest in career development theory, research, and practice increased. In the early 1970s, state guides for integrating career development into the school curriculum were developed. The idea of implementing career development through the curriculum did not originate with these models. As discussed in Chapter 2 of this text, Jesse B. Davis had outlined such a curriculum by as early as 1914. Of more immediate interest, however, are Tennyson, Soldahl, and Mueller's (1965) *The Teacher's Role in Career Development* and the Airlie House Conference in May 1966 on the topic *Implementing Career Development Theory and Research Through the Curriculum*, which was sponsored by the National Vocational Guidance Association (Ashcroft, 1966). Also, in the 1960s and early 1970s came the work of theorists and practitioners who advocated for career education or the need to integrate career development concepts into the curriculum. Through these efforts, career development concepts began to be translated into individual outcomes and the resulting goals and objectives began to be arranged sequentially for kindergarten through 12th grade (Gysbers & Henderson, 2012).

In the late 1980s and the 1990s, state school guidance program models were being developed and put into operation because of the work of guidance leaders at the state level and the work of counselors, administrators, and boards of education at the local level (Gysbers & Henderson, 2012). Work on federal legislation for guidance and counseling continued, and several states passed legislation or rules that support the development, implementation, and evaluation of comprehensive guidance and counseling programs in their local school districts. The idea that education and career should be linked was promoted by the National Occupational Information Coordinating Committee (NOICC), and in 1996 their work was consolidated into a single publication (Kobylarz, 1996). In 1994, the **School to Work Opportunities Act** (STWOA) was passed by Congress. This legislation provided the impetus for public schools to develop challenging educational programs for all, to relate academic subject matter to work, to help students identify their interests, and to stimulate students to make educational and career plans. With the continued progression of school improvement and standards-based education, the next logical step was the development of professional standards to assist the field in delivering comprehensive school counseling programs.

ASCA National Model

Standards and competencies that students were expected to gain in the academic, career, and personal/social domains as a result of comprehensive school counseling program were developed in the late 1990s. In 1997, the American School Counselor Association (ASCA) published *Sharing the Vision: The National Standards for School Counseling Programs* (Campbell & Dahir, 1997), which was followed by the publication of *Vision into Action: Implementing the National Standards for School Counseling Programs* (Dahir, Sheldon, & Valiga, 1998). This initiated the development of the **ASCA National Model** in 2003, which has its roots in the work of the NOICC. The ASCA model is comprehensive in scope, preventative in design, and developmental in nature, and is an integral part of the total educational program. A workbook was published in 2004 (ASCA, 2004), and a second edition of the National Model was published in 2005 (ASCA, 2005).

The ASCA model set forth nine standards and competencies (knowledge, attitudes, and skills) that are contained within three broad areas: academic, career, and personal/social development. According to the American School Counselor Association (2017), "school counselors recognize students should demonstrate growth in these domains equally to be successful" (p. 8). In particular, the ASCA Model emphasizes the importance of developing career development competencies in school-age youth in the context of the school counseling program. The three key components of the **ASCA career development standards** are:

- Students will acquire the skills to investigate the world of work in relation to knowledge of self and to make informed career decisions.
- Students will employ strategies to achieve future career goals with success and satisfaction.
- Students will understand the relationship between personal qualities, education, training, and the world of work.

The ASCA standards served an additional purpose. Although school counselors and other professionals engage in helping behaviors designed to foster student academic, career, and social/emotional success, their efforts are not cohesively organized or regularly evaluated (Kolbert et al., 2017). By having a set of standards, competencies and indicators with which to plan the curriculum, implement activity-based interventions, and evaluate student outcomes, they can report the necessary data to stakeholders.

Today, the role and functions of the school counselor are undergoing a paradigm shift as the profession embraces the various components of the ASCA National Model. Considered the next generation of this model, the ASCA **Mindsets and Behaviors for Student Success** (ASCA, 2014) identifies and prioritizes outcomes or the specific attitudes, knowledge, and skills students should be able to demonstrate as a result of a school counseling program. It encourages emphasis on how students perceive themselves in relation to others and how developing their interpersonal capabilities will lead to current and future academic and personal success. A tool is available for schools to help in planning the overall school counseling curriculum (see resource section at the end of the chapter). For example, schools would encourage the following two mindsets that are applicable to the career domain:

- Understanding that postsecondary education and lifelong learning are necessary for long-term career success.
- Positive attitude toward work and learning.

The ASCA National Standards and Mindsets and Behaviors model clarifies the role and functions of public schools. The roles that school counselors should play in fostering students' career development is most recently addressed through ASCA's 2017 official Position Statement on the School Counselor and Career Development to help professionals advocate for their school counseling programs and appropriate school counseling duties (see Appendix B).

National and State Initiatives

National and state efforts have supported the movement for change in the public schools and some are briefly described here. The Carl D. Perkins Vocational and Technical Education Act of 2006 requires states to have programs of study which link academic and technical content. Funding associated with the Act led to renewed interest in the **States' Career Clusters Initiative** (SCCI) which is a collaboration involving state, schools, educators, employers, industry groups, and other stakeholders, originally developed in 1997. The career clusters allow students to identify pathways (of which there are currently 79) from secondary school to two- and four-year colleges, graduate school, and the workplace. The career clusters help motivate young people to achieve academically and pursue their career goals by demonstrating how they can develop a chosen career.

Two national initiatives were instrumental in the reform of public schools. In 2010, President Obama's *Race to the Top* initiative called upon educators to encourage graduates of high school to be career and college ready, regardless of socioeconomic status, race, gender, ethnicity, language background, or ability/disability status (U. S. Department of Education, 2010). This initiative offered bold incentives to states willing to implement systemic reform geared toward improving teaching and learning in America's schools. In 2014, the *Reach Higher* initiative, sponsored by Michelle Obama in conjunction with ASCA, was created to provide support for school counselors and other educators in helping students obtain postsecondary education and employment. Sampson et al. (2011)

suggested that well-organized career development programs have the potential to positively impact the following factors targeted by such initiatives:

- *Retention.* Engaging young people in school participation
- *Achievement.* Inspiring young people to achieve academic results from their schooling (e.g., receiving a high school diploma)
- *Transition.* Enabling young people to make smooth transitions to work
- *Career and Life Success.* Preparing young people to pursue successful careers

States have also answered the call by mandating, through legislation, that students have formal plans in place prior to high school graduation. Similar to individual service plans that have been developed for students with disabilities, **individualized learning plans** (ILPs) are for all students. ISPs are a long-term and comprehensive approach to education and career planning and span multiple grade levels and courses personalized to each student (Solberg, 2014). ILPs empower all students to think early and often about their postsecondary plans, continually check the alignment of their interests and skills with their college and career aspirations, and select academic and extracurricular options that support achievement of these aspirations. The National Collaborative on Workforce and Disability for Youth research indicates that efforts related to developing students' self-exploration, career search, and career planning and management skills through ISPs support the emergence of important social/emotional resiliency skills that in turn produce better academic outcomes (Solberg et al., 2014).

As of 2016, 38 states use ILPs for students and 21 of those states mandate them (U. S. Department of Labor, 2016). For example, Virginia's Academic and Career Plan was mandated by the state in 2013 and includes all students 7th–12th grade. ILPs continuously evolve to include activities and experiences that correspond to the student's progress, guiding learning through phases of self-exploration, career exploration, and career planning and management (Solberg et al., 2018). Such efforts continue to intensify and expand in the first decade of the 21st century as school professionals get students ready for college and work.

As we can see, the direction ASCA and national and state initiatives has taken regarding the promotion of college and career readiness speaks volumes about the importance of developing and delivering comprehensive career development programming in schools. Yet, there appear to be two main issues that circumvent the delivery of career interventions in high schools and that have possible implications for student readiness. First, in a study by Anctil, Smith, Schenck, and Dahir (2012), school counselors gave lower priority to career services with their students than they did academic development and personal-social development; and second, we still have little knowledge about what kind of interventions schools across the country are providing, as there is much variability. Only a few studies to date have investigated career development interventions that commonly occur in American secondary schools (e.g., Dykeman et al., 2003). School counselors need to be more engaged in career service delivery. In addition, data about specificity about interventions in secondary schools is important information for school counselors and policymakers in an era of limited resources (Dykeman et al., 2003). Research gives school counselors and other professionals in school systems concrete guidance on what career development activities can give them the most leverage in promoting student success.

Career and College Readiness

As a human service professional working with adolescents, it is important to know the definition of career and college readiness (CCR) in the context of working with students. Researchers, educators, and policy makers agree that CCR are essential components of a P-12 education (Curry & Milsom, 2017). CCR have a separate focus. Most of the literature on **college readiness** has been written about the characteristics to gain access and succeed at 4-year institutions. Conley (2007) defines college readiness in part as when a student can "understand what is expected in a college course, can cope with the content knowledge that is presented, and can take away from the course the key intellectual lessons and disposition the course was defined to convey and develop" (p. 5-6). There is a plethora of literature on college readiness and creating a college-going culture in high school. This focus on college, however, leaves out or forgets students who will enter employment or the military after graduation. Because of this, Gysbers and Lapan (2009) prefer to use the term career readiness instead of college readiness.

Students who are ready to advance in a job or succeed in training for a new job require the necessary skills to support their transition. Yet there is less distinction today than there used to be between the skills that support college and career readiness, and the career interventions school counselors must develop that expose every student to a broader, more inclusive range of postsecondary options (Erford, 2019). According to Gysbers and Lapan (2009), **career readiness** conveys a more holistic picture of resilient individuals who are active and involved in shaping and directing their lives. Career-ready students have a "proactive, resilient, and adaptive style of interacting in the present and use that style to assertively move towards self-defined career futures that add meaning, purpose, and satisfaction to their lives" (p. 23). Savickas (1997) also addressed career readiness through his concept of **career adaptability** (previously referred to as career maturity). Savickas defined career adaptability as the "readiness to cope with the predictable tasks of preparing for and participating in the work role and with the unpredictable adjustments prompted by changes in work and working conditions" (p. 254). Although the concept of career adaptability is relevant during the adolescent's school-to-work transition, it has evolved to include any time that an individual makes an occupational transition during their life span. Professional organizations and state departments of education have also been instrumental in defining and promoting career readiness.

College and career readiness are increasingly a priority for professional associations and states. Associations not only prepare definitions of CCR but provide leadership for members, public schools and government and advocates for public policy. The Association for Career and Technical Education (ACTE, 2010), which is the largest national education association in the United States for the advancement of education that prepares youth and adults for careers, defines career readiness as involving three major skill areas: core academic skills, employability skills, and technical or job-specific skills. This picks up on **Career and Technical Education** (CTE), which provides the opportunity for students during middle and high school years to complete college coursework and offer hands-on learning in the work world.

CTE programs frequently offer both academic and career-oriented courses. Many programs provide work experience through internships, job shadowing, on-the-job training, and industry-certification opportunities. Research shows that work-based learning helps students apply and extend classroom learning, gain motivation and understanding, explore careers, and develop critical understanding of the work environment (Alfeld, Charner, Johnson, & Watts, 2013). Students who see the links between what they are learning in school and career as well as work opportunities beyond high school are more likely to attend to their class work and build a positive mental image of their future (Hoyt, 2005).

Nearly all states are beginning to implement career and college ready content standards and are in the process of developing new aligned assessment systems to measure whether their students have the knowledge and critical skills they need to be ready for tomorrow's jobs. Many state departments of education have defined or are in the process of defining CCR for secondary students. For example, the **Virginia College and Career Readiness Initiative** (VDE, 2010) has articulated that the purpose of CCR is to:

- Ensure that college and career-ready learning standards in reading, writing, and mathematics are taught in every Virginia high school classroom.
- Strengthen students' preparation for college and the work force before leaving high school.

Although Virginia is in the process of defining CCR, other states have already created definitions of readiness (see Mishkind, 2014 for state definitions). For example, the Ohio Department of Education has adopted a definition of CCR (U. S. Department of Education, 2013) which is summarized below:

Ohio's college and career ready definition is to ensure all students 'Start Ready and Graduate Ready' from their PreK–12 learning environment, qualified for success in a degree or credential-granting post-secondary education program, without remediation, and advanced training for a career of choice. Student readiness for college and careers includes: content knowledge, readiness behaviors, and college and career survival skills which is the acquisition of knowledge and skills needed to navigate successfully within the world of higher education and world of work.

Over the past several years, state departments of education have begun to require local boards of education to adopt policies on career advising for their public-school districts (see Appendix C for an example of a state policy). Keep in mind that each state's system is unique, with different governance structures and policy and program priorities. Nevertheless, the task of increasing the focus of school counseling programs on CCR may prove challenging, due to the increase in testing responsibility some school counselors face, and the challenge of teachers unwilling to relinquish instructional time for school counselors to provide career interventions (Zunker, 2016).

Career Theory and Assessment for Schools

Several career development theories and career assessment tools can be successfully applied when working with adolescents. A few specific theories can benefit school counselors the most as their practical application with adolescents are well-documented in the literature. Three career theories we will revisit briefly in this section are Super's life-span, life-space theory, Holland's theory of vocational personalities and work environments, and Lent, Brown, and Hackett's social cognitive career theory (see Chapter 4 of this text for a review). Career assessment results provide professional school counselors and others with concrete self-information to help students increase self-awareness and exploration that can guide them in the career planning process. Once such programs are devised, other theories can be applied as long as they are appropriate to the age level.

Career Theories

Super's Life-Span, Life-Space. Perhaps the most important approach in this context is the use of a developmental theory such as that of Super's Life-Span, Life-Space approach. Super's theory helps the school counselor devise career programs that are appropriate to children's age levels (Neukrug, 2012). Super's approach considers career counselling and development an ongoing process that begins in early childhood but encompasses and permeates the entire lifespan. Theorists and practitioners alike agree that career counseling-related processes and activities commence in childhood (Hartung, 2013).

Adolescents require a certain degree of career maturity, also referred to as career adaptability. The essence of the developmental perspective for high school youth is that "youth cope better with the STW [school-to-work] transition if they have developed the awareness of the choices to be made and of the information and planning that bear on these choices" (Savickas, 1999, p. 326-327). Career maturity or adaptability refer to the cognitive competencies evident in students who are planful, future-oriented, and involved. As you may remember from Chapter 4, Super (1990) emphasized that students are in the career exploration stage of career development, which highlights planning and exploring as well as developing cognitive competencies and behavioral skills. As such, students who are career adaptable develop greater job-seeking readiness and adjust more quickly to the world-of-work. A few examples of activities will be presented in the next section of this chapter.

Holland's Theory. The theory of vocational personalities and work environments by Holland can be applied beginning in middle school as students begin to examine who they are and which talents they possess. As discussed in Chapter 4, the underlying assumption of person-environment (trait-and-factor) career theories is that individuals seek out environments that are congruent with their characteristics. Holland's theory is based on personality styles through which one can categorize people and occupations. In Holland's (1997) terms, people "search for environments that will let them exercise their skills and abilities, express their attitudes and values, and take on agreeable problems and roles" (p. 4). Many assessment tools based on trait-and factor or person-environment model have been developed for schools to use. A simple and inexpensive approach to helping students understand how the person-environment model by Holland works can be learned through playing the **Party Game** created by Richard Bolles (2018) (see resource section at the end of this chapter).

According to person-environment career theorist, fit needs to be fully recognized for youth transitioning from school to work. Although this is critical for work-bound youth, it can be applied to college-bound youth as well. Traditionally, schools have focused on the environment or on helping students develop skills required by employers, rather than on the person's side (Swanson & Fouad, 1999). As Swanson & Fouad suggest, it is important for students to understand that, although improving their abilities may help them secure a job, understanding the rewards provided by a work environment will help them stay in a job. Thus, introducing person-environment career theories into career and college readiness interventions can help student make sense of their own interests, abilities, and values and improve the quality of decisions they make.

Social-Cognitive Career Theory. SCCT (Lent, Hackett, & Brown, 1996) is closely related to Krumboltz's learning theory of career counseling. It focuses more on how cognitive factors guide students career decisions rather than their interests. How students' think about and make meaning of the world is important to high school students as they begin to examine the realities of work or college and to look at how they may fit in. Based in Bandura's (1977) social learning theory, SSCT emphasizes the interplay between three key variables: self-efficacy, outcome expectations, and goals. Because this theory is comprehensive in scope, we will focus on self-efficacy that lend itself to practical application in the schools.

The confidence one has in their ability to successfully perform a given task or set of tasks is referred to as **self-efficacy**. What people accomplish depends, in part, on how they interpret and apply their abilities (Bandura, 1986). These beliefs about personal capabilities are responsive to environmental conditions (e.g., How supportive is the art teacher? How tough is the basketball competition?). There are four primary sources of self-efficacy: (a) performance accomplishments, (b) vicarious experiences, (c) verbal persuasion, and (d)

183

emotional arousal. The most robust source of self-efficacy is performance accomplishments. That is, successful performance enhances self-efficacy beliefs. For example, if a student does well in biology, it will influence his or her confidence and expectations of success for taking more biology classes in the future. These will in turn lead to the student creating personal performance goals. This process is the same when making a career choice. Over time, a student's career self-efficacy beliefs about their performance accomplishments can make certain career choice paths attractive and viable and render other options less appealing (Lent, 2013). Students will likely encounter problems when they either don't possess sufficient ability to succeed at a given task or when they greatly misconstrue their self-efficacy (Lent, Brown, & Hackett, 2002).

Career self-efficacy is also influenced by social persuasion and vicarious learning or modeling. These things can influence career self-efficacy and thus an individual's career interests and choices. Social persuasion is facilitated through encouragement or positive feedback. In vicarious learning, if a student watches the performance behaviors of others such as an adult-role model, and the consequence for that role-model's behavior is positive, then the experience will create the expectation that the student will succeed if they persist in their behaviors.

In later grades, self-efficacy is related to a person's past performance/abilities, such that overconfidence and underconfidence in one's actual abilities can be detrimental to performance attainment. Bandura (1986) postulates that self-efficacy beliefs determine the amount of effort a person will expend, how long he or she will persist in a given activity in the face of obstacles, as well as one's ultimate performance. Overconfident students may set unrealistic or unattainable goals, often resulting in disappointment and frustration because they did not possess the requisite skills or knowledge to be successful. Underconfident students tend to exert less effort, give up more quickly, and set minimally challenging goals for themselves (Lent, Brown, & Hackett, 1994). The anxiety that many of these students' experiences before engaging in tasks can prevent them from achieving success. If a student is not very motivated to explore careers, then a school counselor could develop interventions to explore those issues or challenge faulty thinking. Interventions designed to promote educational/vocational and life outcomes must create learning experiences that build self-confidence or efficacy beliefs (Solberg, Howard, Blustein, & Close, 2002).

Career Assessment

It is through formal and informal assessments that students begin to learn about themselves and their interests, skills, and values related to the world of work. Results from career assessments provide professional school counselors and others with a starting point for guiding students in the career planning process. School counselors must remain current in their knowledge about which career assessments are suitable for use with school-aged youth. A variety of formal assessments appropriate for use with students in grades 9-12 include:

- Kuder Career Interests Assessment; Kuder Skills Confidence Assessment; Kuder Work Values Assessment
- Super's Work Values Inventory
- Self-Directed Search
- Strong Interest Inventory
- O*NET Interest Profiler; O*NET Ability Profiler; O*NET Work Importance Locator
- CAPS (Abilities); COPES (Values); COPS (Interests)

School counselors typically use classroom lessons and small group activities to present relevant career information and administer career assessments. Lessons and group activities are typically incorporated into the school's online career exploration programs. Popular online career exploration programs include Bridges, Career Cruising, and Naviance. Free online career exploration programs are available through College Board, and some state departments of education (see resource section at the end of this chapter).

Developmental Concerns and Career Readiness

Many adolescents' understandings about themselves, the careers that are available to them, and the nature of different jobs are formed during their high school years. These years are filled with many developmental transitions in the social, physical, emotional, cognitive, and educational areas of life and are interrelated with and greatly influence career and college readiness. A key turning point in one's self-understanding involves identity development. Identity in early to late adolescence is particularly important because it influences other areas of development such as career readiness (Skorikov & Vondracek, 1998). For example, as adolescents advance in their identity development, they tend to have positive attitudes and an openness to a variety of occupations. Also, the quality of one's identity development is related to a greater sense of self-efficacy in decision-making and a clearer understanding of personal interests (Nauta & Kahn, 2007). Because vocational identity evolves in both an educational context and a broader social context (Vondracek & Skorikov, 2007), we will focus on some of the basic developmental issues involving identity and self-efficacy and present some approaches for helping adolescents become college and career ready throughout 9th to 12th grade.

9th Grade Career Readiness

Developmental transitions are a regular part of students' development. The ninth-grade transition is a critical time for a student's future outcomes. By the eighth grade, a student's academic skills and coursework should be on target, or they run the risk of being left behind with limited postsecondary options (Arrington, 2000). The U. S. Department of Education (1997) suggest that career guidance efforts have a significant impact on students during middle school. As Niles and Harris-Bowlsbey (2017) asserted, "the transition to high school offers opportunities for actively engaging students in career development interventions that can strengthen their academic motivation, bolster their self-esteem, and help them to make connections between their school experiences and their future academic and career opportunities" (p. 326). Thus, attention to the unique needs of ninth-grade students is paramount to helping them adjust to the increasing academic demands of high school (McCallumore & Sparapani, 2010). Facilitating the successful transition to ninth grade often begins with specific instruction in **self-regulatory skills** such as effective study habits, goal-setting, and time management (Curry & Milsom, 2017). School professionals also help students in this grade explore self and careers so that they can continue to narrow down their choices throughout their high school experience.

To prompt exploration and planning, career theorists recommend that school counselors and teachers offer students "anticipatory guidance" to foster planning attitudes, competencies, and activities. According to Savickas (1999), one of the many effective orientation techniques is to discuss with students the items on the *Career Maturity Inventory-Form C* (CMI; Crites & Savickas, 2011) rather than use it as an assessment device (see resource section at the end of this chapter). Teaching the CMI concentrates on fostering career adaptability (career maturity) or the cognitive competencies and behavioral skills that student may use to develop work choice and work adjustment competencies. An example of such activity deals with how "Work is Different from School." This lesson seeks to orient students to the world-of-work by familiarizing student with ten distinctions between school and work. The distinctions are found in the

Appendix D of this text and can be used by school counselors, teachers, and career professionals with students in grades 9-10 in groups or individually (Savickas & Crites, 1981).

10th Grade Career Readiness

Tenth grade is a time when school professionals help students to examine the intrapersonal and interpersonal factors that affect their academic and career choices. These factors involve developing a healthy sense of identity (intrapersonal) and exploring the world-of-work environment (interpersonal). These students are similar to ninth graders as they may still struggle to develop an identity through their relationship with their peers. School professionals cannot assume that career plans developed in tenth grade will remain stable throughout high school years. Nevertheless, career strategies are provided to help student to think more concretely about career and college planning activities (Curry & Milsom, 2017). By the end of tenth grade, students should start preparing for their future careers and postsecondary educational choices, which means narrowing down their choices and engaging in activities that will help them move forward.

Tenth grade is also a good time to identify students with low career-self efficacy. Self-efficacy is relevant for mid-adolescents because it influences an individual's intentions or goals; students may limit career and college possibilities based on what they think they can or cannot do (Lent et al., 1994). This is important until graduation. Students who show a decreased commitment to academics or have adequate abilities but low confidence in their abilities in a performance context display low career self-efficacy. As discussed previously, self-efficacy is increased through various ways including vicarious learning such as exposure to role models. For this reason, connecting students with career-role models based on similar cultures is important for school professionals to provide mentoring opportunities (Curry & Milsom, 2017).

Role models and mentors are important relationships to facilitate for students during tenth grade. In addition, students are most influenced by individuals with whom they feel a connection based on some salient characteristics (Bandura, 1977). Role models are often created when both parties having similar cultural attributes, but sometimes students connect with certain people of other cultures for various reasons such as those individuals being athletes or television personalities. School professionals can partner with various organizations and groups in their local community to recruit adult mentors or successful alumni to speak to student groups or pair with specific students.

11th Grade Career Readiness

Eleventh grade is a time when most students start to acknowledge that high school graduation is around the corner. Students grow increasingly aware of the relationship between educational achievement and career planning as the need to choose postsecondary options becomes more immediate. Students start to shift their thinking and take school more seriously. They may worry about being involved in enough activities to boost their college applications and become more willing to engage in activities to prepare them for their future in work, college, or the military. Students who are still undecided about their future may start to feel pressured from peers and parents to make a choice and other may be unmotivated and withdrawn.

According to Erikson (1968), starting at around age 13 and continuing into the early 20s, adolescents are entering the stage of **identity versus role confusion**. While some students develop a healthy sense of identity, many will struggle. Finding a meaningful sense of career direction is what most challenges young people who are struggling to form a clear sense of identity. Adolescents grapple with questions such as "Who am I, and where am I going in life?" Many things go into identity formation, including a sense of awareness about one's interest, strengths, weakness, and beliefs.

Although identity development begins in early adolescence, it becomes increasingly intense and important for school counselors to be cognizant of during eleventh grade. Since Erikson developed his theory about adolescent identity versus role confusion, researchers such as Marcia (1987) elaborated that adolescents cope with their identity development in a variety of ways. His popular model was originally developed to be used with late adolescents. Marcia developed a taxonomy that comprises four **identity statuses**: achieved, moratorium, foreclosed, and diffused (see Figure 11.1). The presence or absence of a sense of commitment (to life goals and values) and exploration (active questioning and exploration) combine to produce four possible identity statuses. During this time, an adolescent explores and commits to various domains such as career, family, religion, and politics. As depicted in the figure, the degree to which an adolescent resolves the tasks associated with exploration and commitment determines one of the four identity statuses (Marcia, 1987):

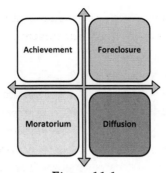

Figure 11.1
Marcia's Four Identity Statuses

- *Achievement.* Exploration and commitment present. Successful achievement of a sense of identity.
- *Moratorium.* Exploration present, and commitment absent. Active struggling for a sense of identity.
- *Foreclosure.* Exploration absent, and commitment present. Unquestioning adoption of parental, peer, or societal values.
- *Diffusion.* Exploration present, and commitment absent. Absence of struggle for identity with no obvious concern about it.

Being aware of the impact of identity development on the career development of adolescents is important during the last two years of high school. This provides professionals an opportunity to be aware of those students who may benefit from activities to facilitate healthy development. It is important to note that identity statuses are not fixed but may change to a different status for some adolescents over time as they struggle with their identity formation. Also, an adolescent can have characteristics of an identity status in one domain, and characteristics of another identity status in a different domain.

Identity moratorium often characterize students who are actively exploring but have not committed to a role. This is ideal for middle school through ninth grade as students are keeping their career options open through exploratory activities, but for some late adolescents exploring without a commitment can continue into early adulthood during the early college years. In a study by Skorikov and Vondracek (1998), there was a higher percentage of identity moratorium and achieved adolescents within the career domain than in any other domain. Moratorium is not necessarily unhealthy, as some adolescents need time to gain a healthy sense of identity and find a sense of belonging. However, it can be a difficult time for students and their families as adolescents may begin to differentiate from views and beliefs of their families, which may cause strain on the family system (Bowen, 1976).

Identity foreclosed often characterize students who are committed to an identity role but did so with minimal or no exploration. It is not uncommon for students during this time to follow career options their peers are pursuing. Also, some students may adopt the values and goals of their parents or communities, and in some cases, this can be considered a culturally chosen identity status. Entering the family business without considering whether it fits one's interests or values is an example of foreclosure.

Identity diffuse often characterize students who are without a plan or are resistant to or ambivalent about participating in career or college readiness activities. Such students are often not worried about receiving low grades (Curry & Milsom, 2017). They are usually unmotivated and withdrawn. Identity diffusion is also related to depression and at-risk behavior in adolescents. During this time, Curry and Milsom suggest that school professionals provide encouragement to students to be proactive and intentional in identifying their strengths.

Recognizing the impact of identity development on career development during adolescence is important for school professionals to know; interventions and activities can be provided to facilitate this process. During eleventh grade, school professionals should select activities that focus on helping students take concrete steps toward pursuing their plans. Because factors encompassing vocational personality are evident in the activities in which people engage, school professionals can help students identify strengths through their activities and hobbies. Work and extracurricular experiences help high school students increase their understanding of the need for positive attitudes toward work and learning and developing more sophisticated interpersonal skills. For example, work-based learning activities and technical training in career and technical education programs can help students evaluate their self-characteristics within an occupational context and understand how academic knowledge is applied to workplace settings. Community resources that expose students to a variety of career options, such as local employment administrators, local university admission officers, community members, recent graduates, job shadowing, summer enrichment programs, and informational interviews, can have an impact on student identity and career development.

12th Grade Career Readiness

Developing readiness for the transition to college or work is an important focus of career development intervention in high school. Although many students during the twelfth grade can articulate their interests and abilities and identify future career and postsecondary educational goals, some are still uncertain about who they are and who they want to become, or are avoidant with regards to decision making. According to Niles and Harris-Bowlsbey (2017), "many students default to enrolling in college while possessing no clear goal and, often, lacking in the academic readiness to succeed" (p. 327). For these adolescents, the importance of peers and the experimentation with various roles continues. As they move closer to completion, a sense of urgency to plan can set in.

Some students may make plans in haste, based on pressure from peers, partners, or family, and others may avoid making decisions altogether, due to apprehension and anxiety. These students experience **indecision,** usually enacted as confusion, procrastination, or impulsivity and lack a sense of control or responsibility over their career futures. Savickas (2013) states, "control involves interpersonal self-discipline and the processes of being conscientious, deliberate, organized, and decisive in performing vocational developmental tasks and making occupational transitions" (p. 160). Helping students by allowing them to have a familiar face or support system present can make decision-making less intimidating. The confusion that many high-school seniors experience related to their identities, exerting their independence, considering making plans with their romantic partners in mind, and going to college, work, or the military suggests that interventions should be designed to help them, and their parents, navigate this transition to life after high school (Curry & Milsom, 2017).

School professionals can help student gain a sense of control over their futures. During this time, a focus on clarifying and prioritizing values by administering values inventories can help students narrow down college choices and motivate them (Curry & Milsom, 2017). For example, English teachers can infuse future planning by having students write an autobiography that would reflect their life at age 25 or 30. They can discuss what they will be doing, how they got there, what their strengths are, and other accomplishments along the way. In addition, encouraging college curiosity through clarifying the differences between 2- and 4-year colleges, visiting colleges virtually or in person, talking to a recruiter, involving peers in the process for sharing information about colleges, and attending college fairs can all be helpful. For students not going to college, they will need assistance in developing career-related skills such as resume-writing, drafting cover letters, developing interview skills, networking, and approaching the job search process (as discussed in Chapter 7 of this text).

Schools are an important place for individuals to start exploring different career opportunities. To ensure students future career success, schools must offer diverse curricula and educational options. Having a diverse curriculum and educational opportunities allow students to have wide-ranging opportunities to develop skills and competencies for the world of work (Curry, 2017).

Conclusion

This chapter focused on career and college readiness for grades 9 through 12. We began with the role of the school counselor in helping students develop relevant skills and knowledge. A brief overview of the history of career and college readiness in schools was presented, along with prominent initiatives that currently impact career and college readiness for students. Next, we distinguished between college and career readiness and looked at several career theories and assessment tools relevant for use with a high school population. Last, developmental issues involving identity and self-efficacy as well as approaches for helping adolescents become college and career ready were discussed.

Key Chapter Terms

School Counselors' Role Statement	Career Adaptability
School to Work Opportunities Act	Career and Technical Education
ASCA National Model	Virginia College & Career Initiative
ASCA Career Standards	Party Game
Mindsets & Behaviors for Success	Self-Efficacy
States' Career Clusters Initiative	Self-Regulatory Skills
Individualized Learning Plans	Identity versus Role Confusion
College Readiness	Identity Statuses
Career Readiness	Indecision

Web Resources
Note that website URLs may change over time.

ASCA
ASCA Mindsets and Behaviors: Program and Planning Tool
https://www.schoolcounselor.org/asca/media/asca/ASCA%20National%20M
odel%20Templates/M-BProgramPlanningTool.pdf

ASCA National Model: A Framework for School Counseling Programs.
https://www.schoolcounselor.org/asca/media/asca/ASCA%20National%20M
odel%20Templates/ANMExecSumm.pdf

Guidance Counselors or School Counselors: How the Name of the Profession
Influences Perceptions of Competence
https://www.schoolcounselor.org/asca/media/asca/Careers-
Roles/ResearchReport-Zyromski.pdf

Career and Technical Education
Association for Career & Technical Education
https://www.acteonline.org/

CTE Today - Overview of CTE
https://www.acteonline.org/wp-content/uploads/2018/03/CTE_Today_Fact-
Sheet_January2018.pdf

CTE: Readiness for all Careers
https://www.acteonline.org/wp-
content/uploads/2018/05/ReadinessForAllCareers-FactSheet.pdf

Virginia Department of Education & Career Development
Virginia's Career View - Career Information Delivery System for Grades K-8
https://www.vaview.org/

National Career Readiness Initiatives
Race to the Top
https://obamawhitehouse.archives.gov/issues/education/k-12/race-to-the-top

Reach Higher
https://obamawhitehouse.archives.gov/reach-higher

School Online Career Programs
Bridges
https://www.xap.com

Career Cruising
https://public.careercruising.com/en

Naviance
https://www.naviance.com

College Board
https://bigfuture.collegeboard.org/?navId=www-cp

Webinars
2015 ASCA: Academic Habits and College and Career Readiness
https://www.youtube.com/watch?v=5gK00Z7NWPU

2016 ASCA: Youth Apprenticeship: A Work-Based Learning Opportunity
https://www.youtube.com/watch?v=UnNnAgIVdGY&feature=youtu.be

2017 ASCA: Career Conversations to Promote Academic Career Development
https://www.youtube.com/watch?v=lFpPrkEvSw4&feature=youtu.be

Videos
Life After High School: How School Counselors Assist Students with Career
and College Planning
http://bit.ly/qHqqLY

Career Games
Party Game – by Richard Bolles Based on Holland's Theory
https://career.berkeley.edu/sites/default/files/pdf/Plan/PartyGame2.pdf

Facilitator's Guide to Party Game
https://www.wright.edu/sites/www.wright.edu/files/page/attachments/careers
ervices-hollandparty-facilitator-guide_0.pdf

Lost in Islands Exercise
https://www.utoledo.edu/success/career/pdfs/Holland_Lost-
RIASECIslandsExercise.doc

Career Theory, Development, and Appraisal

Career Instruments
Career Maturity Inventory-Form C
http://www.vocopher.com/ms/cmic/cmi_c_master.pdf

Student Career Construction Interview
http://www.vocopher.com/ms/scci/SCCI_Master.pdf

Career Clusters Activity
http://www.educationplanner.org/students/career-planning/find-careers/career-clusters.shtml

Career Clusters Interest Survey
https://careertech.org/student-interest-survey

Chapter 12

ETHICAL ISSUES IN CAREER SERVICES

"...it's tricky to figure out whether it's better to learn on the job while being supervised, or to refer the client to another helper. It might take a bit of reflection and a wise decision in these circumstances."
~Edward S. Neukrug, 2017, p. 252

CHAPTER HIGHLIGHTS
The Need for Ethical Codes
Ethical Dimensions in Providing Career Services
Knowing Your Ethical Values
Models for Solving Ethical Dilemmas
NOHS Ethical Standards & Using Multiple Codes
Ethical Considerations in Career Testing & Assessment
Ethics in Internet-Based Career Services

Pamela is a young professional working in a college academic advising center. She recently graduated with a bachelor's degree in human services and has now been working for several months as an academic advisor assisting students. Pamela is an avid social media user with active profiles on several platforms. One Sunday morning while enjoying a cup of coffee and scrolling through her Facebook news feed, Pamela comes across a picture of some friends attending a pool party the previous evening. She "likes" the picture and comments "Looks like you had a wild time! Wish I was there..." As Pamela takes a closer look at the picture, she notices one of the people is a current student of hers named James. Pamela is concerned because James will likely get an automatic notification that she, his advisor, commented and "liked" the photo. Pamela starts to panic—will he now be able to see her account and her personal posts? If so, how would she respond? Pamela wonders if she should inform her supervisor or if she should just lay low and hope it blows over.

Human service professionals may encounter situations like the above vignette that require a process of ethical decision-making. Most people will find themselves caught at one time or another in a struggle between their moral codes and their emotional desires or feelings, and these difficult situations can often lead to a breaking down of moral behavior (Martin & Stoner, 1996). Moreover, we may use our emotions to justify our unethical behavior during these conflicts. A person's ethical codes keeps them on a good moral track, and although there are certainly times when people will be driven by passion or will need to follow their hunches, in a professional role emotions and desires serve people best when they don't lead the decision-making process. Thus, helpers need to be knowledgeable about the ethical standards of their profession and competent in applying soundly ethical decision-making skills.

In this chapter, we provide working definitions of some typical terms human service professionals will encounter wrestling with the topic of ethics. We then discuss the need for codes of ethics and present some typical ethical conflicts that human service professionals may come across when providing career interventions. Because knowing your own values is a starting point for providing career services, we also present some strategies for practitioner self-awareness. Next, we briefly discuss three models of ethical decision-making and provide a process for determining if professional duties are within one's scope of practice. Presented are challenges in and approaches to ethical decision-making when referring to multiple codes of ethics and professional standards. This chapter concludes with ethical considerations in testing and assessment, and some ethical guidelines in providing internet-based career services.

Human service professionals must have a clear understanding of ethical language. The following provides working definitions of some typical terms encountered when discussing the topic of ethics:

- *Ethics.* **Ethics** refer to a set of standards or rules of right and wrong that prescribe what individuals ought to do, usually in terms of rights, obligations, benefits to society, fairness, or specific virtues. Ethics also refers to the explicit philosophical study of moral values and rules and to the development of one's ethical standards.

- *Ethical.* To be **ethical** means to follow the dictates of a set of standards that a particular group has determined to be ethically right.
- *Ethical Standards.* **Ethical standards** are sets of principles or codes of conduct that guide individuals or groups through ethical or professional decision-making (National Organization for Human Services, 2015). Standards provide guidelines of expected conduct, encourage excellence in practice, guide professional in decision-making, and promote public understanding and confidence in the profession.
- *Laws.* **Laws** are rules and principles of conduct that have been derived from court decision, approved by government, and established by local customs. Legal rules and ethical standards are generally complimentary, but they serve different purposes.
- *Moral.* **Moral** is related to the principles of right or wrong as they apply to an individual's behavior. A person can have a moral code that can be based on ethical standards or not.
- *Professional Standards.* **Professional standards** documents are often regarded as prescribing minimal behavioral requirements that professional are expected to follow in a given field. They are guidelines for the actions necessary to provide appropriate service to clients.

The aforementioned terms do not cover the span of ethical language but provides a foundation for the development of knowledge and skills relevant to ethical-decision making for the human service professional. Keep these terms in mind as we discuss ethical dimensions in providing career services.

The Need for Ethical Codes

The establishment of ethical guidelines in the helping professions began during the midpoint of the twentieth century. In 1953, the American Psychological Association (APA) published its code of ethics. Not long after, in 1960, the National Association of Social Workers (NASW) adopted its code, and in 1961, the American Counseling Association (ACA) developed its ethical code. Because ethical standards are to some degree a mirror of change in society, the associations' guidelines have undergone a number of major revisions over the years to reflect society's ever-changing values (see ACA, 2014; APA, 2003; NASW, 2008).

In general, a **code of ethics** is a set of guidelines developed for professions that help guide the behavior of practitioners. It sets boundaries, defines values, and provides expectations for professional conduct. Human service professionals have a main code of ethics developed by the National Organization for Human Services (2015). There are also two other organizations for career services providers that maintain a code of ethics: The National Career Development Association (2015a) and the Center for Credentialing and Education (2015). Jordan and Marinaccio (2017) state that most codes of ethics in the helping professions serve five main purposes:

1. Enables the organization to clarify to current and future members, and to those served by their members, the nature of ethical responsibilities held in common by its members.
2. Helps support the mission of the organization.
3. Establishes principles that define ethical behaviors and practices of association members.
4. Serves as an ethical guide designed to assist members in constructing a professional course of action that best serves those providing career services and promotes that values of the profession.
5. Serves as a guide for those receiving career services so that they may understand what to expect from working with a professional and their rights and responsibilities as consumers of career services.

Although ethical codes can be of considerable assistance in a professional's ethical decision-making process, there are limitations to the use of such a code. Several limitations are noted below (Corey, Corey, & Callanan, 2011; Dolgoff, Loewenberg, & Harrington, 2009; Remley & Herlihy, 2010):

- Codes don't address some dilemmas and offer no clear guidelines for how to handle those issues.
- There can be conflicts within the same code, between the code and the law, and between the code and a counselor's value system.
- It can be difficult to enforce ethical violations in the codes.
- The public is often not involved in the code development process, and public interests are not always taken into consideration.
- Codes do not always address the latest issues.

It is not possible for an ethical code or standard to provide an unambiguous answer to every potential ethical question (Niles & Harris-Bowlsbey, 2017). For example, in some cases, ethical codes or standards may be in conflict with laws. If resolution can't be achieved, professionals must adhere to the requirements of all applicable federal, state, local, and/or institutional laws, regulations, and procedures. There will also be occasions when human service professionals providing career services will need to consult a trusted professional colleague or supervisor to provide an assessment of the proper action in response to an ethical dilemma.

Ethical Dimensions in Providing Career Services

The following ethical challenges, adapted from Spokane (1991), shed light on some typical ethical conflicts that human service professionals may face when delivering career interventions.

- *Pressure to See as Many Clients as Possible.* Because of budget cuts, streamlining of services, and other circumstances, practitioners may face extreme pressure from their agencies and supervisors to serve large numbers of clients. Although professionals must often respond appropriately to agency needs, the client's needs should determine the length and intensity of the career services provided.

- *Indiscriminate Testing.* Human service professionals may use assessments inappropriately. This may be due to a lack of training for the helper, client anticipation to find out answers to problems, and/or insufficient conceptualization of the client's issues or career service area identified. In addition, to identifying the proper tool, the practitioner should provide the client with a list of options for testing procedures and the cost, if any.

- *Informational Interviews.* Sometimes human service professionals will set up informational interviews or job shadowing experiences with businesses or contacts. In this case, practitioners should obtain a written release from their client prior to discussing the client with any third party.

- *Exaggerated Claims of Effectiveness.* Although many career interventions result in positive outcomes for clients, some may have negative results or results that are less than hoped for. Human service professionals should not guarantee positive outcomes such as "this inventory will find you the perfect job!" They should balance the objective information from outcome research regarding the intervention's effectiveness with the client's motivation for career services and personal change.

- *Client Follow-Up.* When clients miss one or more sessions without notifying the helping professional, reasonable follow-up contact with the client should take place. Missing appointments may be a sign of an obstacle that is impeding the success of the interventions. Practitioners should contact the client directly and invite them to discuss the situation and to problem solve as needed.

- *Note-Taking and Record-Keeping.* Human service professionals should write brief post session notes and retain copies of all the client's assessment results, interpretations, correspondence, and reports. Notes should be saved and eventually archived for the period of time required by professional licensing laws and/or organizational policies. In addition, because records may be subpoenaed by the courts, practitioners should ensure that all notes and written communications are professional and abide by the ethical standards of the profession.

- *Referral.* Human service professionals should only provide career services within their scope of practice (i.e., training, knowledge, and competence). When they are faced with clients and situations for which they do not possess the necessary skills, knowledge, or competence, practitioners should refer clients to professionals who can meet their needs, and they should have available a list of such professionals for these clients.

- *Setting Fees.* Some career services typically billed include career and organizational consultation, testing and scoring, on-site counseling, program evaluation, manuscript evaluation, supervision for interns or for trainees, videotaped mock interviews, resume and cover letter preparation, report writing, expert testimony, and others. A common complaint regarding setting fees is the practice of charging excessive fees for career services. We suggest that career service providers consider setting fees that are within the range of those fees charged by human services colleagues and other career professionals within the community.

- *Third-Party Reimbursement.* Some helping professionals may be licensed counselors, social workers, or psychologists who are eligible for reimbursement from third-party insurers. Although career services are not reimbursable, some counseling and psychotherapy with a career focus may be if the level of intrapersonal distress, depression, or anxiety calls for an integrated approach to career intervention.

Human service professionals are likely to encounter a number of ethical and legal issues during their work. To avoid unethical practice in career interventions, helpers must be sensitive to the assumptions underlying their personal values, their client's values, the career interventions model, and the values being disseminated at the national level (Niles & Harris-Bowlsbey, 2017).

Knowing Your Ethical Values

Almost every aspect of human behavior is influenced by your personal values. As such, a discussion of ethics and ethical decision-making would not be complete without considering the influence of our own personal values. Value assumptions underlie all questions related to ethical behavior in career development interventions (Niles & Harris-Bowlsbey, 2017). When values pertain to the attitudes and beliefs concerning what is right or wrong in a helping relationship, they may be referred to as **ethical values**. Bergin (1985) suggests, "values are orienting beliefs about what is good for the clients and how that good should be achieved" (p. 99). Thus, ethical values influence an individual's behavior and decision-making process in regard to what is right and wrong. According to Niles and Harris-Bowlsbey (2017), the need for helping professionals to clearly understand their own values is a starting point for providing career services and is an ethical issue within career services.

Human service professionals should be aware of how their personal values influence their work with clients. When you take time to clarify and define your values, you can make ethical decisions with more confidence. Tjeltveit (1986, pp. 515-537) suggests several strategies for minimizing the likelihood of counselors behaving in ways that are insensitive to clients' values. These strategies for **ethical-values awareness** help you become cognizant of your values and can be a useful exercise by entry-level human service professionals:

1. Become informed about the variety of values held in society
2. Be aware of your own values
3. Present value options to client in an unbiased manner
4. Be committed to clients' freedom of choice
5. Respect clients with values that differ from your own
6. Consult with others when necessary
7. Consider referring clients to another helping professional when substantial moral, religious, or political value differences exist

Being aware of your ethical values help you develop **ethical sensitivity**. Welfel and Kitchener (1992) noted that the first step in ethical action, "interpreting the situation as a moral one, involves the recognition that one's actions affect the welfare of another" (p. 179). Rest (1984) discussed ethical sensitivity:

> a person realizes that she/he could do something which would affect the interests, welfare, or expectations of other people. (Realizing that one's actions might be violating some moral norm or principle is one of the ways that a person might realize his/her actions affects the interests, welfare, or expectations of others). (p. 21)

To help increase your awareness of your own values (Strategy 2), you can self-administer the free *Personal Values Assessment* available via the resource section at the end of this chapter. It is vital that human service professionals engage in professional reflection about their own values and how those values affect their work with clients.

Models for Solving Ethical Dilemmas

When professionals are faced with ethical dilemmas that are difficult to resolve, they should engage in a carefully considered ethical decision-making process. While there is no single ethical decision-making model that is most effective, human service professionals are expected to be familiar with a credible model of decision-making. In search of a more flexible and comprehensive approach to resolving ethical dilemmas, models of decision-making have been devised in the helping professions. These models can be theoretical/philosophical, practice-based, and/or related to special populations and issues. Although there have been several ethical decision-making models developed by prominent scholars (see Cottone & Claus, 2000 for a review), we will focus on and briefly discuss three specific models: Problem-solving model, principle-based model, and a relational view of ethical decision-making.

Problem-Solving Model to Resolve Ethical Dilemmas

Scholars have developed models to aid helping professionals think purposefully and systematically about ethical dilemmas. **Problem-solving ethics models** are practice-based and particularly helpful for beginning helping professionals. We briefly present the problem-solving model developed by Welfel (2015) which provides the helper with a 10-step practical approach to ethical decision-making. Welfel stressed that the helping professional gathers information and consults with others regarding the dilemma but must deliberate alone before making an informed decision. The problem-solving **model for ethical decision-making** is presented in Table 12.1.

Table 12.1	
Model for Ethical Decision-Making	
1.	Develop ethical sensitivity
2.	Clarify facts, stakeholders, and the sociocultural context of the case
3.	Define the central issues and available options
4.	Refer to professional standards and relevant laws/regulations
5.	Search out ethics scholarship
6.	Apply ethical principles to the situation
7.	Consult with supervisors and respected colleagues
8.	Deliberate and decide
9.	Inform supervisor, and document decision-making process and actions
10.	Reflect on the experience

Using Principles to Resolve Ethical Dilemmas

There are also moral models to guide the decision-making process. **Moral models** are based on moral principles and include principle ethics models. Ethical principles can provide a more solid framework for decision-making than ethical codes (VanHoose, 1986). The principle ethics model proposed by Kitchener (1986) revolves around six **principles of ethical decision-making** (Table 12.2). Kitchener suggests that the following six principles provide the primary rationale for the context of codes of ethics in helping professions: *autonomy, beneficence, fidelity, justice, nonmaleficence,* and *veracity.*

Table 12.2	
Foundational Ethical Principles	
Autonomy	Protecting the independence, self-determination, and freedom of choice of clients
Beneficence	Actively doing good for society; promoting positive growth
Fidelity	Maintaining trust; keeping confidentiality and being committed to the client
Justice	Providing equal and fair treatment to all clients
Nonmaleficence	Doing no harm; avoiding actions that put clients at risk
Veracity	Ensuring truthfulness, honesty, and transparency in the context of helping relationship

It is important to distinguish between the ethical codes of a profession and the moral principles model. Primarily, ethical codes inform professional as to *what* behaviors are ethical or unethical; ethical principles explain *why* behaviors have been so labeled (Welfel, 2015). In applying ethical principles, Forester-Miller and Davis (1996) suggested, "Decide which principles apply to the specific situation, and determine which principle takes priority for you in this case" (p. 3). When questions arise pertaining to proper practice, these principles can be used to help guide the human services practitioner identify appropriate actions. An additional self-test can be used if you find lingering feelings of doubt, discomfort, or uncertainty after resolving an ethical dilemma. These feelings may signal compromises made along the way that led to compromised ethical outcomes for the situation (Makela & Perlus, 2017). If these feelings remain, take time to reflect and seek appropriate consultation with supervisors or a respected colleague. Use this opportunity to better prepare for future encounters.

A Relational View of Ethical Decision-Making

An in-depth discussion of postmodern ethics is beyond the scope of this chapter, but we will briefly describe the **relational view of ethical decision-making**. This framework is based in a postmodern view, or more specifically, social constructionism (Cottone, 2001; Guterman & Rudes, 2008). Because social constructionism recognizes that knowledge is social, intersubjective, and language-based, viewing ethical dilemmas in a traditional way can be problematic and often results in using language that is embedded in one's culture and society but is not helpful for specific dilemma. Practitioners operating from a traditional perspective tend to seek a single, correct interpretation of any given ethics code, whereas practitioners who adhere to a postmodern perspective tend to see information in ethics codes as intersubjective, changeable, and open to interpretation (Guterman & Rudes, 2008). One must review and be aware of potential cultural and generational differences relating to the dilemma. A behavior or practice that could be completely ethical in one setting could be discriminatory in another setting. Thus, a human service practitioner operating from a postmodern stance would take context, meaning, and relationship into consideration when making ethical decisions.

Scholars who embrace a postmodern perspective believe there is a need for an ethical decision-making process—but from a relational viewpoint. Essentially, this kind of ethical decision-making takes a relational view of reality rather than placing responsibility on the individual decision-maker (Cottone, 2001). Although fully aware of ethical guidelines, postmodern practitioners rely on ethical decision-making through a process of dialogue between practitioner and client (and supervisors and others in the client's world). Guterman and Rudes (2008) suggested that "a code of ethics not be considered a fixed text but, rather, a fluid and socially constructed document" (p. 143).

Role Boundaries Analysis in Ethical Decision-Making

When examining the issues involved in ethical decision-making, it can be helpful to examine the roles and duties you are expected to perform. You may sometimes be asked to do things which are not in your job description. **Role boundary analysis** is a process of determining if professional duties are within one's scope of practice and whether or not they may pose an ethical dilemma. Hoppin and Splete (1996) have provided guidelines to determine what duties are within one's scope of practice, and what helpful or unhelpful in analyzing ethical situations:

- *When Activities are Within Your Role.* When an activity you have been asked to perform is clearly within your role (your scope of practice), and you know how to do it (you have the right level of skill, training, and experience), then you may proceed with the task. If the activity is within your role, but you don't know how to do it or are unsure, you should not proceed until you have been properly trained and/or supervised.

- *When Activities are Clearly Outside of Your Role.* When an activity you have been asked to perform is clearly outside your role, but you know how to do it, then you must seek consultation and/or supervision before you can proceed with the task. To determine if the task is outside your scope of practice, consult the state licensing board if applicable, and peruse the policy manual for the organization for which you work. If the activity or task is outside your role, and you don't know how to do it, you should not proceed.

- *When You are Unsure if Activities are Within Your Role.* When you are unsure if an activity you have been asked to perform is within your role, but you know how to do it, then you must seek consultation and/or supervision before you can proceed with the task. You will likely need permission to determine if you could add the task to your role. If you are unsure if an activity or tasks is within your role, and you don't know how to do it, or how to do it adequately, you should not proceed until you seek consultation and/or additional training and supervision.

NOHS Ethical Standards & Using Multiple Codes

As mentioned previously, human service professionals have a main code of ethics developed by the National Organization for Human Services. The complete NOHS 2015 Ethical Standards are listed in Appendix E of this book. Nevertheless, there are a several standards we would like to highlight below:

- STANDARD 7: Human service professionals ensure that their values or biases are not imposed upon their clients.

- STANDARD 12: Human service professionals are aware of local, state, and federal laws. They advocate for change in regulations and statutes when such legislation conflicts with ethical guidelines and/or client rights. Where laws are harmful to individuals, groups, or communities, human service professionals consider the conflict between the values of obeying the law and the values of serving people and may decide to initiate social action.

- STANDARD 26: Human service professionals seek the training, experience, education, and supervision necessary to ensure their effectiveness in working with culturally diverse individuals based on age, ethnicity, culture, race, ability, gender, language preference, religion, sexual orientation, socioeconomic status, nationality, or other historically oppressive groups. In addition, they will strive to increase their competence in methods which are known to be the best fit for the population(s) with whom they work.

- STANDARD 36: Human service professionals hold a commitment to lifelong learning and continually advance their knowledge and skills to serve clients more effectively.

There are times, however, when career professionals may desire ethical guidance targeted toward their specific work environments and tasks. They will perhaps be looking for depth to complement the breath of the NOHS code of ethics. Due to the nature of their work, many professional's identity with more than one professional association or credentialing agency, making familiarization with multiple codes of ethics and standards of practice a professional necessity (Makela & Perlus, 2017). There are several professional associations that publish codes of ethics and whose foci relate to the work of professionals providing career services (see resource section at end of this chapter). Because other professional organizations provide more specific ethical codes for the delivery of career services, we suggest that human service professionals providing career services consider additional codes of ethics that go beyond the scope of the NOHS codes. These can include their state, regional, or national associations, as well as relevant licensure and certification boards.

Nevertheless, a challenge in ethical decision-making can occur when engaging multiple codes of ethics and professional standards. Although there is no single remedy for addressing such ethical conundrums, however, by considering the various components of ethical decision-making strategies emerge in which these multiple sources of information become useful when considering options. Makela and Perlus (2017) suggested that helping professionals reflect on the following steps if they perceive contradictory information because of using multiple codes of ethics:

1. Ask yourself: How is your definition informed by each code of ethics or professional standards that you are referencing? What information might you want to gather to inform your reflections?
2. Identify the ethical principles discussed earlier that may be relevant to the situation. Do you perceive conflicts between any of these principles?
3. Tune into your own feelings about the dilemma. Are they influencing your objectivity?
4. Consider your obligations and relationships to different codes of ethics and professional standards documents. Which documents are you bound to follow due to licensure, certification, or membership?
5. Identify your desired outcomes for the situation, and consider your potential actions as they are informed by each code or standard.
6. Document the process that you take to resolve your ethical dilemma. This can help you in future situations and justify that you used good judgment and a fitting strategy to resolve an ethical dilemma.

It may be helpful to explore similarities and differences between documents titled "code of ethics" and those titled "professional standards." Two distinctions can be made between these document types. First, professional standards documents are often regarded as prescribing minimal behavioral requirements that professional are expected to follow in a given field; the actions necessary for appropriate service to clients (Makela & Perlus, 2017). In contrast, with a code of ethics, although minimal requirements are also included, the intention is often to go beyond the baseline prescriptions and include aspirational principles that practitioners are encouraged to continually strive for throughout their practice (Welfel, 2015). It is important to recognize that one document type is not necessarily better than the other. Both provide useful contributions to human service professionals providing career services.

Remember that codes of ethics and professional standards are ever evolving resources. They represent the current thinking of a group of professionals who work under a set of circumstances (Makela & Perlus, 2017). One benefit of reflecting on documents from multiple professional association is that you are introduced to different perspective on ethical dilemmas that professional providing career service may encounter in day-to-day practice. These perspectives provide an opportunity to learn from each other and in the end will help you become competent at ethical decision-making.

Ethical Considerations in Career Testing & Assessment

Human service professionals who administer tests and assessments for the purpose of assisting clients with career concerns have the same ethical obligations as practitioners who administer tests and assessments for mental health purposes. Practitioners have two sets of people to whom they have ethical obligations: test developers and test takers (Welfel, 2015). Because tests are copyrighted, test users have a duty to protect the security of the tests from theft and unwarranted use. This obligation means that test users must keep testing materials in their possession and refrain from copying or otherwise disseminating test items in inappropriate ways. The ethical responsibilities of professionals who administer test are extensive and are discussed in other sources. In general, human service professionals must refrain from using instruments inappropriately because clients may not receive the assistance they truly need and deserve. In particular, we provide several obligations that human services practitioners have toward test takers:

- The human service practitioner must be competent in administering and interpreting results of tests and assessment instruments. **Determinants of competence** include careful review of test manuals, understanding the instrument's validity, reliability, and norms as provided by the publisher, knowing the strengths and limitations of the instrument used, proper application of instrument with diverse populations, and a period of supervised experience in its use (Welfel, 2015).

- Practitioners do not use data or results from assessments that are obsolete or outdated for the current purpose.

- Practitioners inform clients of the purpose and nature of all aspects of their involvement in testing and assessment.
- Practitioners must carefully read the results of the test or assessment reports and consult with a supervisor when needed.
- Practitioners must take care when purchasing assessments, being sure to purchase only from credible sources.

Ethics in Internet-Based Career Services

Most human service professionals acknowledge the potential of the Internet as a source of information that can be accessed by people who might not have access to other sources of the information. **Distance career counseling** involves the provision of brief or longer-term individual counseling to clients via the telephone or the web that is often augmented using career assessments and information available on the Internet. Common modes of distance career counseling include encrypted mail, phone calls, and Skype or other video calling services. Although there are advantages and limitations to online career services, this discussion focuses on the ethical and practical considerations surrounding career development counseling via the Internet. We list several guidelines for providing to client's career services over the internet adapted from NCDA Code of Ethics Section F (2015a) and Sampson and Osborn (2015). These guidelines can limit potential ethical issues a human services professional may encounter when offering internet-based career services:

- The qualifications of the provider must be clearly stated on the site.
- The cost of services provided must be clearly stated.
- The provider must appropriately screen clients to determine whether they can benefit from using the online services provided.
- Providers who use online instruments must investigate the psychometric characteristics of the measures, methods of interpretation, and that the instruments are current and unbiased.
- The provider should keep an active role in the design of online career counseling services including consistency, recoverability and control over the system's data flow, and extended user guidance and assistance.
- The provider must make every attempt to protect confidentiality and data security, ensure transparency and equitable treatment of clients, and meet any legal and ethical requirements for the use of online resources.
- The provider must provide periodic support for the client via telephone contact or videoconferencing to increase intimacy of communication.

- The provider must refer clients to local practitioners when needed.
- Providers must inform clients of the privacy policies followed by the provider, so that they can determine the risks involved in the delivery of online career services.

The use of the Internet to provide career services grows each day. With its increase in use, human service professionals are constantly presented with new ethical issues in service delivery. Human service professionals are encouraged to read the paper on the ethical use of social networking sites in career services published by The National Career Development Association (2015b) (see resource section at the end of this chapter). The paper provides a comprehensive synthesis of current professional conversations in the literature about the use of social networking technologies (SNT) in practice by career professionals and those in related helping professions. As Welfel (2015) noted, acting ethically means being as competent as declared, considering the client's welfare as primary, using power responsibly, and conducting oneself so as to enhance the credibility and reputation of the profession.

Conclusion

This chapter defined some typical terms human service professionals will come across when discussing the topic of ethics. The need for ethical codes was discussed along with some typical ethical conflicts that human service professionals may encounter when providing career interventions. Because awareness of one's personal values are a starting point for providing ethical career services, we presented some strategies for self-awareness. We discuss three models of ethical-decision making, and a process of determining if professional duties are within one's scope of practice. Challenges in and approaches to ethical decision-making when engaging multiple codes of ethics and professional standards was discussed. This chapter concluded with ethical considerations in testing and assessment, and ethics in providing internet-based career services. Human services professional providing career services have a duty to fulfill their promise to help and protect the public from unprincipled practitioners.

Key Chapter Terms

Ethics	Ethical Sensitivity
Ethical	Problem-Solving Ethics Models
Ethical Standards	Model for Ethical-Decision Making
Laws	Moral Models
Morals	Principles of Ethical-Decision Making
Professional Standards	Relational View of Ethical-Decision Making
Code of Ethics	Role Boundary Analysis
Ethical Values	Determinants of Competence
Ethical-Values Awareness	Distance Career Counseling

Web Resources

Note that website URLs may change over time.

Personal Values Assessment
https://www.valuescentre.com/our-products/products-individuals/personal-values-assessment-pva

Codes of Ethics of Various Professional Organizations
American Counseling Association
https://www.counseling.org/resources/aca-code-of-ethics.pdf

American Mental Health Counselors Association
http://www.amhca.org/learn/ethics

American Psychological Association
https://www.apa.org/ethics/code/

American School Counselor Association
https://www.schoolcounselor.org/asca/media/asca/Ethics/EthicalStandards2016.pdf

Commission on Rehabilitation Counselor Certification
https://www.crccertification.com/filebin/pdf/ethics/CodeOfEthics_01-01-2017.pdf

Career Theory, Development, and Appraisal

National Association of Social Workers
https://www.socialworkers.org/About/Ethics/Code-of-Ethics/Code-of-Ethics-English

National Career Development Association
https://www.ncda.org/aws/NCDA/asset_manager/get_file/3395

National Organization for Human Services
https://www.nationalhumanservices.org/ethical-standards-for-hs-professionals

The Association for Addiction Professionals
https://www.naadac.org/code-of-ethics

Chapter 13

21ST CENTURY CHANGES FOR WORK AND CAREER SERVICES

"People are 'meaning-makers' and word-munchers. They use language and action to make meaning out of daily activities. The most important personal meanings are relational. They are constructed through interactions with others and with aspects of the surrounding world."

~R. Vance Peavy, 1995, p. 1.

CHAPTER HIGHLIGHTS
A New Social Arrangement in Work and Career
Features of Precarious Work
Toward Meaning Making in Work
Message of Postmodern Thought for Career Counseling

As society continues to move from the high modernity of the 20th century to the postmodernity of the 21st century, career practitioners must be prepared to help individuals cope with an uncertain and rapidly changing occupational structure. The nature of work and the meaning of career have been restructured and reinvented over the last three decades. Shaped by a global economy and propelled by information technology, the new social arrangement is characterized by uncertain, unpredictable, and risky employment opportunities as perceived by the worker (Kalleberg, 2009). In addition, organizational restructuring has increasingly altered the mutual expectations between employee and employer, making it difficult for workers to anticipate and adapt to the changing demands of the new psychological contract (Conway & Briner, 2005). Consequently, many companies today expect their employees to take responsibility for the direction and evolution of their own career pathways (Arthur & Rousseau, 1996). As established paths and societal narratives disappear, individuals are forced to assume increased responsibility for managing their own lives and careers. This leaves some feeling anxious, depressed, and frustrated.

As we discussed in Chapter 3 of this book, career counseling can be viewed as a career service area that integrates process-oriented counseling skills and places the practitioner's attention to the subjective experience of the client. Savickas (2011) defined career counseling as the use of "psychological methods to foster self-exploration as a prelude to choosing and adjusting to work" (p. 151). This includes helping a client with personal meaning-making, exploring and processing emotions and thoughts, using language to foster a therapeutic conversation, revising one's sense of identity, and viewing career and work concerns as being embedded in one's cultural context. Given the complexity of the interventions, career counseling requires advanced training and supervision to provide effective help to clients.

The purpose of the chapter is not to discuss techniques of career counseling intervention, but to illustrate why we need more professionals trained in career counseling, especially postmodern approaches, and how career assessment and intervention has been adapting to the changing nature of work. We first discuss the new social arrangement in work and career, and then introduce the concept of precarious work along with several of its defining features. Next, we introduce you to the importance of constructing meaning-making in helping clients with their career issues, and we conclude with four features of culture and context in postmodern thought which have shaped career counseling in the 21st century.

A New Social Arrangement in Work and Career

New social arrangements of work in the United States during the last few decades have made career progression more difficult for many people. Organizational restructuring for lower costs and greater efficiencies has resulted in layoffs, unanticipated transfers, offshoring (i.e., contracting out the performance of service sector activities to businesses located beyond U.S. borders), career destabilization, and nonstandardized work contracts (Inkson & Elkin, 2008). Yet, for many people, such transformation results in what Kalleberg (2009) denoted as **precarious work** or "employment that is uncertain, unpredictable, and risky from the point of view of the worker" (p. 2). Standing (1999) described sources of work insecurity as those which include loss of a job or fear of losing a job, lack of alternative employment opportunities, and diminished freedom to obtain and maintain skills and to advance in a position. According to Standing, possible **effects of insecurity** include a sense of oppression and exploitation, demoralization, demotivation, and ill health. In the past, precarious work was often described in terms of a dual labor market, with unstable and uncertain jobs concentrated in the secondary labor market (i.e., low-skilled, low-wage jobs requiring relatively little training with high labor turnover). Today, precarious work and insecurity have spread to the primary sector of the economy (i.e., higher grade, higher status, and better-paid jobs) and have become much more pervasive and generalized.

According to data from the *Current Population Survey*, a joint effort between the Bureau of Labor Statistics and the Census Bureau, employment in white-collar occupations accounts for more than one half of total U.S. employment. Some 9 out of 10 white-collar workers are employed in the service sector (e.g., as cooks and servers, cleaners and maintenance workers, hairdressers, child care workers, and police and firefighters), and these jobs represent about four-fifths of total U.S. employment (Levine, 2005). This changing mix of occupations is reflected in a decline in blue-collar jobs and an increase in high- and low-wage white-collar occupations. Nevertheless, many white-collar workers also have experienced a transformation in secure employment due to organizational restructuring. Whether this uncertainty affects more white- or blue-collar workers, we are witnessing a transformation in which occupation and employment no longer serve to grade and group people to the extent or in the same way that was possible under industrialism. Our interest is in helping human services and career professionals increase their understanding of the impact of this postmodern transformation on individuals today.

Features of Precarious Work

Three primary features characterize the difficulty individuals encounter with precarious work. First, permanent jobs increasingly are in short supply in the United States, and this forces workers to be part of a *temporary workforce.* Jobs during the industrial period were, for the most part, characterized by a **standardized employment** model: Individuals worked full-time for a single employer and had opportunities to advance gradually in responsibility and pay (Kalleberg & Leicht, 2002). Today many firms are organized around a **nonstandardized employment** model, which is a form of flexibility that advocates for a small group of core workers in managerial positions who are augmented by an adjustable number of peripheral and external employees who make up a contingent and temporary workforce (Arabandi, 2015; Kalleberg,

2009). Peripheral and external workers have also been called independent contractors, casual, contract, freelance, part-time, atypical, adjunct, consultant, and self-employed. This type of flexibility reduces vertical hierarchies while increasing horizontal management practices within an organization, providing fewer workers with an opportunity for advancement (Arabandi, 2015).

The second feature of the transformation of work arrangements describes the *general decline in the average length of time workers remain with their employers*. Rather than developing a stable life based on secure employment, most workers today change jobs every 5 years (Bureau of Labor Statistics, 2015). The general assumption has been that a "career" consisted of a succession of permanent, full-time, five-days-a-week, 9-to-5 jobs, which was a value held within hierarchical societies. Savickas (2019) refers to this new employment market as a **"gig economy"** which views career as "selling services and skills to a series of employers who need projects completed" (p. 5). Now individuals can expect to occupy at least 11 jobs during their lifetime, in part because of being a displaced worker. In particular, the average person born in the later years of the baby boom in the United States (1957–1964) held an average of 11.7 jobs between age 18 and age 48, with nearly half of these jobs being held before age 25 (Bureau of Labor Statistics, 2015). Moreover, among jobs started by 40- to 48-year-olds, the Bureau reported that 32% ended in less than a year, and 69% ended in fewer than 5 years. Related to this decline in the length of employment is the change in psychological contracts between employees and employers.

A salient trend confronting the contemporary workforce is the new employment relationship between workers and their employers. This has been referred to by industrial-organizational scholars as to the **psychological contract** (Rousseau, 1998). Long-term employment with one organization has become increasingly rare as growing numbers of individuals are willing to move from job to job. In the 1950s, there was primarily a **relational implicit contract** (legal in the case of unions) between employee and employer. Workers traded their work hours, labor, and commitment for what was frequently a lifetime job or at least the steady income and job security geared to seniority.

Today the psychological contract has been largely replaced by a new contract. As an emerging **transactional explicit contract** becomes noticeable, fewer workers can count on guaranteed job security, regardless of their occupational status (Conway & Briner, 2005). For many peripheral workers today, hiring is based in an "at-will" employment relationship, which is predominant in almost all U.S. states. An employer can terminate an at-will employee at any time for any reason, except an illegal one, or for no reason without being legally liable; also, an employer can change the terms of the employment relationship with no notice and no consequences (Stone, 2007). Workers increasingly feel like independent contractors who have to chart their career paths. As a result, fewer workers now offer total loyalty to their employers.

The third primary feature of the increased prevalence of precarious work involves a *change in standardized work hours*. Paid work is no longer based on holding a position but on producing a **project** (Savickas, 2011). With projects, workers shift from one assignment to another. Their work schedules change as well, and they are expected to adjust their hours accordingly. Work begins as a project and ends as a product. This work role unpredictability has had subsequent effects on the family, community, and leisure role. Technology and flexibility have intensified work to such an extent that overwork has become highly valued in American culture (Sweet & Meiksins, 2008). For example, if employees do not spend long hours in the office, or are not available when requested they fear it might be interpreted as a lack of commitment to the job and might reflect negatively on their aspirations for promotion. Job insecurity and nonstandardized work contracts have heightened anxiety about job loss and unemployment while also placing increased demands on workers' performance and productivity (Crowley, Tope, Chamberlain, & Hodson, 2010). As one can infer, these new, 21st-century workplace arrangements require updated career interventions to help people keep pace with the changing structure of work.

Toward Meaning-Making in Work

The transformation in the world of work that has occurred during postmodern times has made career choices more difficult. In a postmodern era, identities no longer provide meaning as they once did, and this makes occupational commitments problematic (Richardson, 2015). Commitment to an occupational choice is increasingly difficult due to a lack of stability in social structures. As suggested by Savickas et al. (2009), "Clients and counselors should not concentrate on choice in a world where there is much uncertainty and fewer choices. Instead, they should concentrate on meaning-making through intentional processes in the ongoing construction of lives" (p. 246). Yet, meaning is embedded in the context of the client. As Peavy (2004) stated, "ideas, perspectives, and meanings profoundly influence our actions and form the basis for negotiating and communicating with others" (p. 8). Career practitioners can facilitate meaning-making through self-authoring, autobiography, and other forms of narrative career counseling (see Busacca & Rehfuss, 2017 for meaning-making career interventions). Some individuals lack a stable framework and may benefit from collaboration with career services providers who understand the occupational landscape of the 21st century.

A Message of Postmodern Thought for Career Counseling

Postmodernism has, in part, influenced the way we think about career counseling. The message of postmodern thought provides the assumptions underlying postmodern career counseling. In this section, we first provide a brief contrast between two epistemologies: realism and constructivism. Second, we discuss the concept of meaning and how it is personally and socially constructed. Last, we explain how cultural context has become increasingly essential as individuals further disconnect from the established paths and narratives that once guided their career progression. We have included a guide table (see Table 13.1) that highlights and distinguishes the conceptual and pragmatic shift from traditional career services provided during the modern era to the needed postmodern career counseling of today. Many of the terms in this table are in bold for the reader and for instructional purposes throughout this chapter.

Underlying Assumptions

An important aspect of philosophical inquiry as it applies to career counseling concerns the study of how ideas and meanings are generated. Each of the career theories discussed in Chapter 4 of this book originates from a point of view or **epistemology** that encompasses shared assumptions, common understandings, and collective values (Savickas, 2015). This epistemology validates the source of knowledge or what we know about career issues, counseling orientations, and interventions. Scholars tend to refer to epistemologies when discussing postmodern career counseling. A brief look at two epistemological foundations—realism and constructivism—illustrates the assumptions underlying the constructivist and social constructionist perspectives.

For most of the 20th century, the career field embraced realism. The foundational assumption of **realism** (also called modernism) is that actual reality, with enduring properties, exists and is independent of those who observe it (Erwin, 1999). That is, reality represents what we know. Realism, as applied to counseling, denotes that practitioners can objectively observe clients and come to know particular truths about them. A practitioner uses a map, theory, hypothesis, idea, table, or other representation of the objective world. Once a client's experience is understood, the practitioner can draw on a map to impart an intervention. For example, vocational guidance emphasizes norm-based inventories such as the STRONG and Self-Directed Search. Realism in counseling and psychology also relies on quantitative research and psychometrics. The critique of modernism does not challenge its validity but the omission of the process. That is, it leaves out the mapmaker (the subject) who may bring something critical to the picture (Wilber, 2000). Consequently, the postmodern movement has increasingly offered vigorous challenges to the basic assumptions of modernism (Sexton, 1997).

The way the term postmodern is used has become so convoluted that many individuals are confused about its exact meaning. **Postmodernism** is at the leading edge of today's cultural evolution. In general, a postmodernist would believe that individuals construct meaning or perceive their reality or truth (Neimeyer & Stewart, 2000). The goal of postmodernity in the social and behavioral sciences can be expressed as an attempt to be more inclusive and to conscientiously avoid marginalizing the many voices and viewpoints that modernity has often overlooked (Wilber, 2000). This contrasts with the modernist assumption that an external and objective meaning can be discovered. The influence of various offshoots of postmodern thought, such as psychological constructivism (e.g., Maturana & Varela, 1988) and social constructionism (e.g., Berger & Luckmann, 1966), has gained significance in recent years.

Since the 1980s, the field of career services has increasingly infused its theories and practices with the epistemologies of psychological constructivism and social constructionism. Both epistemologies emphasize subjectivity, appreciate multiple perspectives, acknowledge multiple truths, value interpretive or qualitative research, and emphasize context (Watson & McMahon, 2004). As a response to the modernist tradition, which highlighted the notion of the self-contained individual with measurable traits, the postmodern conceptualization of career represents a unique interaction of self and social experience (Young & Collin, 2004). Both constructivism and social constructionism emphasize certain features of postmodern thought.

The similarities between psychological constructivism and social constructionism are much greater than their differences. The postmodern era describes a world that is in part a construction or an interpretation in which meaning is context-dependent. Both schools of thought view reality as relative to social interaction and the social context rather than as completely objective and waiting to be discovered. The words constructivism and constructionism have been frequently used interchangeably in the literature, with constructivism often referring to both. This text will present the terms as separate and distinct. **Constructivism** is a perspective that arose in developmental and cognitive psychology, whereas **constructionism** is derived from multidisciplinary sources such as sociology, literary studies, and postmodern approaches. Constructivism focuses on meaning-making and construing the social and psychological worlds through individual cognitive processes, or how we develop meaning. Constructivism postulates a highly individualistic approach with minimal reference to social interaction, context, and discourse, which Young and Collin (2004) asserted are important factors that make self-reflection and meaning-making possible. This limitation is being addressed by social constructionism, which emphasizes that the social and psychological worlds are made real (constructed) through social processes and interaction.

It may be useful to think of psychological constructivism and social constructionism as windows or perspectives for how practitioners view and approach a client's experience and reality. These two perspectives have emerged relatively recently and are still evolving (Young & Collin, 2004); they can be placed on a continuum with offshoots and variations. We do not recommend viewing these perspectives as mutually exclusive, however, because ambiguity exists. Thus, postmodern career models and methods may be rooted in one of these perspectives or in both. Although models focus on different aspects and have different names, they all originate from either a constructivist or social constructionist epistemology, or both, or may be classified as a variant. Given these assumptions, both perspectives concentrate on meaning-making.

The Construction of Meaning

Individuals build their careers by imposing meaning on their vocational behavior. Certainly, many individuals identify the work role as an important source of meaning in their lives (Baum & Stewart, 1990). For individuals who view their work as having more than just economic value, purpose is considered to be at the center of their career satisfaction (Kosine, Steger, & Duncan, 2008). To succeed in a postmodern world of work, *personal meaning* must be present because it structures an individual's career as it plays out across the various jobs a worker can expect to occupy during her or his work life. Individuals must identify a purpose for doing the work they do to maintain their motivation. As Savickas (2019) noted, meaning is embedded within intentions, and intention denotes having a purpose in mind as one acts. At a general level, **meaning** can be defined as "the sense made of, and significance felt regarding, the nature of one's being and existence" (Dik & Duffy, 2012, p. 65). Postmodern career counseling theories values the concept of meaning at their core and demonstrate how meaning is personally construed and socially constructed.

The emphasis on personal meaning draws inspiration and support from the constructivist perspective. According to Young and Collin (2004), meaning-making results from constructing the social and psychological worlds through individual cognitive processes. Likewise, social constructionists emphasize that the social and psychological worlds are made real through social processes and interaction. Postmodern career models and methods informed by these epistemologies facilitate the meaning-making process for clients. The practitioner explores how clients can elaborate on and evaluate their meanings relative to their intentions, rather than attempting to match people to occupations based on their decisions.

Postmodern career counseling also distinguishes meaning-making from **matchmaking**. During the assessment phase, the matching model uses an individual's interests, values, and other traits to match the individual with suitable occupations. If their traits are similar to an occupation, then it will be a good fit; if not, then it will be a poor fit. From a postmodern perspective, however, these individual variables do not exist for the client; they exist within the counselor's objective view. Thus, postmodern career practitioners rely more on autobiography, meaning-making, and qualitative assessment than on interest inventories and guidance techniques (Savickas, 1993). Qualitative career assessment as an idiographic subjective process is the preferred method of assessment. Qualitative career assessment is grounded in constructivism, with a focus on meaning-making and an understanding that the client's contextual experiences are continually evolving (Whiston & Rahardja, 2005). Many of the traditional career theories, in the realist or modernist tradition, do not support the individual's meaning-making process. These traditional interventions aim to help clients discover meaning that they are not yet aware of but that is already present.

In contrast, postmodern career models and methods help clients create personal meaning. Meaning-making, through dialogue and relationship with the practitioner, becomes an objective framed in terms of how it can be useful for the client. The central intervention goal of career counseling is **narratability**—helping clients reflect on and retell their own stories to foster meaning (Savickas, 2019). The narrative helps clients create alternative meanings and new knowledge that open up possibilities. The postmodern concepts of personal meaning-making extend to language as well.

Use of Language

The power of language in constructing meaning offers an important contribution to postmodern career counseling. Practitioners view language not as a tool for uncovering a client's true self, or solely as a reflection of clients' subjective perceptions, but as an active process in constructing identity and meaning in therapeutic conversations (Watson, 2011). As such, language is viewed in a relational rather than a conventional sense. The strategic use of language to elicit new meanings, expand perspectives, and encourage change is central to the postmodern perspective. Bird's (2004) concept of relational language-making positions the self of the client in relation to his or her feelings, thoughts, characteristics, personality traits, and actions. For example, **externalizing** a problem helps the client perceive the problem as separate from the identity of the person (Madigan, 2011). So, a client may use totalizing language such as, "I am a failure at work." The traditional counselor would help the client view failure as a separate problem with a life of its own.

In externalizing, however, the postmodern practitioner helps move the client's words and phrases from individual contexts of meaning toward a relational language in a collaborative way. This use of language can significantly reframe the client's self-critical comment. The practitioner may respond, "The failure, letdown feelings you notice in relation to your employer not providing you with an interview for the full-time position..." In this case, a shift from meaning construed *by self* to meaning construed *in a relationship* provides a form of inquiry that locates the client's interaction and experiences within the contextual environment that has shaped the self (Watson, 2011). Thus, the use of language goes from reflecting reality to producing reality and meaning.

Culture and Context

Postmodern career counseling embraces all expressions of diversity. Whether clients are from ethnic minority populations, are immigrants from other countries, live in the Little Italy of a major city, are military veterans, or are transgender students attending a university, career counseling addresses the individual's culture and context (i.e., contextual influences and interactions that make and remake the individual). Culture and context become increasingly essential as the labor force grows more diverse (Arabandi, 2015). It is important to revisit and elaborate upon the four features of culture and context in postmodern career counseling. These features provide a unique perspective from which to work with clients who experience difficulty in work and career.

First, *the dialogue in multicultural career counseling has evolved from a monocultural to a pluralistic perspective of culture.* The postmodern perspective includes not only race and ethnicity but also gender, sexual orientation, disability, age, religion, and spirituality—along with multiple or intersectional identities. Recall that the term intersectionality refers to the assumption that one cannot understand any one of these identities in isolation; they must be considered in combination (Cole, 2009). Intersectionality draws attention to diversity within categories. Nevertheless, both the constructivist and social constructionist principles go beyond group membership. Although the influence of social and political forces on clients' lives and careers is important, the focus of counseling emphasizes the meaning and interpretations of culture rather than the experiences of clients fixed to group membership (Arthur, 2006). Thus, career practitioners take a **universalistic stance**, which assumes that every client has a unique cultural background embedded in and influenced by culture and context.

The second feature *views individual career behavior as relative to the contexts in which it occurs.* Career theories have been informed by mechanism, organism, or both (Collin & Young, 1986). A mechanistic worldview explains phenomena in mechanical terms; a organismic worldview sees human development as an orderly, maturational, unfolding process. Practitioners who ascribe to the latter view believe individuals can be studied separately from their environments; consequently, the contexts within individuals' work become less important than their actions (Watson, 2006). Contextualism opposes both of these views.

Contextualism is reflected in social constructionist epistemology. It considers knowledge about us that is derived from social interaction and the active nature of individuals. This differs from the organismic model, which takes a passive view of people and asserts that some unfolding developmental process underlies change. Contexts provide the influences and interactions that make and remake the individual. Contextual variables (i.e., socializing agents) that influence a client include electronic media, peer group, neighborhood, community, house of worship, school, family, technology, workplace, print media, the arts, and sports. For example, two clients may grow up in the same town and culture but have vastly different contextual exposures, expectations, and perspectives. Context also consists of multiple complex connections and interrelationships, the significance of which is interpreted from the client's perspective (Young, Valach, & Collin, 2002). Career practitioners who value a contextual worldview understand development and change as resulting from an ongoing process of interaction between the client and his or her environment (Ford, 1987; Steenbarger, 1991).

The third feature *examines the links between culture and social justice through discourse analysis.* **Discourse analysis** moves beyond social constructionism by not only acknowledging the construction of phenomena through language but by underscoring how language is ruled by the hierarchies of discourse, including structures of power, ideology, and knowledge (Stead & Bakker, 2010). This view of culture moves from the dominant social discourse concerned with power relations to more contextual processes concerned with local occurrences of behavior. That is, counselors shift the focus from society's story for how people should live and work in the United States to the client's individual story. Blustein (2006) postulated that many traditional career theories and models appear irrelevant to some groups because they remain based on cultural assumptions that emphasize freedom of choice, affluence, the centrality of the work role, and notions of career success. The social justice perspective requires that practitioners encourage clients to give voice to their experiences of oppression and to examine how dominant discourses have framed their career experiences (Blustein, Schultheiss, & Flum, 2004). For example, approaches that use narrative or autobiographical methods empower clients from traditionally oppressed groups, because this exploration broadens and validates their perspective. Some of the postmodern career models and methods in Busacca and Rehfuss (2017) emphasize the development of narratives in one's local context.

The fourth feature *explores the ways work is rooted in a relational context.* **Relational theory** builds on the social constructionist perspective, which proposes that people learn about themselves, their social world, and culture through relationships (Blustein, 2011). The relational understanding of work and career enriches traditional career counseling practice by acknowledging the potential adaptive function of interpersonal connection in approaching career transitions, career choice, and work traumas (e.g., Schultheiss, 2003). Yet some multicultural theories have persisted in their use of value orientation models, which are deeply entrenched in individualistic dominant discourses. For example, postmodernists have challenged constructs such as locus of control and the Western concept of individualism and self-reliance in the workplace (Kvale, 1992). According to Jordan (1991), an appreciation of the importance of relational interdependence provides recognition and acknowledgment of the importance of turning to others for support rather than relying solely on oneself and seeking the independence expected from society's new metanarrative. Through relational career assessment, practitioners can facilitate an exploration of how clients' relational and work worlds intersect to gain a rich understanding of how clients connect and interact with others and how these connections are interdependent with their work lives (Schultheiss, 2005).

Table 13.1		
Parameters for Distinguishing Career Counseling During Modern and Postmodern Eras		
Parameter	*Modernity*	*Postmodernity*
Era	1900–1980's	1980's–present
Philosophy		
World View	Mechanism; organicism	Contextualism, holism
Epistemology	Realism	Psychological constructivism, social constructionism
Employment		
Socioeconomic Era	Industrial and corporate	Information and global
Labor Market	Permanent workers	Contingent workers
Employment Contracts	Standardized jobs	Non-standardized assignments
Elements of Counseling		
Career Services	Vocational guidance, career education, career development, placement	Career counseling
Focus of Counseling	Objective career; maturity, occupational fit, decision making, developmental tasks	Subjective career; adaptability, meaning, purpose, usefulness, stories, themes, identities, agency, self-authoring; context
Nature of Assessment	Quantitative; interpreting scores, statistical, norms-referenced, linear	Qualitative; professional judgment, nonstatistical, flexible, open ended
Adapted from: Busacca, L. A., & Rehfuss, M. C. (2017). Postmodern career counseling: A new perspective for the 21st century. In L. A. Busacca & M. C. Rehfuss (Eds.), *Postmodern Career Counseling: A handbook of culture, context, and cases* (p. 8). Alexandria, VA: American Counseling Association.		

Conclusion

Postmodern career counseling offers a new paradigm with which to comprehend the diversity in individuals' career behavior. New social provisions of work in the United States during the last few decades have made career progression for people more challenging. PCC is a much-needed career service area that keeps up with the pace of this transformation and meets the needs of clients through models and methods that emphasize meaning-making and purpose. In our changing world of work, we advise human services and career professionals to acknowledge the third paradigm for career services that address the needs of adults who must make frequent transitions among jobs, occupations, and organizations.

Source: Busacca, L. A., & Rehfuss, M. C. (2017). Postmodern career counseling: A new perspective for the 21st century. In L. A. Busacca & M. C. Rehfuss (Eds.), *Postmodern Career Counseling: A handbook of culture, context, and cases* (pp. 1-19). Alexandria, VA: ACA. Reproduced by permission of publisher.

Key Chapter Terms

Precarious Work	Postmodernism
Effects of Insecurity	Constructivism
Standardized Employment	Constructionism
Nonstandardized Employment	Meaning
Gig Economy	Matchmaking
Psychological Contract	Narratability
Relational Implicit Contract	Externalizing
Transactional Explicit Contract	Universalistic Stance
Project	Contextualism
Epistemology	Discourse Analysis
Realism	Relational Theory

Web Resources

Note that website URLs may change over time.

Life-Design Counseling Manual
http://www.vocopher.com/LifeDesign/LifeDesign.pdf

Video-Dr. Mark Savickas "Unplugged." Demonstrates a narrative method.
https://www.youtube.com/watch?v=AVgylt9cHy0

Appendix A

Success Formula Components
Using the Holland Types

Realistic	Investigative	Artistic
Work with tools	Solve problems	Be independent
Think with my hands	Work with science	Share feelings
Make or repair things	Work with math	Be sensitive
Use mechanical ability	Use logic	Paint
Apply physical skill	Research ideas	Play an instrument
Work outdoors	Figure out how things	Write
Work with animals	work	Apply artistic flair
Work with nature	Read	Decorate
Demonstrate skill	Analyze situations	Design
Social	**Enterprising**	**Conventional**
Help others	Make decisions	Be precise
Work with people	Convince others	Be a part of a team
Provide a service	Lead a group	Record data
Be outgoing and pleasant	Use power	Type
Help children	Act with enthusiasm	Organize materials
Assist the elderly	Sell things	Have a set routine
Teach	Be the center of attention	Know what is expected
Counsel	Be dynamic	Carry out orders
Advise	Have a lot of variety	Work with a partner

Adapted from: Savickas, M. L. (2009). Career-style counseling. In T. Sweeny (Ed.), *Adlerian counseling and psychotherapy: A practitioner's approach* (5th ed., pp. 183-207). Muncie, IN: Accelerated Development Press. Reproduced with permission by Mark L. Savickas.

Instructions:

Goal: Help students and clients state their success formula.

Procedures: Select the three roles that best characterize the client. Then ask the client to complete the following sentence with one phrase from each of the three roles clusters: "I feel successful and satisfied when I _____." The client picks the phrases and together with the helper arranges them into a success sentence that she or he can use to identify and evaluate prospective occupations.

Appendix B

American School Counselor Association
The School Counselor and Career Development
Position Statement, 2017

School counselors play a critical role in students' career development by:

- Introducing careers and the world of work in lower elementary grades
- Providing opportunities to engage students in "life roles including learner and worker" (Gysbers, 2013)
- Providing learning and experiential opportunities for students to acquire behaviors and skills for career readiness (Gysbers, 2013)
- Working with students to identify their interests, abilities, specific career clusters (Stipanovic, 2010) and postsecondary plans (many states mandate an academic/career action plan as a graduation requirement)
- Help understand the connection between school and world of work
- Helping students plan the transition from school to postsecondary education and/or the world of work (ASCA, 2014)
- Advising students on multiple postsecondary pathways (e.g., college, career-specific credentials and certifications, apprenticeships, military, service-year programs, full-time employment with a family-supporting wage) (Chicago Public Schools Multiple Postsecondary Pathways Framework)
- Connecting to early college programs (e.g., dual credit/dual enrollment)
- Collaborating with administration, teachers, staff and decision makers to create a postsecondary-readiness and college-going culture
- Providing and advocating for individual pre-K through postsecondary students' college and career awareness through exploration and postsecondary planning and decision making, which supports students' right to choose from the wide array of options after completing secondary education
- Identifying gaps in college and career access and the implications of such data for addressing both intentional and unintentional biases related to college and career counseling
- Working with teachers to integrate career education learning in the curricula
- Providing opportunities for all students to develop the mindsets and behaviors necessary to learn work-related skills, resilience, perseverance, an understanding of lifelong learning as a part of long-term career success, a positive attitude toward learning and a strong work ethic
- Recognizing and supporting essential developmental factors key to future successes, such as self-efficacy and identity, motivation and perseverance (Savitz-Romer & Bouffard, 2013)

229

Appendix C

Ohio Board of Education
Policy on Career Advising in Schools

Many state departments of education now require local boards of education to adopt policies on career advising for their public-school districts. The DOE's have developed model career advising policies that districts can customize based on local resources and needs.

For example, the Ohio Board of Education adopted a policy on career advising beginning with the 2015-2016 school year. The policies are to be updated at least once every two years and specify how the district will do all of the following:

- Provide students with grade-level examples that link their schoolwork to one or more career fields;
- Create a plan to provide career advising to students in grades six through twelve;
- Provide additional interventions and career advising for students who are identified as at risk of dropping out of school;
- Train its employees on how to advise students on career pathways, including training on advising students using online tools;
- Develop multiple, clear academic pathways through high school that students may choose in order to earn a high school diploma;
- Identify and publicize courses that can award students both traditional academic and career-technical credit;
- Document the career advising provided to each student for review by the student, the student's parent, guardian, or custodian, and future schools that the student may attend;
- Prepare students for their transition from high school to their post-secondary destinations, including any special interventions that are necessary for students in need of remediation in mathematics or English language arts.

Appendix D

Career Decision Making: Teaching the Process Differences Between School and Work

School	Work
Membership	
Non-Optional Each student belongs in the school and is assured of a place. Teachers accept the students assigned to their classes	*Optional* Worker are free to enter or leave employment. Employers are free to hire and fire or lay off employees.
Status	
Devalued Each student should be evaluated for what she/her does, not for what she/he is. Stereotypes and prejudices are possible.	*Evaluated* Workers are often evaluated by class, education, race, sex, age nationality, and religions. Bias may limit worker's opportunities to express competence.
Interpersonal Relationships	
Sympathetic Cooperation Each student should expect teachers to help her/him. Students should try to help each other.	*Competitive Striving* Workers should not expect supervisors to help them. Workers should expect co-workers to be guarding their own self-interests (e.g., holding the job, raises, promotions).
Morality	
Uniform Moral Code Each student should do what is considered right. Students and teachers should trust each other.	*Ethical Neutrality* Each worker should be free to lead her/his life without co-workers "sticking their noses in." Workers and supervisors may not trust each other.
Goals	
Personality Growth Each student should have an opportunity for a wide range of experiences to develop her/his full potential.	*Work Persistence* Each worker should learn to stay with a job. If a worker seeks a variety of different jobs, she/her may be considered unstable, unreliable, and unable to hold a job.
Success	
Self-Fulfillment	*Company's Fulfillment* A successful worker is one who makes significant contributions to the

A successful student is one who actualizes her/his potential and expresses her/himself to the fullest.	organization's goals, sometimes at the personal expense (e.g., neglects family and personal leisure time).
Means to Advance	
Clear Each student is expected to advance to the next grade. The means are clear, and support is offered.	*Ambiguous* Only better workers can advance. The means to advancement is often ambiguous and little to no help is offered because workers should do it on their own.
Supervisory Authority	
Weak Teachers have limited authority to direct student's academic progress. The authority they do possess should be exercised in the best interests of the students.	*Strong* Supervisors have extensive authority to direct workers. This authority may be exercised with self-centered motives.
Consequences	
Student-Centered Consequences (e.g., punishment) are used for the student's own good. When applied, it is often temporary and artificial.	*Employer-Centered* Consequences are used for the good of the company/organization. When applied, it is often real and drastic (e.g., written up, demotion, lost wages, separated from employment, transferred to new city)
Movement	
Uni-Directional & Regular Student usually advance each year. At worst, one may be retained at a grade level for a second year.	*Bi-Directional & Slow* Workers move only intermittently. Usually, workers are held in positions for years, especially part-time workers. When movement does occur, it can either be promotions or demotion.

Adapted from: Savickas, M. L., & Crites, J. O. (1981). *Career decision making: Teaching the process* (pp. 19-21). Rootstown, OH: NEOUCOM. Reproduced with Permission by Mark. L. Savickas.

Appendix E

Ethical Standards for Human Services Professionals
National Organization of Human Services adopted 2015

Preamble

Human services is a profession developed in response to the direction of human needs and human problems in the 1960's. Characterized by an appreciation of human beings in all of their diversity, human services offers assistance to its clients within the context of their communities and environments. Human service professionals and those who educate them promote and encourage the unique values and characteristics of human services. In so doing, human service professionals uphold the integrity and ethics of the profession, promote client and community well-being, and enhance their own professional growth.

The fundamental values of the human services profession include respecting the dignity and welfare of all people; promoting self-determination; honoring cultural diversity; advocating for social justice; and acting with integrity, honesty, genuineness and objectivity.

Human service professionals consider these standards in ethical and professional decision making. Conflicts may exist between this code and laws, workplace policies, cultural practices, credentialing boards, and personal beliefs. Ethical-decision making processes should be employed to assure careful choices. Although ethical codes are not legal documents, they may be used to address issues related to the behavior of human service professionals.

Persons who use this code include members of the National Organization for Human Services, students in relevant academic degree programs, faculty in those same programs, researchers, administrators, and professionals in community agencies who identify with the profession of human services. The ethical standards are organized in sections around those persons to whom ethical practice should be applied.

Responsibility to Clients

STANDARD 1 Human service professionals recognize and build on client and community strengths.

STANDARD 2 Human service professionals obtain informed consent to provide services to clients at the beginning of the helping relationship. Clients should be informed that they may withdraw consent at any time except where denied by court order and should be able to ask questions before agreeing to the services. Clients who are unable to give consent should have those who are legally able to give consent for them review an informed consent statement and provide appropriate consent.

STANDARD 3 Human service professionals protect the client's right to privacy and confidentiality except when such confidentiality would cause serious harm to the client or others, when agency guidelines state otherwise, or under other stated conditions (e.g., local, state, or federal laws). Human service professionals inform clients of the limits of confidentiality prior to the onset of the helping relationship.

STANDARD 4 If it is suspected that danger or harm may occur to the client or to others as a result of a client's behavior, the human service professional acts in an appropriate and professional manner to protect the safety of those individuals. This may involve, but is not limited to, seeking consultation, supervision, and/or breaking the confidentiality of the relationship.

STANDARD 5 Human service professionals recognize that multiple relationships may increase the risk of harm to or exploitation of clients and may impair their professional judgment. When it is not feasible to avoid dual or multiple relationships, human service professionals should consider whether the professional relationship should avoided or curtailed.

STANDARD 6 Sexual or romantic relationships with current clients are prohibited. Before engaging in sexual or romantic relationships with former clients, friends, or family members of former clients, human service professionals carefully evaluate potential exploitation or harm and refrain from entering into such a relationship.

STANDARD 7 Human service professionals ensure that their values or biases are not imposed upon their clients.

STANDARD 8 Human service professionals protect the integrity, safety, and security of client records. Client information in written or electronic form that is shared with other professionals must have the client's prior written consent except in the course of professional supervision or when legally obliged or permitted to share such information.

STANDARD 9 When providing services through the use of technology, human service professionals take precautions to ensure and maintain confidentiality and comply with all relevant laws and requirements regarding storing, transmitting, and retrieving data. In addition, human service professionals ensure that clients are aware of any issues and concerns related to confidentiality, service issues, and how technology might negatively or positively impact the helping relationship.

Responsibility to the Public and Society

STANDARD 10 Human service professionals provide services without discrimination or preference in regard to age, ethnicity, culture, race, ability, gender, language preference, religion, sexual orientation, socioeconomic status, nationality, or other historically oppressed groups.

STANDARD 11 Human service professionals are knowledgeable about their cultures and communities within which they practice. They are aware of multiculturalism in society and its impact on the community as well as individuals within the community. They respect the cultures and beliefs of individuals and groups.

STANDARD 12 Human service professionals are aware of local, state, and federal laws. They advocate for change in regulations and statutes when such legislation conflicts with ethical guidelines and/or client rights. Where laws are harmful to individuals, groups, or communities, human service professionals consider the conflict between the values of obeying the law and the values of serving people and may decide to initiate social action.

STANDARD 13 Human service professionals stay informed about current social issues as they affect clients and communities. If appropriate to the helping relationship, they share this information with clients, groups and communities as part of their work.

STANDARD 14 Human service professionals are aware of social and political issues that differentially affect clients from diverse backgrounds.

STANDARD 15 Human service professionals provide a mechanism for identifying client needs and assets, calling attention to these needs and assets, and assisting in planning and mobilizing to advocate for those needs at the individual, community, and societal level when appropriate to the goals of the relationship.

STANDARD 16 Human service professionals advocate for social justice and seek to eliminate oppression. They raise awareness of underserved population in their communities and with the legislative system.

STANDARD 17 Human service professionals accurately represent their qualifications to the public. This includes, but is not limited to, their abilities, training, education, credentials, academic endeavors, and areas of expertise. They avoid the appearance of misrepresentation or impropriety and take immediate steps to correct it if it occurs.

STANDARD 18 Human service professionals describe the effectiveness of treatment programs, interventions and treatments, and/or techniques accurately, supported by data whenever possible.

Responsibility to Colleagues

STANDARD 19 Human service professionals avoid duplicating another professional's helping relationship with a client. They consult with other professionals who are assisting the client in a different type of relationship when it is in the best interest of the client to do so. In addition, human service professionals seek ways to actively collaborate and coordinate with other professionals when appropriate.

STANDARD 20 When human service professionals have a conflict with a colleague, they first seek out the colleague in an attempt to manage the problem. If this effort fails, the professional then seeks the assistance of supervisors, consultants, or other professionals in efforts to address the conflict.

STANDARD 21 Human service professionals respond appropriately to unethical and problematic behavior of colleagues. Usually this means initially talking directly with the colleague and if no satisfactory resolution is achieved, reporting the colleague's behavior to supervisory or administrative staff.

STANDARD 22 All consultations between human service professionals are kept private, unless to do so would result in harm to clients or communities.

Responsibility to Employers

STANDARD 23 To the extent possible, human service professionals adhere to commitments made to their employers.

STANDARD 24 Human service professionals participate in efforts to establish and maintain employment conditions which are conducive to high quality client services. Whenever possible, they assist in evaluating the effectiveness of the agency through reliable and valid assessment measures.

STANDARD 25 When a conflict arises between fulfilling the responsibility to the employer and the responsibility to the client, human service professionals work with all involved to manage the conflict.

Responsibility to the Profession

STANDARD 26 Human service professionals seek the training, experience, education and supervision necessary to ensure their effectiveness in working with culturally diverse individuals based on age, ethnicity, culture, race, ability, gender, language preference, religion, sexual orientation, socioeconomic status, nationality, or other historically oppressive groups. In addition, they will strive to increase their competence in methods which are known to be the best fit for the population(s) with whom they work.

STANDARD 27 Human service professionals know the limit and scope of their professional knowledge and offer services only within their knowledge, skill base, and scope of practice.

STANDARD 28 Human service professionals seek appropriate consultation and supervision to assist in decision-making when there are legal, ethical or other dilemmas.

STANDARD 29 Human service professionals promote cooperation among related disciplines to foster professional growth and to optimize the impact of inter-professional collaboration on clients at all levels.

STANDARD 30 Human service professionals promote the continuing development of their profession. They encourage membership in professional associations, support research endeavors, foster educational advancement, advocate for appropriate legislative actions, and participate in other related professional activities.

STANDARD 31 Human service professionals continually seek out new and effective approaches to enhance their professional abilities and use techniques that are conceptually, or evidence based. When practicing techniques that are experimental or new, they inform clients of the status of such techniques as well as the possible risks.

STANDARD 32 Human service professionals conduct research that adheres to all ethical principles, institutional standards, and scientific rigor. Such research takes into consideration cross-cultural bias and is reported in a manner that addressed any limitations.

STANDARD 33 Human service professionals make careful decisions about disclosing personal information while using social media, knowing that they reflect the profession of human services. In addition, they consider how their public conduct may reflect on themselves and their profession.

Responsibility to Self

STANDARD 34 Professionals are aware of their own cultural backgrounds, beliefs, values, and biases. They recognize the potential impact of their backgrounds on their relationships with others and work diligently to provide culturally competent service to all of their clients.

STANDARD 35 Human service professionals strive to develop and maintain healthy personal growth to ensure that they are capable of giving optimal services to clients. When they find that they are physically, emotionally, psychologically, or otherwise not able to offer such services, they identify alternative services for clients.

STANDARD 36 Human service professionals hold a commitment to lifelong learning and continually advance their knowledge and skills to serve clients more effectively.

Responsibility to Students

STANDARD 37 Human service educators develop and implement culturally sensitive knowledge, awareness, and teaching methodologies.

STANDARD 38 Human service educators are committed to the principles of access and inclusion and take all available and applicable steps to make education available to differently-abled students.

STANDARD 39 Human service educators demonstrate high standards of scholarship in their scholarship, pedagogy, and professional service and stay current in the field by being members of their professional associations, attending workshops and conferences, and reviewing and/or conducting research.

STANDARD 40 Human service educators recognize and acknowledge the contributions of students to the work of the educator in such activities as case material, grants, workshops, research, publications, and other related activities.

STANDARD 41 Human service educators monitor students' field experiences to ensure the quality of the placement site, supervisory experience, and learning experience towards the goals of personal, professional, academic, career, and civic development. When students experience potentially harmful events during field placements, educators provide reasonable investigation and response as necessary to safeguard the student.

STANDARD 42 Human service educators establish and uphold appropriate guidelines concerning student disclosure of sensitive/personal information which includes letting students have fair warning of any self-disclosure activities, allowing students to opt-out of in-depth self-disclosure activities when feasible, and ensuring that a mechanism is available to discuss and process such activities as needed.

STANDARD 43 Human service educators are aware that in their relationships with students, power and status are unequal. Human service educators are responsible to clearly define and maintain ethical and professional relationships with student; avoid conduct that is demeaning, embarrassing or exploitative of students; and always strive to treat students fairly, equally and without discrimination.

STANDARD 44 Human service educators ensure students are familiar with, informed by, and accountable to the ethical standards and policies put forth by their program/department, the course syllabus/instructor, their advisor(s), and the Ethical Standards of Human Service Professionals.

From: National Organization for Human Services (2015). *Ethical Standards for Human Services Professionals*. Portland, OR: NOHS. Reproduced by Permission.

References

Preface

Adler, A. (1927/1954). *Understanding human nature* (W. B. Wolf, Trans.). Fawcett Premier. (Original work published 1927).

Anderson, M., Goodman, J., & Schlossberg, N. K. (2012). *Counseling adults in transition: Linking Schlossberg's theory with practice in a diverse world* (4th ed.). New York, NY: Springer Publishing.

Ansbacher, H. L., & Ansbacher, R. R. (1956). *The individual psychology of Alfred Adler: A systematic presentation in selections of his writings.* New York, NY: Basic Books.

Baum, S. K., & Stewart, R. B. (1990). Sources of meaning through the lifespan. *Psychological Reports, 67,* 3–14.

Baumeister, R. F. (1991). *Meanings of life.* New York, NY: The Guilford Press.

Baumeister, R. F. (1999). Self-concept, self-esteem, and identity. In V. J. Derlega, B. A. Winstead, & W. H. Jones (Eds.), *Personality: Contemporary theory and research* (2nd ed., pp. 339-375). Belmont, CA: Wadsworth.

Bellair, P. E., & Roscigno, V. J. (2000). Local labor-market opportunity and adolescent delinquency. *Social Forces, 78* (4), 1509-1538

Blustein, D. L. (2006). *The psychology of working: A new perspective for career development, counseling, and public policy.* Mahwah, NJ: Lawrence Erlbaum.

Blustein, D. L. (2008). The role of work in psychological health and well-being: A conceptual, historical, and public policy perspective. *American Psychologist, 63* (4), 228-240.

Blustein, D. L. (2011). A relational theory of working. *Journal of Vocational Behavior, 79,* 1–17.

Blustein, D. L. (2013). The Psychology of Working: A New Perspective for a New Era. In D. L. Blustein (Ed.), *The Oxford Handbook of the Psychology of Working* (pp. 3-18). New York, NY: Oxford University Press

Budd, J. W. (2011). *The thought of work.* Ithica, NY: ILR Press.

Busacca, L. A. (2002). Career problem assessment: A conceptual schema for counselor training, *Journal of Career Development, 29,* (2), 129-146.

Busacca, L. A., & Rehfuss, M. C. (2017). Postmodern career counseling: A new perspective for the 21st century. In L. A. Busacca & M. C. Rehfuss (Eds.), *Postmodern Career Counseling: A handbook of culture, context, and cases* (pp. 1-19). Alexandria, VA: American Counseling Association.

Carlson, J., & Englar-Carlson, M. (2017). *Adlerian psychotherapy.* Washington, DC: American Psychological Association.

Cohen, B. N. (2003). Applying existential theory and intervention to career decision-making. *Journal of Career Development, 29,* 195-209.

Council for Standards of Human Service Education. (2015). *Accredited programs.* Retrieved from http://www.cshse.org/accredited.html

Dice, T. F., & Rehfuss, M. C. (2017). Human Services Students' Preferences for Master's Level Training. *Journal of Human Services, 37,* 41-53.

Dik, B. J., Byrne, Z. S., & Steger, M. F. (2013). Introduction: Toward an integrative science and practice of meaningful work. In B. J. Dik, Z. S. Byrne, & M. F. Steger (Eds.), *Purpose and meaning in the workplace* (pp. 3-14). Washington, DC: American Psychological Association.

Dreikurs, R. R. (1989). *Fundamentals of Adlerian psychology.* Chicago, IL: Alfred Adler Institute.

Fouad, N. A. (2007). Work and vocational psychology: Theory, research, and applications. *Annual Review of Psychology, 58,* 543-564.

Frankl, V. E. (1984). *Man's search for meaning.* New York, NY: Pocket Books.

Fritzsche, B. A., & Parrish, T. J. (2005). Theories and research on job satisfaction. In S. D. Brown & R. W. Lent (Eds.), *Career development and counseling: Putting theory and research to work.* (pp. 180-202). Hoboken, NJ US: John Wiley & Sons Inc.

Giddens, A. (1991). *Modernity and self-identity: Self and society in the late modern age.* Cambridge, MA: Polity Press.

Hackett, G. (1993). Career counseling and psychotherapy: False dichotomies and recommended remedies. *Journal of Career Assessment, 1,* 105-117.

Hartung, P. J. (2002). Cultural context in career theory and practice: Role salience and values. *The Career Development Quarterly, 51,* 12-25.

Herr, E. L., Cramer, S. H., & Niles, S. G. (2004). *Career guidance and counseling though the life span: Systematic approaches* (6th ed.). Boston, MA: Pearson/Allyn & Bacon.

Hollis, J. (2005). *Finding meaning in the second half of life.* New York, NY: Penguin Group.

Johnson, K. F., Sparkman-Key, N., & Kalkbrenner, M. T. (2017). Human service students' and professionals' knowledge and experiences of interprofessionalism: Implications for education. *Journal of Human Services, 37*(1), 5-13.

Juntunen, C. (2006). The psychology of working: The clinical context. *Professional Psychology: Research and Practice, 37* (4), 342-350.

Kalleberg, A. L. (2009). Precarious work, insecure workers: Employment relations in transition. *American Sociological Review, 74,* 1–22.

Keyes, C. L. M., & Waterman, M. B. (2003). *Dimensions of well-being and mental health in adulthood.* In M. H. Bornstein, L. Davidson, C. L. M. Keyes & K. A.

Krumboltz, J. D. (1993). Integrating career and personal counseling. *The Career Development Quarterly, 42,* 143-148.

LaPointe, K. (2010). Narrating career, positioning identity: Career identity as a narrative practice. *Journal of Vocational Behavior, 77,* 1–9.

Lent, R. W., & Brown, S. D. (2013). Understanding and facilitating career development in the 21st century. In S. D. Brown & R. W. Lent (Eds.), *Career development and counseling: Putting theory and research to work* (2nd ed., pp. 1-26). Hoboken, NJ: John Wiley & Sons, Inc.

Lucas, R.E., Clark A.E., Georgellis, Y. and Diener E. (2004). Unemployment alters the set-point for life satisfaction. *Psychological Science, 15*, 8-13.

Moser, K., & Schuler, H. (2004). Is involvement a suppressor of the job satisfaction-life satisfaction relationship? *Journal of Applied Social Psychology, 34* (11), 2377-2388.

Neff, W. S. (1985). *Work and human behavior* (3rd ed.). NY: Aldine Publishing Company.

Neukrug, E. (2017). *Theory, practice, and trends in human services: An introduction.* Belmont, CA: Cengage Learning.

Niles, S. G, & Harris-Bowlsbey, J. (2017). *Career development interventions* (5th ed.). Boston, MA: Pearson Education, Inc.

Paul, K. I., & Moser, K. (2009). Unemployment impairs mental health: Meta-analyses. *Journal of Vocational Behavior, 74* (3), 264-282

Quick, J. C., & Tetrick, L. E. (Eds.). (2010). *Handbook of occupational health psychology* (2nd ed.). Washington, DC: American Psychological Association.

Rather, D. (2001). The American dream. New York: HarperCollins.

Rosso, B. D., Dekas, K. H., & Wrzesniewski, A. (2010). On the meaning of work: A theoretical integration and review. *Research in Organizational Behavior, 30*, 91-127.

Savickas, M. L. (2019). *Career counseling* (2nd ed.). Washington, DC: American Psychological Association.

Savickas, M. L. (2012). Life design: A paradigm for career intervention in the 21st century. *Journal of Counseling & Development, 90*, 13–19.

Savickas, M. L. (2004). *Meaning and Mattering in Career Construction: The Case of Elaine.* Rootstown, OH: Northeast Ohio Medical University. Retrieved from http://www.cannexus.ca/wp-content/uploads/2014/04/Meaning-and-Mattering-in-Career-Construction-The-Case-of-Elaine-cx10_Dr.-Savickas_A-Demonstration.pdf

Schultheiss, D. E. P. (2003). A relational approach to career counseling: Theoretical integration and practical application. *Journal of Counseling & Development, 81* (3), 301-310.

Schultheiss, D. E. P. (2006). The interface of work and family life. *Professional Psychology: Research and Practice, 37* (4), 334-341.

Sampson, R. J., & Laub, J. H. (1993). *Crime in the making: Pathways and turning points through life.* Cambridge, MA US: Harvard University Press.

Standing, G. (1999). *Global labour flexibility: Seeking distributive justice.* New York, NY: St. Martin's Press.

Steger, M. F., & Dik, B. J. (2010). Work as meaning: Individual and organizational benefits of engaging in meaningful work. In P. A. Linley, S. Harrington, & N. Garcea (Eds.), *Oxford library of psychology. Oxford handbook of positive psychology and work* (pp. 131-142). New York, NY, US: Oxford University Press.

Swanson, J. L. (2012). Work and Psychological Health. In N. A. Fouad & J. A Carter (Eds.), *APA Handbook of Counseling Psychology* (pp. 3-24). Washington, DC: American Psychological Association.

Sweeney, T., & Witmer, J. M. (1991). Beyond social interest: Striving towards optimum health and wellness. *Individual Psychology: The Journal of Adlerian Theory, Research, and Practice, 47,*527-540.

Sweet, S., & Meiksins, P. (2017). *Changing contours of work: Job opportunities in the new economy (3rd ed.).* Thousand Oaks, CA: Sage Publications.

Vinokur, A, Schul, Y., Vuori, J. & Price, R. (2000). Two years after a job loss: Long-term impact of the JOBS program on reemployment and mental health. *Journal of Occupational Health Psychology, 5,* 32-47.

Walsh, K. and Gordon, J. R. (2008), Creating an individual work identity. *Human Resources Management Review, 18,* pp. 46-61.

Whiston, S. C., & Rahardja, D. (2008). Vocational counseling process and outcome. In S. D. Brown & R. W. Lent (Eds.), *Handbook of counseling psychology* (4th ed., pp. 444-461). Hoboken, NJ US: John Wiley & Sons Inc

Wida, E. C. (March 18, 2019). *After overcoming opioid addiction, chef finds solace back in the kitchen.* TODAY. Retrieved from https://www.today.com/food/chef-ashish-alfred-shares-harrowing-story-overcoming-addiction-t150576

Zedeck, S. (1992). Introduction: Exploring the domain of work and family careers. In S. Zedeck (Ed.), *Work, families, and organizations* (pp. 1-32). San Francisco, CA: Jossey-Bass.

Zunker, V. G. (2008). *Career, work, and mental health.* Thousand Oaks, CA: Sage Publications.

Chapter 1

Amundson, N. E., Harris-Bowlsbey, J., Niles, S. G. (2014). *Essential elements of career counseling: Processes and techniques.* New York, NY: Pearson Education, Inc.

Ansbacher, H. L., & Ansbacher, R. R. (1964). *The Individual Psychology of Alfred Adler: A systematic presentation in selections from his writings.* New York, NY: Harper & Row.

Arabandi, B. (2015). Globalization, flexibility and new workplace culture in the United States and India. In A. S. Wharton (Ed.), *Working in America: Continuity, conflict, and change in a new economic era* (4th ed., pp. 69–87). Boulder, CO: Paradigm.

Betz, N. E., & Corning, A. F. (1993). The inseparability of career and personal counseling. *Career Development Quarterly, 42,* 137-142.

Blustein, D. L. (2001). The interface of work and relationships: A critical knowledge base for 21st century psychology. *The Counseling Psychologist, 29,* 179-192.

Blustein, D. L. (2006). The psychology of working: A new perspective for a new era. In D. L. Blustein (Ed.), *The Oxford handbook of the psychology of working,* (pp. 3-18). New York, NY: Oxford University Press.

Brown, D. (2016). *Career information, career counseling, and career development* (11th ed.). Boston, MA: Pearson Education.

Busacca, L. A., Beebe, R. S. & Toman, S. M. (2010). Life and work values of counselor trainees: A national survey. *The Career Development Quarterly, 59,* 2-18.

Busacca, L. A., & Rehfuss, M. C. (2017). Postmodern career counseling: A new perspective for the 21st century. In L. A. Busacca & M. C. Rehfuss (Eds.), *Postmodern Career Counseling: A handbook of culture, context, and cases* (pp. 1-19). Alexandria, VA: American Counseling Association.

Cochran, L. (1997). *Career counseling: A narrative approach.* Thousand Oaks, CA: Sage Publications

Diambra, J. F. (2001). Human services: The past as prelude. In T. McClam & M. Woodside (Eds.), *Human service challenges in the 21st century* (pp. xvii-xxii). Birmingham, AL: Ebsco Media.

Dik, B. J., & Duffy, R. D. (2009). Calling and vocation at work: Definitions and prospects for research and practice. *Counseling Psychologist, 37,* 424-450.

Egan, G. (2013). *The skilled helper: A problem management and opportunity development approach to helping* (10th ed.). Belmont, CA: Brooks Cole.

Freeman, S. C. (1990). C. H. Patterson on client-centered career counseling: An interview. *The Career Development Quarterly, 38,* 291-301.

Freud, S. (1930). *Civilization and its Discontents. Standard Edition,* Vol. 21. London, England: Hogarth Press.

Gallup. (2017). *State of the American workplace.* New York, NY: Gallup, Inc.

Gelso, C. (2009). The real relationship in a postmodern world: Theoretical and empirical explorations. *Psychotherapy Research, 19,* 253-264.

Gordon, V. N. (2006). *Career advising: An academic advisors guide.* Hoboken, NJ: Wiley.

Hazler, R. J., & Kottler, J. A. (2005). *The emerging professional counselor: Student dreams to professional realities* (2nd ed.). Alexandria, VA: American Counseling Association.

Herr, E. L., Cramer, S. H., & Niles, S. G. (2004). *Career guidance and counseling through the life span: Systematic approaches* (6th ed.). Boston, MA: Allyn & Bacon.

Hoffman, M. (2000). *Empathy and moral development.* Cambridge, UK: Cambridge University Press.

Krumboltz, J. D. (1993). Integrating career and personal counseling. *Career Development Quarterly, 42,* 143-148.

National Alliance of Direct Support Professionals. (2011). Making a world of difference in people's lives: Community Support Skill Standards. Retrieved from https://www.nadsp.org/library/csss.html

National Career Development Association (2011). *NCDA 2011 Harris Interactive Survey on Working America.* Retrieved from https://www.ncda.org/aws/NCDA/pt/sd/news_article/48270/_PARENT/l ayout_details/false

National Career Development Association (2018a). Competencies addressed in the NCDA FCD Curriculum. Retrieved from https://www.ncda.org/aws/NCDA/pt/sp/facilitator_overview_competencies

National Career Development Association (2018b). *NCDA facilitating career development training.* Retrieved from https://www.ncda.org/aws/NCDA/pt/sp/facilitator_overview#1

Neault, R. (2011, September). Career flow: A hope-centered approach to achieving dreams. *Career Convergence: Web Magazine.* Retrieved from https://www.ncda.org

Niles, S. G. (2011). Career flow: A hope-centered model of career development. *Journal of Employment Counseling, 48,* 173-175.

Quick, J. C., & Tetrick, L. E. (2010). *Handbook of occupational health psychology* (2nd ed.). Washington, DC: American Psychological Association.

Robertson, P. J. (2013). The well-being outcomes of career guidance. *British Journal of Guidance & Counseling, 41,* 254-266.

Rogers, C. R. (1957). The necessary and sufficient conditions of therapeutic personality change. *Journal of Counseling Psychology, 21,* 95-103.

Rogers, C. R. (1980). *A way of being.* Boston, MA: Houghton Mifflin.

Rønnestad, M. H., & Skovholt, T. M. (2003). The journey of the counselor and therapist: Research findings and perspectives on professional development. *Journal of Career Development, 30,* 5-44.

Rounds, J., & Jin, J. (2013). Nature, importance, and assessment of needs and values. In S. D. Brown & R. W. Lent (Eds.), *Career development and counseling: Putting theory and research to work* (2nd ed., pp. 417-448). Hoboken, NJ: John Wiley & Sons, Inc.

Saks, A. M. (2006). Antecedents and consequences of employee engagement. *Journal of Managerial Psychology, 21,* 600-619.

Savickas, M. L. (1998). Career style assessment and counseling. In T. J. Sweeney (Ed.), *Adlerian counseling: A practitioner's approach* (4th ed., pp. 183-207). New York, NY: Routledge.

Savickas, M. L. (2011). *Career counseling.* Washington, DC: American Psychological Association.

Savickas, M. L. (2019). *Career counseling* (2nd ed.). Washington, DC: American Psychological Association.

Schaufeli, W. B., Salanova, M., Gonzalez-Roma, V., & Bakker, A. B. (2002). The measurement of engagement and burnout: A two-sample confirmatory factor analytic approach. *Journal of Happiness Studies, 3*, pp. 71-92.

Sharf, R. S. (2013). *Applying career development theory to counseling* (6th ed.). Belmont, CA: Brooks/Cole.

Skovholt, T. M. (2001). *The resilient practitioner.* Boston, MA: Allyn & Bacon.

Spokane, A. R. (1991). *Career interventions.* Englewood Cliffs, NJ: Prentice-Hall.

Super, D. E., (1990). Career and life development. In D. Brown & L. Brooks (Eds.), *Career choice and development: Applying contemporary theories to practice* (2nd ed., pp. 197-261). San Francisco, CA: Jossey-Bass.

Zunker, V. G. (2008). *Career, work, and mental health: Integrating career and personal counseling.* Los Angeles, CA: Sage.

Zunker, V. G. (2016). *Career counseling: A holistic approach* (9th ed.). Boston, MA: Cengage Learning.

Chapter 2

Applebaum, H. (1998). *The American work ethic and the changing work force: An historical perspective.* Westport, CT: Greenwood Press.

Arthur, M. B., & Rousseau, D. M. (Eds.). (1996). *The boundaryless career: A new employment principle for a new organizational era.* Oxford, England: Oxford University Press.

Aubrey, R. F. (1977). Historical development of guidance and counseling and implications for the future. *Personnel and Guidance Journal, 55,* 288-295.

Busacca, L. A., & Rehfuss, M. C. (2017). Career counseling in postmodern times: Emergence and narrative conceptions. In L. A. Busacca & M. C. Rehfuss (Eds.), *Postmodern career counseling: A handbook of culture, context, and cases* (pp. 23-36). Alexandria, VA: American Counseling Association.

Davis, J. B. (1956). *The saga of a schoolmaster: An autobiography.* Boston, MA: Boston University Press.

Giddens, A. (1991). *Modernity and self-identity: Self and society in the late modern age.* Cambridge, MA: Polity Press.

Guichard, J. (2015). From vocational guidance and career counseling to life design dialogues. In L. Nota & J. Rosier (Eds.), *Handbook of life design: From practice to theory and from theory to practice* (pp. 11-25). Boston, MA: Hogrefe.

Herr, E. L. (2001). Career development and its practice: A historical perspective. *The CDQ: Special Millennium Issue, 49* (3), 196-211.

Inkson, K., & Elkin, G. (2008). Landscape with travelers: The context of careers in developed nations. In J. A. Athanasou & R. van Esbroeck (Eds.), *International handbook of career guidance* (pp. 69–94). Dordrecht, The Netherlands: Springer.

Kalleberg, A. L. (2009). Precarious work, insecure workers: Employment relations in transition. *American Sociological Review, 74,* 1–22.

Kuhn, T. S. (1962). *The structure of scientific revolutions.* Chicago, IL: University of Chicago Press.

Maccoby, M. (1983). *The leader: A new face for American management.* New York, NY: Ballantine Books.

Parsons, F. (1909). *Choosing a vocation.* Boston, MA: Houghton-Mifflin.

Pope, M. (2000). A brief history of career counseling in the United States. *The Career Development Quarterly, 48,* (194-211).

Richards, L. S. (1881). *Vocophy: The new profession.* Malboro, MA: Bratt Brothers.

Richardson, M. S. (1996). From career counselling to counseling/psychotherapy and work, jobs, and career. In M. L. Savickas & W. B. Walsh (Eds.), *Handbook of career counseling theory and practice* (pp. 347–360). Palo Alto, CA: Davies-Black.

Richardson, M. S. (2015). Agentic action in context. In R. A. Young, J. F. Domene, & L. Valach (Eds.), *Counseling and action: Toward life-enhancing work, relationships, and identity* (pp. 51–68). New York, NY: Springer.

Robinson, C. C. (1922). *The find yourself idea: A friendly method of vocational guidance for older boys.* New York, NY: Association Press.

Savickas, M. L. (2008). Helping people choose jobs: A history of the guidance profession. In J. A. Anthanasou & R. Van Esbroeck (Eds.). *International Handbook of Career Guidance* (pp. 97-113). Dordrecht, The Netherlands: Springer.

Savickas, M. L. (2009). Pioneers of the vocational guidance movement: A centennial celebration. *The Career Development Quarterly, 57,* 194-198.

Savickas, M. L. (2019). *Career counseling* (2nd ed.). Washington, DC: American Psychological Association.

Standing, G. (1999). *Global labour flexibility: Seeking distributive justice.* New York, NY: St. Martin's Press.

Super, D. E. (1957) *The psychology of careers.* New York, NY: Harper.

Whiteley, J. M. (1984). *Counseling psychology: A historical perspective.* Schenectady, NY: Character Research.

Williamson, E. G. (1965). *Vocational counseling.* New York, NY: McGraw-Hill.

Zinn, H. (2003). *A people's history of the United States.* New York, NY: HarperCollins.

Chapter 3

Allen, J. E., Jr. (1970, February). *Conference for all as the goal for secondary education.* Paper presented at the meeting of the National Association of Secondary School Principals, Washington, DC.

Bedi, R. P. (2004). The therapeutic alliance and the interface of career counseling and personal counseling. *Journal of Employment Counseling, 41,* 126–135.

Busacca, L. A. (2002). Career problem assessment: A conceptual schema for counselor training. *Journal of Career Development, 29,* 129-146.

Busacca, L. A., & Rehfuss, M. C. (2017). *Postmodern career counseling: A handbook of culture, contexts, and cases.* Alexandria, VA: American Counseling Association.

Busacca, L. A., & Taber, B. J. (2002). The Career Maturity Inventory-Revised: A preliminary psychometric investigation. *Journal of Career Assessment, 4,* 441–455.

Crites, J. O., & Savickas, M. L. (1996). Revision of the career maturity inventory. *Journal of Career Assessment, 4,* 131–138.

Crites, J. O., & Savickas M. L. (2011). Career Maturity Inventory-Form C. Retrieved from http://www.vocopher.com/ms/cmic/CMI_C_Master.pdf

Cummings, A. L., Hallberg, E. T., Martin, J., Slemon, A., & Hiebert, B. (1990). Implications of counselor conceptualizations for counselor education. *Counselor Education and Supervision, 30,* 120–134.

Evans, R., Hoyt, K., Mackin, E., & Mangum, G. (1972). *Career education: What it is and how to do it.* Salt Lake City, UT: Olympus Publishing Company.

Granvold, D. K. (1996). Constructivist psychotherapy. *Families in Society, 77,* 345–359.

Harmon, L. W., Hansen, J., Borgen, F. H., & Hammer, A. L. (1994). *Strong interest inventory: Applications and technical guide.* Palo Alto, CA: Consulting Psychologist Press.

Hartung, P. J. (2013). Career as story: Making the narrative turn. In W. B. Walsh, M. L. Savickas, & P. J. Hartung (Eds.), *Handbook of vocational psychology* (4th ed., pp. 33–52). New York, NY: Routledge.

Herr, E. L. (1996). Toward the convergence of career theory and practice: Mythology, issues, and possibilities. In M. L. Savickas & W. B. Walsh (Eds.), *Handbook of career counseling theory and practice* (pp. 13–35). Palo Alto, CA: Davies-Black.

Holland, J. L. (1997). *Making vocational choices: A theory of vocational personalities and the work environments (3rd ed.).* Odessa, FL: Psychological Assessment Resources.

Holland, J. L., Powell, A. B., & Fritzsche, B. A. (1994). *The self-directed search professional user's guide.* Odessa, FL: Psychological Assessment Resources.

Hoyt, K. B. (1972). *Career education: What it is and how to do it.* Salt Lake City, UT: Olympus Publishing Co.

Hoyt, K. B. (2005). *Career education: History and future.* Tulsa, OK: National Career Development Association.

Liptak, J. J. (1991). The fourth alternative: Leisure search and planning. *Journal of Employment Counseling, 28,* 57–62.

Nevill, D. D., & Super, D. E. (1986) *The Salience Inventory: Theory, application and research.* Palo Alto, CA: Consulting Psychologist Press.

Savickas, M. L. (1991). Improving career time perspective. In D. Brown & L. Brooks (Eds.), *Techniques of career counseling* (pp. 236–249). Boston, MA: Allyn & Bacon.

Savickas, M. L. (1996). A framework for linking career theory and practice. In M. L. Savickas & W. B. Walsh (Eds.), *Handbook of career counseling theory and practice* (pp. 191-208). Palo Alto, CA: Davies-Black.

Savickas, M. L. (2008). Helping people choose jobs: A history of the guidance profession. In J. A. Anthanasou & R. Van Esbroeck (Eds.), *International Handbook of Career Guidance* (pp. 97-113). Dordrecht, The Netherlands: Springer.

Super, D. E. (1957). *The psychology of careers.* New York, NY: Harper & Row.

Super, D. E. (1980). A life-span, life-space approach to career development. *Journal of Vocational Behavior, 16,* 282–298.

Super, D. E., Savickas, M. L., & Super, C. M. (1996). The life-span, life-space approach to career. In D. Brown, L. Brooks (Eds.), *Career choice and development: Applying contemporary theories to practice, 3rd Ed.* (pp. 121–178). San Francisco: Jossey-Bass.

Super, D. E., Thompson, A. S., Lindeman, R. H. (1988). *The Adult Career Concerns Inventory.* Palo Alto, CA: Consulting Psychologists Press.

Chapter 4

Anderson, M. L., Goodman, J., & Schlossberg, N. K. (2012). *Counseling adults in transition* (4th ed.). New York, NY: Springer.

Bandura, A. (1971). *Social learning theory.* Morristown, NJ: General Learning Press.

Cochran, L. (1997). *Career counseling: A narrative approach.* Thousand Oaks, CA: Sage.

Gottfredson, G. D., & Holland, J. L. (1996). *Dictionary of Holland occupational codes* (3rd ed.). Odessa, FL: Psychological Assessment Resources.

Gysbers, N. C., Heppner, M. J., & Johnston, J. A. (2014). *Career counseling: Holism, diversity, and strengths.* Alexandria, VA: American Counseling Association.

Hartung, P. J., & Blustein, D. L. (2002). Reason, intuition, and social justice: Elaborating on Parsons career decision-making model. *Journal of Counseling and Development, 80,* 41-47.

Holland, J. L. (1959). A theory of vocational choice. *Journal of Counseling Psychology, 6,* 35–45.

Holland, J. L. (1997). *Making vocational choices: A theory of vocational personalities and work environments* (3rd ed.). Odessa, FL: Psychological Assessment Resources.

Krumboltz, J. D. (1975). A social learning theory of career decision making. In A. M. Mitchell, G. B. Jones, & J. D. Krumboltz (Eds.), *A social learning theory of career decision making* (pp. 13-39). Palo Alto, CA: American Institutes for Research.

Krumboltz, J. D. (2005). Don't let theories boggle your mind. In S. G. Niles & J. Harris-Bowlsbey (Eds.), *Career development interventions in the 21st century* (p. 34). Upper Saddle River, NJ: Pearson Education.

Krumboltz, J. D., & Levin, A. S. (2010). *Luck is no accident: Making the most of happenstance in your life and career* (2nd ed.). Oakland, CA: New Harbinger.

Mitchell, L. K. & Krumboltz, J. D. (1996). Krumboltz's learning theory of career choice and development. In D. Brown, & L. Brooks (Ed.), *Career choice and development* (3rd ed., pp. 233-280). San Francisco, CA: Jossey-Bass.

Mitchell, L. K., Levin, A. S., & Krumboltz, J. D. (1999). Planned happenstance: Constructing unexpected career opportunities. *Journal of Counseling & Development, 77*, 115-124.

Miller-Tiedeman, A. L. (1988). *LIFECAREER: The quantum leap into a process theory of career.* Vista, CA: Lifecareer Center.

Miller-Tiedeman, A. L. (1999). *Learning, practicing, and living the new careering.* Philadelphia, PA: Accelerated Development

Peterson, G. W., Sampson, J. P., Jr., Lenz, J. G., & Reardon, R. C. (2002). Becoming career problem solvers and decision makers: A cognitive information processing approach. In D. Brown (Ed.), *Career choice and development* (4th. ed., pp. 312-369). San Francisco, CA: Jossey-Bass.

Rayman, J., & Atanasoff, L. (1999). Holland's theory and career intervention: The power of the hexagon. *Journal of Vocational Behavior, 55*, 114-126.

Reardon, R. C., & Lenz, J. G. (1998). *The Self-Directed Search and related Holland career materials: A practitioner's guide.* Odessa, FL: Psychological Assessment Resources, Inc.

Rounds, J., & Jin, J. (2013). Nature, importance, and assessment of needs and values. In S. D. Brown & R. W. Lent (Eds.), *Career development and counseling: Putting theory and research to work* (2nd ed., pp. 417-448). Hoboken, NJ: John Wiley & Sons, Inc.

Sampson, J. P., Jr., Reardon, R. C., Peterson, G. W., & Lenz, J. G. (2004). *Career counseling and services: A cognitive information processing approach.* Pacific Grove, CA: Brooks/Cole.

Savickas, M. L. (1995). Constructivist counseling for career indecision. *Career Development Quarterly, 43*, 363-373.

Savickas, M. L. (2001). Toward a comprehensive theory of careers: Dispositions, concerns, and narratives. In F. T. L. Leong & A. Barak (Eds.), *Contemporary models in vocational psychology: A volume in honor of Samuel H. Osipow.* Manwah, NJ: Erlbaum.

Savickas, M. L. (2005). The theory and practice of career construction. In S. D. Brown & R. W. Lent (Eds.), *Career development and counseling: Putting theory and research to work* (pp. 42-70). Hoboken, NJ, US: John Wiley & Sons Inc.

Savickas, M. L. (2015). Career counseling paradigms: Guiding, developing, and designing. In P. Hartung, M. Savickas, & W. Walsh (Eds.), *The APA handbook of career interventions* (pp. 129–143). Washington, DC: APA Press.

Sharf, R. S. (2013). *Applying career development theory to counseling* (6th ed.). Belmont, Ca: Brooks/Cole.

Strong, E. K., Jr. (1955). *Vocational interests 18 years after college.* Minneapolis, MN: University of Minnesota Press.

Super, D. E. (1980). A life-span, life-space approach to career development. *Journal of Vocational Behavior, 16,* 282-298.

Super, D. E. (1990). A life-span, life-space approach to career development. In D. Brown, L. Brooks & Associates, *Career choice and development* (2nd ed., pp. 197-261). San Francisco, CA: Jossey-Bass.

Young, R. A., & Collin, A. (2004). Introduction: Constructivism and social constructionism in the career field. *Journal of Vocational Behavior, 64,* 373–388.

Chapter 5

American Counseling Association. (2014). *ACA code of ethics.* Retrieved from https://www.counseling.org/resources/aca-code-of-ethics.pdf

American Educational Research Association, American Psychological Association, & National Council on Measurement in Education. (2014). *Standards for educational and psychological testing.* Washington, DC: American Educational Research Association.

Arulmani, G. (2014). Assessment of interest and aptitude: A methodologically integrated approach. In G. Arulmani, A. J. Bakshi, F. T. L. Leong, & A. G. Watts (Eds.), *Handbook of career development: International perspectives* (pp. 609–629). Dordrecht, The Netherlands: Springer.

Association for Assessment in Counseling and Education. (2012). *Standards for multicultural assessment* (4th ed.). Alexandria, VA: Author.

Brown, D. (2002). The role of work values and cultural values in occupational choice, satisfaction, and success. In D. Brown & Associates, *Career choice and development* (4th ed., pp. 465-509). San Francisco, CA: Jossey-Bass.

Brown, D. (2016). *Career information, career counseling, and career assessment* (11th ed.). Boston, MA: Pearson Education, Inc.

Brown, S. D., & McPartland, E. B. (2005). Career interventions: Current status and future directions. In W. B. Walsh & M. L. Savickas (Eds.), *Handbook of vocational psychology: Theory, research, and practice* (3rd ed., pp. 195–226). Mahaw, NJ: Lawrence Erlbaum.

Busacca, L. A., & Rehfuss, M. C. (2017). *Postmodern career counseling: A handbook of culture, context, and cases.* Alexandria, VA: American Counseling Association.

Dawis, R., Goldman, S., & Sung, Y. (1992). Stability and change in abilities for a sample of young adults. *Educational and Psychological Measurement, 52,* 457–465.

Flores, L. Y., Spanierman, L. B., & Obasi, E. M. (2003). Ethical and professional issues in career assessment with diverse racial and ethnic groups. *Journal of Career Assessment, 11,* 76-95.

Heppner, M. J., & Heppner, P. P. (2003). Identifying process variables in career counseling: A research agenda. *Journal of Vocational Behavior, 62,* 429–452.

Holland, J. L., Daiger, D. C., & Power, P. G. (1980). *My Vocational Situation.* Palo Alto, CA: Consulting Psychologist Press, Inc.

Leong, F. T. L., & Hartung, P. J. (2000). Cross-cultural career assessment: Review and prospects for the new millennium. *Journal of Career Assessment, 8,* 391-401.

Lamprecht, J. C. (2002). Career assessment skills. In K. Maree & L. Ebersöhn (Eds.), *Lifeskills and career counselling* (pp. 119–127). Sandown, South Africa: Heinemann.

McAuliffe, G. (2013). Culture and diversity defined. In G. McAuliffe (Ed.), *Culturally alert counseling: A comprehensive introduction* (2nd ed., pp. 3–20). Thousand Oaks, CA: Sage.

Metz, A. J., & Jones, J. E. (2013). Ability and aptitude assessment in career counseling. In S. Brown & B. Lent (Eds.), *Career development and counseling: Putting theory and research to work* (2nd ed., pp. 449-476). Hoboken, NJ: John Wiley & Sons.

National Organization for Human Services (2015). *Ethical Standards for Human Services Professionals.* NOHS. Retrieved from https://www.nationalhumanservices.org/ethical-standards-for-hs-professionals

Neukrug, E., & Fawcett, R. (2015). *Essentials of testing and assessment: A practical guide for counselors, social workers, and psychologists* (3rd ed.). Pacific Grove, CA: Cengage Learning.

Parsons, F. (1909). *Choosing a vocation.* Boston, MA: Houghton-Mifflin.

Salomone, P. R., (1982). Difficult cases in career counseling: II–The indecisive client. *Journal of Counseling & Development, 60,* pp. 496-500.

Stoltz, K. B., & Barclay, S. R. (in press). *A comprehensive guide to career assessment* (7th ed.). Broken Arrow, OK: National Career Development Association.

Strong, E. K., Jr. (1955). *Vocational interests 18 years after college.* Minneapolis, MN: University of Minnesota Press.

Watson, M. & McMahon, M. (2014). Making Meaning of Quantitative Assessment in Career Counseling through a Storytelling Approach. In G...

Worthington, R., L., Flores, L. Y., & Navarro, R. L. (2005). Career development in context: Research with people of color. In S. D. Brown & R. W. Lent (Eds.), *Career development and counseling: Putting theory and research to work* (pp. 225-252). Hoboken, NJ: Wiley.

Whiston, S. C. (2017). *Principles and applications of assessment in counseling* (5th ed.). Boston, MA: Cengage Learning.

Whiston, S. C., & Rahardja, D. (2005). Qualitative career assessment: An overview and analysis. *Journal of Career Assessment, 13,* 371-380.

Wood, C., & Hays, D. (2013). *A counselor's guide to career assessment instruments* (6th ed.). Tulsa, OK: National Career Development Association.

Wood, C., & Scully, Z. (2017). Postmodern career assessment: Advantages and considerations. In L. A. Busacca & M. C. Rehfuss (Eds.), *Postmodern career counseling: A handbook of culture, context, and cases* (pp. 77-88). Alexandria, VA: American Counseling Association.

Chapter 6

Association of Computer-Based Systems of Career Information (2009). *Consumer guide for evaluating career information and services.* Retrieved from https://ncda.org/aws/ACRP/asset_manager/get_file/37672

Brown, D. (2016). *Career information, career counseling, and career assessment* (11th ed.). Boston, MA: Pearson Education, Inc.

Busacca, L. A. (2002). Career problem assessment: A conceptual schema for counselor training. *Journal of Career Development, 29,* 129-146.

Duggan, M. H., & Jurgens, J. C. (2007). *Career interventions and techniques: A complete guide for human services professionals.* Boston, MA: Pearson Education, Inc.

Gysbers, N. C., Heppner, M. J., & Johnston, J. A. (2014). *Career counseling: Holism, diversity, and strengths* (4th ed.). Alexandria, VA: American Counseling Association.

Jordan, A. L., & Marinaccio, J. N. (Eds.). (2017). *Facilitating career development: An instructional program for career development facilitators and other career development providers.* (4th ed.). Broken Arrow, OK: National Career Development Association.

Kirk, J. J. (2000). Web-assisted career counseling. *Journal of Employment Counseling, 37,* 146-159.

National Career Development Association (1991). *Guidelines for the preparation and evaluation of career and occupational information literature.* Retrieved from https://ncda.org/aws/NCDA/asset_manager/get_file/3399

National Career Development Association (2018). *Internet sites for career planning.* Retrieved from https://www.ncda.org/aws/NCDA/pt/sp/resources

Salomone, P. R. (1989). Are "occupational" and "career" information synonymous? *The Career Development Quarterly, 38,* 3-5.

Savickas, M. L. (1996). A framework for linking career theory and practice. In M. L. Savickas & W. B. Walsh. (Eds.). *Handbook of career counseling theory and practice* (pp. 191–208). Palo Alto, CA: Davies-Black.

Sukiennik, D., & Raufman, L. (2016). *The career fitness program: Exercising your options* (11th ed.). Boston, MA: Pearson.

Chapter 7

Asher, D. (2011). *Cracking the hidden job market: How to find opportunity in any economy.* Berkeley, CA: Ten Speed Press.

Bolles, R. N. (2018). *What color is your parachute? 2019: A practical manual for job-hunters and career-changers.* New York, NY: Ten Speed Press.

Busacca, L. A. (2002). Career problem assessment: A conceptual schema for counselor training. *Journal of Career Development, 29,* 129-146.

CareerBuilder.com (2017). *Number of employers using social media to screen candidates at all-time high, finds latest CareerBuilder study.* Retrieved from http://press.careerbuilder.com/2017-06-15-Number-of-Employers-Using-Social-Media-to-Screen-Candidates-at-All-Time-High-Finds-Latest-CareerBuilder-Study

Davis III, C.H.F., Deil-Amen, R., Rios-Aguilar, C., & González Canché, M.S. (2012). *Social media and higher education: A literature review and research directions.* Report printed by the University of Arizona and Claremont Graduate University.

Duggan, M. H., & Jurgens, J. C. (2007). *Career interventions and techniques: A complete guide for human services professionals.* Boston, MA: Pearson Education, Inc.

Kluemper, D. H., Rosen, P. A., & Mossholder, K. N. (2012). Social networking websites, personality ratings, and the organizational context: More than meets the eye? *Journal of Applied Social Psychology, 42,* 1143-1172.

National Career Development Association (2018). *Internet sites for career planning.* Retrieved from https://www.ncda.org/aws/NCDA/pt/sp/resources

National Career Development Association. (1997). *NCDA guidelines for the use of the internet for provision of career information and planning services.* Retrieved from http://www.ncda.org/aws/NCDA/pt/sp/guidelines_internet

Nell, A. (2014). Using social media in career counseling. In N. C Gysbers, M. J. Heppner, & J. A. Johnston (Eds.), *Career counseling: Holism, diversity, and strengths* (4th ed., pp. 289-300). Alexandria, VA: American Counseling Association.

Right Management (2013). *Networking, not internet cruising, still lands most jobs for those in career transition.* Retrieved from https://www.right.com/wps/wcm/connect/right-us-en/home/thoughtwire/categories/talent-work/networking-not-internet-cruising-still-lands-most-jobs-for-those-in-career-transition

Rutledge, P. A. (2012). *Sams teach yourself LinkedIn in 10 Minutes* (3rd Ed.). New York, NY: Sams Publishing.

Quigley, K. (2013). *Recruiters increasingly adopt marketing tactics in fierce competition to hire, 2013 Jobvite social recruiting survey show.* Retrieved from http://recruiting.jobvite.com/company/press-releases/2013/recruiters-increasingly-adoptmarketing-tactics-2013-jobvite-social-recruiting-survey-shows/

Smith, A., & Anderson, M. (2018, March). *Social media use in 2018.* Pew Research Center. Retrieved from http://www.pewinternet.org/2018/03/01/social-media-use-in-2018/

Stollak, M., Vandenberg, A. S., Felhofer, N., & Sutherland, P. (2014). How social media is influencing the job search process. *Journal of Management and Marketing Research, 15,* 1-7.

Sukiennik, D., & Raufman, L. (2016). *The career fitness program: Exercising your options* (11th ed.). Boston, MA: Pearson.

U. S. Department of Labor, Bureau of Labor Statistics. (2015). *Fifty years of looking at changes in people's lives.* Spotlight on Statistics. Retrieved from https://www.bls.gov/spotlight/2015/fifty-years-of-looking-at-changes-in-peoples-lives/home.htm

Yate, M. (2017). *Knock 'em dead 2017: The ultimate job search guide.* Avon, MA: Adams Media.

Chapter 8

Arredondo, P. (1999). Multicultural counseling competencies as tools to address oppression and racism. *Journal of Counseling and Development, 77,* 102-108.

American Psychological Association (2015). *APA dictionary of psychology* (2nd ed.). Washington, DC: APA.

Baruth, L. G., & Manning, M. L. (2016). *Multicultural counseling and psychotherapy: A lifespan approach* (6th ed.). New York, NY: Routledge,

Berry, J. W. (2002). Conceptual approaches to acculturation. In K. M. Chun, P. B. Organista, & G. Marin (Eds.), *Acculturation: Advances in theory, measurement, and applied research* (pp. 17-37). Washington, DC: American Psychological Association.

Blustein, D. L. (2011). A relational theory of working. *Journal of Vocational Behavior, 79,* 1–17.

Blustein, D. L., Schultheiss, D. E. P., & Flum, H. (2004). Toward a relational perspective of the psychology of careers and working: A social constructionist analysis. *Journal of Vocational Behavior, 64,* 423–440.

Brown, D. (2002). The role of work values and cultural values in occupational choice, satisfaction, and success. In D. Brown & Associates, *Career choice and development* (4th ed., pp. 465-509). San Francisco, CA: Jossey-Bass.

Busacca, L. A., & Rehfuss, M. C. (2017). Postmodern career counseling: A new perspective for the 21st century. In L. A. Busacca & M. C. Rehfuss (Eds.), *Postmodern Career Counseling: A handbook of culture, context, and cases* (pp. 1-19). Alexandria, VA: American Counseling Association.

Carter, R. T., & Forsyth, J. (2010). Reactions to racial discrimination: Emotional stress and help-seeking behaviors. *Psychological Trauma: Theory, Research, Practice, and Policy, 2,* 183-191.

Chudek, M., Muthukrishna, M. & Henrich, J. (2016). Cultural Evolution. In D. M. Buss (Ed.), *Handbook of Evolutionary Psychology* (2nd ed., p. 749-769). Hoboken, NY: John Wiley & Sons.

Cole, E. R. (2009). Intersectionality and research in psychology. *American Psychologist, 64,* 170-180.

Collins, S., & Arthur, N. (2007). A framework for enhancing multicultural counselling competence. *Canadian Journal of Counseling, 41,* pp. 31-49.

Cushner, K. H., McClelland, A., & Safford, P. (2015). *Human diversity in education: An intercultural approach* (8th ed.). New York, NY: McGraw Hill.

Diemer, M. A., & Ali, S. R. (2009). Integrating social class into vocational psychology: Theory and practice implications. *Journal of Career Assessment, 17,* 247-265.

Fassinger, R. E. (2008). Workplace diversity and public policy: Challenges and opportunities for psychology. *American Psychologist, 63,* 252-268.

Flores, L. Y. (2014). Empowering life choices: Career counseling in the context of race and class. In N. C. Gysbers, M. J. Heppner, & J. A. Johnston (Eds.), *Career counseling: Holism, diversity, and strengths* (4th ed., pp. 51-77). Alexandria, VA: American Counseling Association.

Fouad, N. A., & Bingham, R. P. (1995). Career counseling with racial and ethnic minorities. In W. B. Walsh & S. H. Osipow (Eds.), *Handbook of vocational psychology: Theory, research, and practice* (2nd ed., pp. 331-365). Manwah, NJ: Erlbaum.

Fouad, N. A., & Kantamneni, N. (2013). The role of race and ethnicity in career choice, development, and adjustment. In S. D. Brown & R. W. Lent (Eds.), *Career development and counseling: Putting theory and research to work* (2nd ed., pp. 215-243). Hoboken, NJ: John Wiley & Sons, Inc.

Grothaus, T., McAuliffe, G., Danner, M., & Doyle, L. (2013). Equity, advocacy, and social justice. In G. McAuliffe (Ed.), *Culturally alert counseling: A comprehensive introduction* (2nd ed., pp. 45–73). Los Angeles, CA: Sage Publications.

Gysbers, N. C., Heppner, M. J., & Johnston, J. A. (2014). *Career counseling: Holism, diversity, and strengths.* Alexandria, VA: American Counseling Association.

Helms, J. E., & Piper, R. E. (1994). Implications of racial identity theory for vocational psychology. *Journal of Vocational Behavior, 44,* 14-136

Katz, J. (1985). The sociopolitical nature of counseling. *The Counseling Psychologist, 13,* 615-624.

Kiselica, M. S. (1999). Confronting my own ethnocentrism and racism: A process of pain and growth. *Journal of Counseling and Development, 77,* 14–17.

Marlowe, F. W. (2002). Why the Hadza are still hunter-gatherers. In S. Kent (Ed.), *Ethnicity, Hunter-Gatherers, and the "Other": Association or assimilation in Africa* (pp 247-275). Washington DC: Smithsonian Institution Press.

Marlowe, F. W. (2010). *The Hadza: Hunter-Gatherers of Tanzania.* Berkeley, CA: University of California Press.

McAuliffe, G. (2008). What is culturally alert counseling? In G. McAuliffe (Ed.), *Culturally alert counseling: A comprehensive introduction* (pp. 2–44). Los Angeles, CA: Sage Publications.

McAuliffe, G. (2013a). Culture: Clarifications and complications. In G. McAuliffe (Ed.), *Culturally alert counseling: A comprehensive introduction* (2nd ed., pp. 25-43). Los Angeles, CA: Sage Publications.

McAuliffe, G. (2013b). Culture and diversity defined. In G. McAuliffe (Ed.), *Culturally alert counseling: A comprehensive introduction* (2nd ed., pp. 3–20). Los Angeles, CA: Sage Publications.

McAuliffe, G. J., & Emmett, J. (2017). The postmodern impulse and career counselor preparation. In L. A. Busacca & M. C. Rehfuss (Eds.), *Postmodern Career Counseling: A handbook of culture, context, and cases* (pp. 37-50). Alexandria, VA: American Counseling Association.

Miller, M. J., & Brown, S. D. (2005). Counseling for career choice: Implications for improving interventions and working with diverse populations. In S. D. Brown & R. W. Lent (Eds.), *Career development and counseling: Putting theory and research to work* (pp. 441-465). Hoboken, NJ: John Wiley & Sons Inc.

National Organization for Human Services (2015). *Ethical Standards for Human Services Professionals.* Retrieved from https://www.nationalhumanservices.org/ethics#clients

Neukrug, E. S. (2012). *The world of the counselor: An introduction to the counseling profession* (4th ed.). Belmont, CA: Brooks/Cole.

Neukrug, E. S. (2017). *Theory, practice, and trends in human services: An introduction* (6th ed.). Boston, MA: Cengage Learning.

Neukrug, E. S., & Milliken, T. (2008). Activities to enhance the cultural competence of human services students. *Human Service Education, 28*, 17-28.

Niles, S. G, & Harris-Bowlsbey, J. (2017). *Career development interventions* (5th ed.). Boston, MA: Pearson Education, Inc.

Padilla, A. M., & Borsato, G. N. (2008). Issues in culturally appropriate psychoeducational assessment. In L. A. Suzuki & J. G. Ponterotto (Eds.), *Handbook of multicultural assessment: Clinical, psychological, and educational applications* (pp. 5-21). San Francisco, CA: Jossey-Bass.

Pedersen, P. B. (1991) Multiculturalism as a generic approach to counseling. *Journal of Counseling and Development, 70,* 6-12.

Ponterotto, J. G., & Benesch, K. F. (1988). An organizational framework for understanding the role of culture in counseling. *Journal of Counseling and Development, 66,* 237-241.

Pope, M. (2012). Embracing and harnessing diversity in the US workforce: What have we learned? *International Journal for Educational and Vocational Guidance, 12,* 17-30.

Power, C. (2015). Hadza gender rituals – epeme and maitoko – considered as counterparts. *Hunter Gatherer Research, 1*(3), 333-358.

Savickas, M. L., & Hartung, P. J. (2012). *My Career Story: An autobiographical workbook for life-career success.* Retrieved from http://www.vocopher.com/CSI/CCI_workbook.pdf

Schultz, E. A., & Lavenda, R. H. (2017). *Cultural anthropology: A perspective on the human condition* (10th ed.). New York, NY: Oxford University Press.

Sewell, H. (2009). *Working with ethnicity, race, and culture in mental health: A handbook for practitioners.* Philadelphia, PA: Jessica Kingsley.

Sharf, R. S. (2013). *Applying career development theory to counseling* (6th ed.). Belmont, CA: Brooks/Cole.

Smedley, A., & Smedley, B. D. (2005). Race as biology is fiction, racism as a social problem is real: Anthropological and historical perspectives on the social construction of race. *American Psychologist, 60*(1), 16-26.

Speight, S. L., Myers, L. J., Cox, C. I., & Highlen, P. S. (1991). A redefinition of multicultural counseling. *Journal of Counseling & Development, 70,* 29-36.

Stead, G. B., & Bakker, T. M. (2010). Discourse analysis in career counseling and development. *The Career Development Quarterly, 59,* 72–86.

Sue, D. W., & Sue, D. (2016). *Counseling the culturally diverse: Theory and practice* (7th ed.). New York, NY: Wiley.

U. S. Census Bureau (2018). *State and country quickfacts.* Retrieved from https://www.census.gov/quickfacts/fact/table/US/PST045218

Watson, M. B., & McMahon, M. (2004). Postmodern (narrative) career counseling and education. *Perspectives in Education, 22,* 169–170.

Woodburn, J. C. (1970). *Hunters and gatherers: The material culture of the nomadic Hadza.* London, England: The British Museum.

Chapter 9

Anderson, M., Goodman, J., & Schlossberg, N. K. (2012). *Counseling adults in transition: Linking Schlossberg's theory with practice in a diverse world* (4th ed.). New York, NY: Springer Publishing.

Andrews, D. A., Bonta, J., & Hoge, R. D. (1990). Classification for effective rehabilitation: Rediscovering psychology. *Criminal Justice and Behavior, 19,* 19–52.

Atuel, H. R., & Castro, C. A. (2019). Military transition process and veteran identity. In E. L. Weiss & C. A. Andrew (Eds.), *American Military Life in the 21st Century Social, Cultural, and Economic Issues and Trends* [Volume 2] (pp. 485-496). Santa Barbara, CA: ABC-CLIO.

Bialik, K. (2017, November). *The changing face of America's veteran population.* Washington, DC: Pew Research Center.

Black, T., Westwood, M. J., & Sorsdal, M. N. (2007). From the front line to the front of the class: Counseling students who are military veterans. In J. A. Lippincott & R. B. Lippincott (Eds.), *Special populations in college counseling: A handbook for mental health professionals* (pp. 3–20). Alexandria, VA: American Counseling Association.

Bonar, T. C., & Domenici, P. L. (2011). Counseling and connecting with the military undergraduate: The intersection of military service and university life. *Journal of College Student Psychotherapy, 25*, 204–219.

Bonta, J., & Andrews, D. A. (2017). *The psychology of criminal conduct* (6th ed.). New York, NY: Routledge.

Bridges, W. (2004). *Transitions: Making sense of life's changes* (2nd ed.). Cambridge, MA: Da Capo Press.

Bureau of Labor Statistics (2017, August). *Number of jobs, labor market experience, and earnings growth among Americans at 50: Results from a longitudinal survey.* [News Release USDL-17-1158]. Retrieved from https://www.bls.gov/news.release/pdf/nlsoy.pdf

Bureau of Labor Statistics (2018a). *Employee tenure in 2018.* [News Release USDL-18-1500]. Retrieved from https://www.bls.gov/news.release/pdf/tenure.pdf

Bureau of Labor Statistics (2018b). *Employment situation of veterans–2017.* [News Release USDL-18-0453]. Retrieved from https://www.bls.gov/news.release/pdf/vet.pdf

Bureau of Labor Statistics (2019). *Workforce Investment Act–Adults and Dislocated Workers Program.* Retrieved from https://www.doleta.gov/programs/general_info.cfm

Carter, R. T., & Forsyth, J. (2010). Reactions to racial discrimination: Emotional stress and help-seeking behaviors. *Psychological Trauma: Theory, Research, Practice, and Policy, 2*, 183-191.

Center for Substance Abuse Treatment (2000). *Integrating Substance Abuse Treatment and Vocational Services.* Treatment Improvement Protocol (TIP) Series, No. 38. HHS Publication No. (SMA) 12-4216. Rockville, MD: Substance Abuse and Mental Health Services Administration.

Duggan, M. H., & Jurgens, J. C. (2007). *Career interventions and techniques: A complete guide for human services professionals.* Boston, MA: Pearson Education, Inc.

Ebberwein, C. A., Krieshok, T. S., Ulven, J. C., & Prosser, E. C. (2004). Voices in transition: Lessons on career adaptability. *Career Development Quarterly, 52*, 292-308.

Eckart, E. & Dufrene, R. L. (2015). Barriers to mental health treatment in the military. *Journal of Military and Government Counseling, 3*, 40-55.

Fassinger, R. E. (2008). Workplace diversity and public policy: Challenges and opportunities for psychology. *American Psychologist, 63*, 252-268.

George, L. K., & Siegler, I. C. (1981). *Coping with stress and coping in later life: Older people speak for themselves.* Durham, NC: Duke University Medical Center.

Goodman, J., Schlossberg, N. K., & Anderson, M. L. (2006). *Counseling adults in transition: Linking practice with theory* (3rd ed.). New York, NY: Springer Publishing Co.

Gunz, H. P., Peiperl, M., & Tzabbar, D. (2007). Boundaries in the study of career. In H. P. Gunz, & M. A. Peiperl (Eds.), *Handbook of career studies* (pp. 471–494). Thousand Oaks, CA: Sage.

Hall, K. C. (2016, August). *From the battlefield to the boardroom: Transferring veterans' skills to the civilian labor market.* The RAND Blog. Retrieved from https://www.rand.org/blog/2016/08/from-the-battlefield-to-the-boardroom-transferring.html

Hardison, C., & Shanley, M. G. (2016). *Essential skills veterans gain during professional military training: A resource for leaders and hiring managers.* Retrieved from https://www.rand.org/pubs/tools/TL160z2-2.html

Hayden, S. C. W., Ledwith, K., Dong, S., & Buzzetta, M. (2014). Assessing the career-development needs of student veterans: A proposal for career interventions. *The Professional Counselor 4,* 129–138.

Homant, R. J., & Dean, D. G. (1988). The effect of prisonization and self-esteem on inmates' career maturity. *Journal of Offender Counseling, Services & Rehabilitation, 12,* 19–40.

Hopson, B. & Adams, J. (1977). Toward and understanding of transitions: Defining some boundaries of transition. In J. Adams, J. Hayes, & B. Hopson (Eds.), *Transition: Understanding and managing personal change* (pp. 1-19). Oxford, England: Allanheld & Osmun.

Houston, M. (2006). *Offender job retention.* Washington, DC: National Institute of Corrections, Office of Correctional Job Training and Placement.

Hudson, F. M. (1999). *The adult years: Mastering the art of self-renewal* (Rev. ed.). San Francisco, CA: Jossey-Bass.

Jenner, B. M. (2017). Student veterans and the transition to higher education: Integrating existing literatures. *Journal of Veterans Studies, 2,* 26-44.

Kalleberg, A. L. (2009). Precarious work, insecure workers: Employment relations in transition. *American Sociological Review, 74,* 1–22.

Kintzle, S., Rasheed, J. M., & Castro, C. A. (2016). *The State of the American Veteran: The Chicagoland Veterans Study.* Retrieved from http://cir.usc.edu/wpcontent/uploads/2016/04/CIR_ChicagoReport_double.pdf

Kirchner, M. J. (2015). Supporting student veteran transition to college and academic success. *Adult Learning, 26*(3), 116–123

Levy Merrick, E. S., Volpe-Vartanian, J., Horgan, C. M., & McCann, B. (2007). Revisiting employee assistance programs and substance use problems in the workplace: Key issues and a research agenda. *Psychiatric Services, 58,* 1262–1264.

Louis, M. R. (1981). Career transitions: Varieties and commonalities. In R. E. Hill, E. L. Miller, & M. A. Lowther (Eds.), *Adult career transitions: Current research perspectives* (pp. 55-73). Ann Arbor, MI: University of Michigan.

Martin, M. E. (2014). *Introduction to human services: Through the eyes of practice settings* (3rd ed.). Boston, MA: Pearson.

Morgan, R. D. (2013). Vocational psychology in corrections: It is about time. *Counseling Psychologist, 4,* 1061–1071.

National Institute on Drug Abuse (2015). *Nationwide Trends.* NIDA. Retrieved from https://www.drugabuse.gov/publications/drugfacts/nationwide-trends

National Institute on Drug Abuse (2017a). *Trends & Statistics.* NIDA. Retrieved from https://www.drugabuse.gov/related-topics/trends-statistics on 2019

National Institute on Drug Abuse (2017b). *Health consequences of drug misuse.* NIDA. Retrieved from https://www.drugabuse.gov/related-topics/health-consequences-drug-misuse

Nightingale, D. S., & Holcomb, P. A. (1997). Alternative strategies for increasing employment. *The Future of Children, 7,* 52– 64.

Pearlin, L., & Schooler, C. (1978). The Structure of Coping. *Journal of health and social behavior. 19,* 2-21.

Rausch, M. A. (2014). Contextual career counseling for transitioning military veterans. *Journal of Employment Counseling 51,* 89–96.

Reger, M. A., Etherage, J. R., Reger, G. M., & Gahm, G. A. (2008). Civilian psychologists in an army culture: The ethical challenge of cultural competence. *Military Psychology, 20,* 21–35.

Robertson, H.C. (2013). Income and support during transition from a military to civilian career. *Journal of Employment Counseling, 50,* 26-33.

Rumann, C. B., & Hamrick, F. A. (2010). Student veterans in transition: Re-enrolling after war zone deployments. *The Journal of Higher Education, 81,* 431- 455.

Schlossberg, N. K. (1984). Counseling adults in transition. New York, NY: Springer.

Sharf, R. S. (2013). *Applying career development theory to counseling* (6th ed.). Belmont, CA: Brooks/Cole.

Stoltz, K. B. (2017). Early recollections with a paroled African American male: A career-focused group approach. In L. A. Busacca & M. C. Rehfuss (Eds.), *Postmodern Career Counseling: A handbook of culture, context, and cases* (pp. 133-146). Alexandria, VA: American Counseling Association.

Strom, T. Q., Gavian, M. E., Possis, E., Loughlin, J., Bui, T., Linardatos, E., & Siegel, W. (2012). Cultural and ethical considerations when working with military personnel and veterans: A primer for VA training programs. *Training and Education in Professional Psychology, 6(2),* 67–75

Tanielian, T., & Jaycox, L. H. (Eds.). (2008). *Invisible wounds of war: Psychological and cognitive injuries, their consequences, and services to assist recovery.* Santa Monica, CA: RAND.

U. S. Department of Justice (2018, April). *Correctional populations in the United States, 2016.* [NCJ 251211, Bulletin]. Retrieved from https://www.bjs.gov/content/pub/pdf/cpus16.pdf

U. S. Department of Housing and Urban Development (2017). *The 2017 Annual Homeless Assessment Report to Congress. Homeless veterans in the United States.* Retrieved from https://www.hudexchange.info/resources/documents/2017-AHAR-Part-2-Section-5.pdf

U. S. Department of Labor (2018). *Workforce Investment Act–Adults and Dislocated Workers Program.* Employment and Training Administration. Retrieved from https://www.doleta.gov/programs/general_info.cfm

U. S. Department of Veterans Affairs (2017, January). *Analysis of VA health care utilization among Operation Enduring Freedom (OEF), Operation Iraqi Freedom (OIF), and Operation New Dawn (OND) Veterans: Cumulative from 1st Qtr FY 2002 through 3rd Qtr FY 2015 (October 1, 2001 – June 30, 2015).* Washington, DC: Author. Retrieved from https://www.publichealth.va.gov/docs/epidemiology/healthcare-utilization-report-fy2015-qtr3.pdf

Varghese, F. P. (2013). Vocational interventions with offenders: Interdisciplinary research, theory, and integration. *Counseling Psychologist, 41,* 1011–1039.

Varghese, F. P., & Cummings, D. L. (2013). Introduction: Why apply vocational psychology to criminal justice populations? *Counseling Psychologist, 41,* 961–989.

Williams, D. (1999). *Life events and career change: Transition psychology in practice.* Paper presented at the British Psychology Society's Occupational Psychology Conference, Blackport, UK.

Wolkstein, E., and Spiller, H. (1998). Providing vocational services to clients in substance abuse rehabilitation. *Directions in Rehabilitation Counseling, 9,* 65–78.

Zinzow, H.M., Britt, T.W., Pury, C.S., Raymond, M., McFadden, A.C., & Burnette, C.M. (2013). Barriers and facilitators of mental health treatment seeking among active-duty army personnel. *Military Psychology, 25,* 514-535.

Zogas, A. (2017, February). *U. S. military veterans' difficult transitions back to civilian life and the VA's response.* Providence, RI: Watson Institute International & Public Affairs, Brown University. Retrieved from https://watson.brown.edu/costsofwar/files/cow/imce/papers/2017/Zogas_Veterans%27%20Transitions_CoW_2.1.17.pdf

Chapter 10

Americans with Disabilities Act of 1990, 42, U. S. C. § 12101 et seq.

Anctil, T. (2017). Action theory of career assessment for clients with chronic illness and disability. In L. A. Busacca & M. C. Rehfuss (Eds.), *Postmodern Career Counseling: A handbook of culture, context, and cases* (pp. 299-310). Alexandria, VA: American Counseling Association.

Barnes, C. (2000). A working social model? Disability, work and disability politics in the 21st century. *Critical Social Policy, 65,* 441-457.

Baron, R. C., & Salzer, M. S. (2002). Accounting for unemployment among people with mental illness. *Behavioral Science and the Law, 20,* 585-599.

Bertoni, D. (2010). *Actions that could increase work participation for adults with disabilities. Highlights of a forum.* Washington, DC: U. S. Government Accountability Office: Eric Document # ED511105.

Bolton, B., & Brookings, J. (1996). Development of a multifaceted definition of empowerment. *Rehabilitation Counseling Bulletin, 39,* 256-264.

Brown, D. (2016). *Career information, career counseling, and career development* (11th ed.). Boston, MA: Pearson Education, Inc.

Bureau of Labor Statistics (2013). *Persons with a disability: Barriers to employment, types of assistance, and other labor-related issues – May, 2012* [News Release]. Retrieved from https://www.bls.gov/news.release/archives/dissup_04242013.pdf

Bureau of Labor Statistics (2018). *Persons with a disability: Labor Force Characteristics–2017* [News Release]. Retrieved from https://www.bls.gov/news.release/pdf/disabl.pdf

Burkhauser, R. V., & Houtenville, A. J. (2010). Employment among working-age people with disabilities: What the latest data can tell us. In E. M. Szymanski and R. M. Parker (Eds.), *Work and disability: Contexts, issues, and strategies for enhancing employment outcomes for people with disabilities* (3rd ed., pp. 49-86). Austin, TX: Pro-ed.

Commission on Rehabilitation Counselor Certification (2019). *Rehabilitation Counseling scope of practice.* Retrieved from https://www.crccertification.com/scope-of-practice

Elliott, T., & Leung, P. (2005). Vocational Rehabilitation: History and practice. In W. B. Walsh & M. L. Savickas (Eds.), *Handbook of Vocational Psychology: Theory, research, and practice* (3rd ed., pp. 319-343), Mahwah, NJ: Lawrence Erlbaum Press.

Erickson, W., Lee, C., von Schrader, S. (2017). Disability statistics from the American Community Survey (ACS). Ithaca, NY: Cornell University Yang-Tan Institute (YTI). Retrieved from www.disabilitystatistics.org

Equal Employment Opportunity Commission (2002). *Enforcement guidance: Reasonable accommodation and undue hardship under the Americans with disabilities act.* Retrieved from https://www.eeoc.gov/policy/docs/accommodation.html

Fabian, E. (2014). Work and disability. In. D. L. Blustein (Ed.) *The Oxford handbook of the psychology of working.* (pp. 185-200). New York, NY: Oxford University Press.

Freedman, R. I. (1996). The meaning of work in the lives of people with significant disabilities: Consumer and family perspectives. *Journal of Rehabilitation, 62,* 49-55.

Harp, H. T. (1994). Empowerment of mental health consumers in vocational rehabilitation. *Psychosocial Rehabilitation Journal, 17,* 83-90.

Houtenville, A. J., & Burkhauser, R. V. (2004). *Did the employment of people with disabilities decline in the 1990's and was the ADA responsible?* Ithaca, NY: Employment and Disability Institute. School of Industrial & Labor Relations, Cornell University.

Jordan, A. L., & Marinaccio, J. N. (Eds.) (2017). *Facilitating career development: An instructional program for career services providers and other career development providers* (4th ed.). Alexandria, VA: National Career Development Association.

Kalleberg, A. L. (2009). Precarious work, insecure workers: Employment relations in transition. *American Sociological Review, 74,* 1-22.

Kosciulek, J. F. (2014). Facilitating the career development of individuals with disabilities through empowering career counseling. In N.C. Gysbers, M. J. Heppner, & J. A. Johnston (Eds.), *Career counseling: Holism, diversity, and strengths* (4th ed., pp. 129-139). Alexandria, VA: American Counseling Association.

Kraus, L., Lauer, E., Coleman, R., & Houtenville, A. (2018). *2017 disability statistics annual report.* Durham, NH: University of New Hampshire. Retrieved from https://disabilitycompendium.org/sites/default/files/user-uploads/2017_AnnualReport_2017_FINAL.pdf

Livneh, H., & Antonak, R. F. (2005). Psychosocial adaptation to chronic illness and disability: A primer for counselors. *Journal of Counseling & Development, 83,* 12-20.

Mashaw, J., & Reno, V.P. (Eds.) (1996). *Balancing security and opportunity: The challenge of disability income policy.* Washington, DC: National Academy of Social Insurance.

Patterson, J., Bruyere, S. M., Szymanski, E., & Jenkins, W. (2011). Philosophical, historical, and legislative aspects of the rehabilitation counseling profession. In R. M. Parker & J. B. Patterson (Eds.), *Rehabilitation counseling: Basics and beyond* (5th ed., pp. 27–53). Austin, TX: Pro-Ed.

Rubin, S. E., Roessler, R., & Rumrill Jr., P. D. (2016). *Foundations of the Vocational Rehabilitation Process* (7th ed.). Austin, TX: PRO-ED.

Sales, A. (2011). *Seeing potential, not disability* (L. Shallcross, Interviewer) *Counseling Today, 54 (2),* 28-35. Retrieved from https://ct.counseling.org/2011/08/seeing-potential-not-disability/

Shallcross, L. (2011, August). Seeing potential, not disability. *Counseling Today.* Retrieved from https://ct.counseling.org/2011/08/seeing-potential-not-disability/

Strauser, D. R. (2014). Introduction to the centrality of work for individuals with disabilities in D. R. Strauser (Ed.), *Career development, employment, and disability in rehabilitation: From theory to practice.* (pp. 1-9). New York, NY: Springer Publishing.

U. S. Equal Employment Opportunity Commission (2002). Enforcement guidance: Reasonable accommodation and undue hardship under the Americans with disabilities act. Retrieved from https://www.eeoc.gov/policy/docs/accommodation.html

Vocational Rehabilitation Act of 1973. *Eligibility and individualized plan for employment.* 29 U. S. C. § 722 (a)(1) et seq.

Williams, G. (2001). Theorizing disability. In G. Albrecht, K. Seelman, & M. Bury (Eds.), *Handbook of disability studies* (pp. 123-144). Thousand Oaks, CA: Sage Publications.

World Health Organization (2001). *The International Classification of Functioning, Disability and Health* (ICF). Geneva, WHO. Retrieved from http://www.who.int/classifications/icf/en/

Chapter 11

Alfeld, C., Charner, I., Johnson, L., & Watts, E. (2013). *Work-based learning opportunities for high school students.* National Institute for Work and Learning. National Research Center for Career & Technical Education. University of Louisville, Louisville, KY: Retrieved from http://www.nrccte.org/sites/default/files/publication-files/nrccte_work-based_learning.pdf

American School Counselor Association. (2004). *The ASCA National Model workbook.* Alexandria, VA: Author.

American School Counselor Association. (2005). *The ASCA National Model: A framework for school counseling programs* (2nd ed.). Arlington, VA: Author.

American School Counselor Association. (n.d.). *The role of the school counselor.* Retrieved from https://www.schoolcounselor.org/asca/media/asca/Careers-Roles/RoleStatement.pdf

American School Counselor Association. (2014). *Mindsets and behaviors for student success: K-12 college- and career-readiness standards for every student.* Retrieved from: https://www.schoolcounselor.org/asca/media/asca/home/MindsetsBehaviors.pdf

American School Counselor Association. (2017). *ASCA positions statements. The School Counselor and Career Development.* Retrieved from https://www.schoolcounselor.org/asca/media/asca/PositionStatements/PositionStatements.pdf

Anctil, T. M., Smith, C. K., Schenck, P., & Dahir, C. (2012). Professional school counselors' career development practices and continuing education needs. *Career Development Quarterly, 60,* 109-121.

Association for Career and Technical Education. (2010). *What is career ready?* Alexandria, VA: Author.

Arrington, K. (2000). Middle grades career planning programs. *Journal of Career Development, 27,* 103-109.

Ashcroft, K. B. (1966). *A report of the invitational conference in implementing career development theory.* Washington, DC: National Vocational Guidance Association.

Baker, S. B., & Gerler Jr., E. R. (2008). *School counseling for the twenty-first century* (5th ed.). Upper Saddle River, NJ: Pearson.

Bandura, A. (1977). *Social learning theory.* Englewood Cliffs, NJ: Prentice Hall.

Bandura, A. (1986). *Social foundations of thought and action: A social cognitive theory.* Englewood Cliffs, NJ: Prentice Hall.

Bolles, R. N. (2018). *What color is your parachute? 2019: A practical manual for job-hunters and career-changers.* New York, NY: Ten Speed Press.

Bowen, M. (1976). Theory in the practice of psychotherapy. In P. J. Guerin (Ed.), *Family therapy* (pp. 42-90). New York, NY: Gardner.

Campbell, C. A., & Dahir, C. A. (1997). *Sharing the vision: The national standards for school counseling programs.* Alexandria, VA: American School Counselor Association.

Carnevale, A. P., Smith, N., & Strohl, J. (2013). *Recovery: Job growth and education requirements through 2020.* Washington DC: Georgetown University Center on Education and the Workforce. Retrieved from https://cew.georgetown.edu/wp-content/uploads/2014/11/Recovery2020.FR_.Web_.pdf

Conley, D. (2007). *Redefining college readiness.* Prepared for the Bill & Melinda Gates Foundation. Retrieved from https://www.epiconline.org/files/pdf/RedefiningCR_Vol3.pdf.

Crites, J. O., & Savickas, M. L. (2011). *The Career Maturity Inventory-Form C.* Author. Retrieved from http://www.vocopher.com/ms/cmic/cmi_c_master.pdf

Curry, J. R., & Milsom, A. (2017). *Career and college readiness counseling in P-12 schools (2nd ed.).* New York, NY: Springer Publishing Company.

Dahir, C. A., Sheldon, C. B., & Valiga, M. J. (1998). *Vision into action: Implementing the national standards for school counseling programs.* Alexandria, VA: American School Counselor Association.

Dykeman, C., Wood, C., Ingram, M. A., Pehrsson, D., Mandsagerand, N., & Herr, E. L. (2003). The structure of school career development interventions: Implications for school counselors. *Professional School Counseling, 6,* 272-278.

Erford, B. T. (2019). *Transforming the school counseling profession* (5th ed.) New York, NY: Pearson Education, Inc.

Erikson, E. (1968). *Identity: Youth and crisis.* New York, NY: Norton.

Gysbers, N. C. (2013). Career-ready students: A goal of comprehensive school guidance programs. *The Career Development Quarterly, 61,* 283-288.

Gysbers, N. C., & Henderson, P. (2012). *Developing and managing your school guidance program* (5th ed.). Alexandria, VA: American Counseling Association.

Gysbers, N. C., & Lapan, R. T. (2009). *Strengths-Based Career Development for School Guidance and Counseling Programs.* Chelsea, MI: Counseling Outfitters, LLC.

Hartung, P. J. (2013). The life-span, life-space theory of careers. In S. D. Brown & R. W. Lent (Eds.), *Career development and counseling: Putting theory and research to work* (2nd ed., pp. 83–113). Hoboken, NJ: John Wiley & Sons.

Holland, J. L. (1997). *Making vocational choices: A theory of vocational personalities and work environments* (3rd ed.). Odessa, FL: Psychological Assessment Resources.

Hoyt, K. B. (2005). *Career education: History and future.* Alexandria, VA: National Career Development Association.

Johnson, L. S. (2000). The relevance of school to career: A study in student awareness. *Journal of Career Development, 26,* 263-276.

Kobylarz, L. (1996). *National career development guidelines: K-adult handbook.* Stillwater, OK: Career Development Training Institute.

Kolbert, J. B., Williams, R. L. Morgan, L. M., Crothers, L. M., & Hughes, T. L. (2017). *Introduction to professional school counseling: Advocacy, leadership, and intervention.* New York, NY: Routledge.

Lent, R. W. (2013). Social cognitive career theory. In S. D. Brown & R. W. Lent (Ed.), *Career Development and Counseling: Putting Theory and Research to Work* (2nd ed., pp. 115-146). Hoboken, NJ: John Wiley & Sons.

Lent, R. W., Brown, S. T., & Hackett, G., (1994). Toward a unifying social cognitive theory of career and academic interest, choice, and performance. *Journal of Vocational Behavior, 45,* 79-122.

Lent, R. W., Brown, S. T., & Hackett, G., (2002). Social cognitive career theory. In D. Brown & Associates (Eds.)., *Career Choice and Development* (4th ed., pp. 255-311). San Francisco, CA: Jossey-Bass.

Lent, R. W., Hackett, G., & Brown, S. T. (1996). A social cognitive view of school-to-work transition. *Career Development Quarterly, 47,* 297-311.

Marcia, J. E. (1987). The identity status approach to the study of ego identity development. In T. Honess & K. Yardley (Eds.), *Self and identity: Perspectives across the lifespan* (pp. 161-171). New York, NY: Routledge.

McCallumore, K. M., & Sparapani, E. F. (2010). The importance of the ninth grade on high school graduation rates and student success in high school. *Education, 130,* 447-456.

Mishkind, A. (2014, September). *Overview: State definitions of college and career readiness.* Washington, DC: American Institutes for Research.

Nauta, M. M., & Kahn, J. H. (2007). Identity status, consistency and differentiation of interests, and career decision self-efficacy. *Journal of Career Assessment, 15,* 55-65.

Neukrug, E. S. (2012). *The world of the counselor: An introduction to the counseling profession* (4th ed.). Belmont, CA: Brooks/Cole.

Niles, S. G., & Erford, B. T. (2019). Promoting career and individual planning in schools. In B. T. Erford (Ed.). *Transforming the School Counseling Profession,* (5th ed., pp. 250-268). New York, NY: Pearson.

Niles, S. G, & Harris-Bowlsbey, J. (2017). *Career development interventions* (5th ed.). Boston, MA: Pearson Education, Inc.

Sampson, J. P., Hooley, T., & Marriot, J. (2011). *Fostering college and career readiness: How career development activities in schools' impact on graduation rates and students' life success.* Florida State University Libraries, Department of Educational Psychology and Learning Systems.

Savickas, M. L. (1997). Career adaptability: An integrative construct for life-span, life-space theory. *The Career Development Quarterly, 45,* 247–259.

Savickas, M. L. (1999). The transition from school to work: A developmental perspective. *Career Development Quarterly, 47,* 326-336.

Savickas, M. (1999). The transition from school to work: A developmental perspective. *Career Development Quarterly, 47,* 326-336.

Savickas, M. L. (2013). Career construction theory and practice. In S. D. Brown & R. W. Lent (Eds.). *Career development and counseling: Putting theory and research to work* (2nd ed., pp. 147-183). Hoboken, NJ: John Wiley & Sons.

Savickas, M. L., & Crites, J. O. (1981). *Career decision making: Teaching the process.* Rootstown, OH: NEOUCOM.

Schenck, P. M., Anctil, T. M., Smith-Klose, C., & Dahir, C. (2012). Coming full circle: Reoccurring career development trends in schools. *The Career Development Quarterly, 60,* 221-230.

Skorikov, V. B., & Vondracek, F. W. (1998). Vocational identity development: Its relationship to other identity domains and to overall identity development. *Journal of Career Assessment, 6,* 13-35.

Solberg, V. S. (2014, December 3). *Individualized career and academic plans: Inspiring all youth to reach higher in pursuit of their career and life goals.* Presentation, Individualized Career and Academic Plan Summit. Retrieved from https://slideplayer.com/slide/13719331/

Solberg, V. S., Howard, K. A., Blustein, D. L., & Close, W. (2002). Career development in the schools: Connecting school-to-work-to-life. *The Counseling Psychologist, 30,* 705-725.

Solberg, V. S., Martin, J., Larson, M., Nichols, K., Booth, H., Lillis, J., & Costa, L. (2018). *Promoting quality individualized learning plans throughout the lifespan: A revised and updated ILP how to guide 2.0.* National Collaborative on Workforce and Disability for Youth, Institute for Educational Leadership. Retrieved from http://www.ncwd-youth.info/wp-content/uploads/2018/03/Promoting-Quality-ILPs-Throughout-the-Lifespan-WEB.pdf

Super, D. E. (1990). A life-span, life-space approach to career development. In D. Brown & L. Brooks (Eds.), *Career choice and development: Applying contemporary theories to practice* (2nd ed., pp. 11-20). San Francisco, CA: Jossey-Bass.

Swanson, J. L., & Fouad, N. A. (1999). Applying theories of person-environment fit to the transition from school to work. *Career Development Quarterly, 47,* 337-347.

Tennyson, W. W., Soldahl, T. A., & Mueller, C. (1965). *The teacher's role in career development.* Washington, DC: National Vocational Guidance Association.

U. S. Department of Education, Office of Vocational and Adult Education (1997). *Getting ready for college early: A handbook for parents of students in the middle and junior high school years.* Washington, DC. Government Printing Office. Retrieved from https://files.eric.ed.gov/fulltext/ED412460.pdf

U. S. Department of Education. (2010). *Race to the top.* Washington, DC: Government Printing Office Retrieved from https://obamawhitehouse.archives.gov/issues/education/k-12/race-to-the-top

U. S. Department of Education. (2013). *Ohio ESEA flexibility request.* Washington, DC: Author. Retrieved from http://www2.ed.gov/policy/eseaflex/approved-requests/ohamendrequest071113.pdf

U. S. Department of Labor. (2016). *Individualized Learning Plans Across the U. S.* Retrieved from https://www.dol.gov/odep/ilp/map/

Virginia Department of Education. (2010, September). *Virginia's College and Career Readiness Initiative.* Author. Retrieved from: http://www.doe.virginia.gov/instruction/college_career_readiness/resources/introductory_briefing.pdf

Vondracek, F. W., & Skorikov, V. B. (2007). Vocational identity. In V. B. Skorikov & W. Patton (Eds.), *Career development in childhood and adolescence* (pp. 143-168). Rotterdam, The Netherlands: Sense Publishers.

Zunker, V. G. (2016). *Career counseling: A holistic approach* (9th ed.). Boston, MA: Cengage Learning.

Chapter 12

American Counseling Association. (2014). *Code of ethics.* Retrieved from https://www.counseling.org/resources/aca-code-of-ethics.pdf

American Psychological Association. (2003). *Ethical principles of psychologists and code of conduct.* Retrieved from http://www.apa.org/ethics/code2002.html

Bergin, A. E. (1985). Proposed values for guiding and evaluating counseling and psychotherapy. *Counseling and Values, 29,* 99-115.

Center for Credentialing and Education (CCE) (2015). *Global Career Development Facilitator Code of Ethics.* Retrieved from https://www.cce-global.org/Assets/Ethics/GCDFcodeofethics.pdf

Corey, G., Corey, M. S., & Callanan, P. (2011). *Issues and ethics in the helping professions* (8th ed.). Belmont, CA: Brooks/Cole.

Cottone, R. R. (2001). A social constructivism model of ethical decision making in counseling. *Journal of Counseling & Development, 79,* 39-45.

Cottone, R. R., & Claus, R. E. (2000). Ethical decision-making models: A review of the literature. *Journal of Counseling & Development, 78,* 275-283.

Dolgoff, R., Loewenberg, F. M., & Harrington, D. (2009). *Ethical decisions for social work practice* (8th ed.). Belmont, CA: Brooks/Cole.

Forester-Miller, H., & Davis, T. (1996). *A practitioner's guide to ethical decision making.* Alexandria, VA: American Counseling Association.

Guterman, J. T., & Rudes, J. (2008). Social constructionism and ethics: Implications for counseling. *Counseling and Values, 52,* 136–144.

Hoppin, J., & Splete, H. (Eds.). (1996). *Curriculum for career development facilitators.* Rochester, MI: Oakland University.

Jordan, A. L., & Marinaccio, J. N. (Eds.). (2017). *Facilitating career development: An instructional program for career development facilitators and other career development providers.* (4th ed.). Broken Arrow, OK: National Career Development Association.

Kitchener, K. S. (1986). Teaching applied ethics in counselor education: An integration of psychological processes and philosophical analysis. *Journal of Counseling and Development, 64,* 306-311.

Makela, J. P., & Perlus, J. G. (2017) *A case study approach to ethics in career development* (2nd ed.). Broken Arrow, OK: National Career Development Association.

Martin, L. L., & Stoner, P. (1996). Mood as input: What we think about how we feel determines how we think. In L. L. Martin & A. Tesser (Eds.), *Striving and feeling: Interactions among goals, affect and self-regulation* (pp. 279–301). Mahwah, NJ: Erlbaum.

National Association of Social Workers. (2017). NASW code of ethics. Retrieved from https://www.socialworkers.org/About/Ethics/Code-of-Ethics/Code-of-Ethics-English

National Career Development Association (2015a). 2015 Code of Ethics. NCDA. Retrieved from https://www.ncda.org/aws/NCDA/asset_manager/get_file/3395

National Career Development Association (2015b). *Ethical use of social networking technologies in career services.* Retrieved from https://ncda.org/aws/NCDA/asset_manager/get_file/110167

National Organization for Human Services (2015). *Ethical Standards for Human Services Professionals.* NOHS. Retrieved from https://www.nationalhumanservices.org/ethical-standards-for-hs-professionals

Neukrug, E. S. (2017). *Theory, practice, and trends in human services: An introduction* (6th ed.). Boston, MA: Cengage Learning.

Niles, S. G, & Harris-Bowlsbey, J. (2017). *Career development interventions* (5th ed.). Boston, MA: Pearson Education, Inc.

Remley, T. P., & Herlihy, B. (2010). *Ethical, legal, and professional issues in counseling* (3rd ed.). Upper Saddle River, NJ: Prentice Hall.

Rest, J. (1984). Research on moral development: Implications for training psychologists. *The Counseling Psychologist, 12,* 19–29

Sampson, Jr., J. P., & Osborn, D. S. (2015). Using information and communication technology in delivering career interventions. In P. J. Hartung, M. L. Savickas, & W. B. Walsh, (Eds). *APA handbook of career intervention, Volume 2: Applications* (pp. 57-70). Washington, DC: American Psychological Association.

Spokane, A. R. (1991). *Career intervention.* Englewood Cliffs, NJ: Prentice-Hall, Inc.

Tjeltveit, A. C. (1986). The ethics of value conversion in psychotherapy: Appropriate and inappropriate therapist influence on client values. *Clinical Psychology Review, 6,* 515-537.

VanHoose, W. H. (1986). Ethical principles in counseling. *Journal of Counseling and Development, 65,* 168-169.

Welfel, E. R. (2015). *Ethics in counseling and psychotherapy: Standards, research, and emerging issues* (6th ed.). Boston, MA: Cengage Learning.

Welfel, E. R., & Kitchener, K. S. (1992). Introduction to the special section: Ethics education: An agenda for the '90s. *Professional Psychology: Research and Practice, 23,* 179-181.

Chapter 13

Arabandi, B. (2015). Globalization, flexibility and new workplace culture in the United States and India. In A. S. Wharton (Ed.), *Working in America: Continuity, conflict, and change in a new economic era* (4th ed., pp. 69–87). Boulder, CO: Paradigm.

Arthur, N. (2006). Infusing culture in constructivist approaches to career counseling. In M. McMahon & W. Patton (Eds.), *Career counseling: Constructivist approaches* (pp. 57–68). New York, NY: Routledge.

Arthur, M. B., & Rousseau, D. M. (Eds.). (1996). *The boundaryless career: A new employment principle for a new organizational era.* Oxford, England: Oxford University Press.

Baum, S. K., & Stewart, R. B. (1990). Sources of meaning through the lifespan. *Psychological Reports, 67,* 3–14.

Berger, P., & Luckmann, T. (1966). *The social construction of reality.* Garden City, NY: Doubleday.

Bird, J. (2004). *Talk that sings: Therapy in a new linguistic key.* Auckland, New Zealand: Edge Press.

Blustein, D. L. (2006). *The psychology of working: A new perspective for career development, counseling, and public policy.* Mahwah, NJ: Erlbaum.

Blustein, D. L. (2011). A relational theory of working. *Journal of Vocational Behavior, 79,* 1–17.

Blustein, D. L., Schultheiss, D. E. P., & Flum, H. (2004). Toward a relational perspective of the psychology of careers and working: A social constructionist analysis. *Journal of Vocational Behavior, 64,* 423–440.

Bureau of Labor Statistics. (2015). *Number of jobs held, labor market activity, and earnings growth among the youngest baby boomers: Results from a longitudinal survey.* Retrieved from http://www.bls.gov/news.release/pdf/nlsoy.pdf

Busacca, L. A., & Rehfuss, M. C. (Eds.) (2017). *Postmodern Career Counseling: A handbook of culture, context, and cases.* Alexandria, VA: American Counseling Association.

Cole, E. R. (2009). Intersectionality and research in psychology. *American Psychologist, 64,* 170–180.

Collin, A., & Young, R. A. (1986). New directions for theories of career. *Human Relations, 39,* 837–853.

Conway, N., & Briner, R. B. (2005). *Understanding psychological contracts at work: A critical evaluation of theory and research.* New York, NY: Oxford University Press.

Crowley, M., Tope, D., Chamberlain, L. J., & Hodson, R. (2010). Neo-Taylorism and work: Occupational change in the post-Fordist era. *Social Problems 57,* 421–447.

Dik, B. J., & Duffy, R. D. (2012). *Make your job a calling: How the psychology of vocation can change your life at work.* West Conshohocken, PA: Templeton Press.

Erwin, E. (1999). Constructivist epistemologies and the therapies. *British Journal of Guidance & Counselling, 27,* 353–365.

Ford, D. (1987). *Humans as self-constructing living systems.* Hillsdale, NJ: Erlbaum.

Inkson, K., & Elkin, G. (2008). Landscape with travelers: The context of careers in developed nations. In J. A. Athanasou & R. van Esbroeck (Eds.), *International handbook of career guidance* (pp. 69–94). Dordrecht, The Netherlands: Springer.

Jordan, J. V. (1991). Empathy, mutuality and therapeutic change: Clinical implications of a relational model. In J. V. Jordan et al. (Eds.), *Women's growth in connection: Writings from the Stone Center* (pp. 283–290). New York, NY: Guilford Press.

Kalleberg, A. L. (2009). Precarious work, insecure workers: Employment relations in transition. *American Sociological Review, 74,* 1–22.

Kalleberg, A. L., & Leicht, K. (2002). The United States. In D. Cornfield & R. Hodson (Eds.), *Worlds of work: Building an international sociology of work* (pp. 87–110). New York, NY: Kluwer Academic/Plenum.

Kosine, N. R., Steger, M. F., & Duncan, S. (2008). Purpose-centered career development: A strengths-based approach to finding meaning and purpose in careers. *Professional School Counseling, 12,* 133–136.

Kvale, S. (Ed.). (1992). *Psychology and postmodernism.* London, England: Sage.

Levine, L. (2005). *Offshoring (a.k.a. offshore outsourcing) and job insecurity among U.S. workers.* Washington, DC: CRS. Retrieved from http://digitalcommons.ilr.cornell.edu/cgi/viewcontent.cgi?article=1243&context=key_workplace

Madigan, S. (2011). *Narrative therapy.* Washington, DC: American Psychological Association.

Maturana, H. R., & Varela, F. J. (1988). *The tree of knowledge: The biological roots of human understanding.* Boston, MA: New Science Library.

Neimeyer, R. A., & Stewart, A. E. (2000). Constructivist and narrative psychotherapies. In C. R. Snyder & R. E. Ingram (Eds.), *Handbook of psychological change: Psychotherapy processes and practices for the 21st century* (pp. 337–357). New York, NY: Wiley.

Peavy, R. V. (1992). A constructivist model of training for career counselors. *Journal of Career Development, 18,* 215-228.

Peavy, R. V. (1995). *Constructivist career counseling.* ERIC Digest. Retrieved from https://www.counseling.org/resources/library/eric%20digests/95-061.pdf.

Peavy, R. V. (2004). *Sociodynamic counseling: A practical approach to meaning making.* Chagrin Falls, OH: Taos Institute.

Richardson, M. S. (2015). Agentic action in context. In R. A. Young, J. F. Domene, & L. Valach (Eds.), *Counseling and action: Toward life-enhancing work, relationships, and identity* (pp. 51–68). New York, NY: Springer.

Rousseau, D. M. (1998). The problem of the psychological contract considered. *Journal of Organizational Behavior, 19,* 665–671.

Savickas, M. L. (1993). Career counseling in the postmodern era. *Journal of Cognitive Psychotherapy, 7,* 205–215.

Savickas, M. L. (2011). *Career counseling*. Washington, DC: American Psychological Association.

Savickas, M. L. (2015). Career counseling paradigms: Guiding, developing, and designing. In P. Hartung, M. Savickas, & W. Walsh (Eds.), *The APA handbook of career interventions* (pp. 129–143). Washington, DC: APA Press.

Savickas, M. L. (2019). *Career counseling* (2nd ed.). Washington, DC: American Psychological Association.

Savickas, M. L., Nota, L., Rossier, J., Dauwalder, J. P., Duarte, M. E., Guichard, J., van Vianen, A. E. M. (2009). Life designing: A paradigm for career construction in the 21st century. *Journal of Vocational Behavior, 75*, 239–250.

Schultheiss, D. E. P. (2003). A relational approach to career counseling: Theoretical integration and practical application. *Journal of Counseling & Development, 81*, 301–310.

Schultheiss, D. E. P. (2005). Qualitative relational career assessment: A constructivist paradigm. *Journal of Career Assessment, 13*, 381–394.

Sexton, T. (1997). Constructivist thinking within the history of ideas: The challenge of a new paradigm. In T. Sexton & B. Griffin (Eds.), *Constructivist thinking in counseling practice, research, and training* (pp. 3–18). New York, NY: Teachers College Press.

Standing, G. (1999). *Global labour flexibility: Seeking distributive justice*. New York, NY: St. Martin's Press.

Stead, G. B., & Bakker, T. M. (2010). Discourse analysis in career counseling and development. *The Career Development Quarterly, 59*, 72–86.

Steenbarger, B. N. (1991). All the world is not a stage: Emerging contextualist themes in counseling and development. *Journal of Counseling & Development, 70*, 288–296.

Stone, K. V. W. (2007). Revisiting the at-will employment doctrine: Imposed terms, implied terms, and the normative world of the workplace. *Industrial Law Journal, 36*, 84–101.

Sweet, S., & Meiksins, P. (2008). *Changing contours of work: Jobs and opportunities in the new economy*. Thousand Oaks, CA: Pine Forge Press.

Watson, M. B. (2006). Career counseling theory, culture and constructivism. In M. McMahon & W. Patton (Eds.), *Career counseling: Constructivist approaches* (pp. 45–56). New York, NY: Routledge.

Watson, M. B. (2011). Postmodern career counseling and beyond. In K. Maree (Ed.), *Shaping the story: A guide to facilitating career counseling* (pp. 73–86). Pretoria, South Africa: Van Schaik.

Watson, M. B., & McMahon, M. (2004). Postmodern (narrative) career counseling and education. *Perspectives in Education, 22*, 169–170.

Whiston, S. C., & Rahardja, D. (2005). Qualitative career assessment: An overview and analysis. *Journal of Career Assessment, 13*, 371–380.

Wilber, K. (2000). *Integral psychology: Consciousness, spirit, psychology, therapy.* Boston, MA: Shambhala.

Young, R. A., & Collin, A. (2004). Introduction: Constructivism and social constructionism in the career field. *Journal of Vocational Behavior, 64,* 373–388.

Young, R. A., Valach, L., & Collin, A. (2002). A contextualist explanation of career. In D. Brown & Associates (Eds.), *Career choice and development* (4th ed., pp. 206–252). San Francisco, CA: Jossey-Bass.

Index

Figures and tables are indicated by "F" and "T" following page numbers.

Career Theory, Development, and Appraisal

Made in the USA
Columbia, SC
27 August 2021